Psychology Today

HERE TO HELP

secrets of
SEXUAL
ECSTASY

Michael S. Broder, Ph.D.
Arlene Goldman, Ph.D.

D0980866

ALPHA

A member of Penguin Group (USA) Inc.

ALPHA BOOKS

Published by the Penguin Group

Penguin Group (USA) Inc., 375 Hudson Street, New York, New York 10014, U.S.A.

Penguin Group (Canada), 10 Alcorn Avenue, Toronto, Ontario, Canada M4V 3B2 (a division of Pearson Penguin Canada Inc.)

Penguin Books Ltd, 80 Strand, London WC2R 0RL, England

Penguin Ireland, 25 St Stephen's Green, Dublin 2, Ireland (a division of Penguin Books Ltd)

Penguin Group (Australia), 250 Camberwell Road, Camberwell, Victoria 3124, Australia (a division of Pearson Australia Group Pty Ltd)

Penguin Books India Pvt Ltd, 11 Community Centre, Panchsheel Park, New Delhi —110 017, India

Penguin Group (NZ), Cnr Airborne and Rosedale Roads, Albany, Auckland, New Zealand (a division of Pearson New Zealand Ltd)

Penguin Books (South Africa) (Pty) Ltd, 24 Sturdee Avenue, Rosebank, Johannesburg 2196, South Africa

Penguin Books Ltd, Registered Offices: 80 Strand, London WC2R 0RL, England

International Standard Book Number: 1-59257-284-7
Library of Congress Catalog Card Number: 2004110015

06   05   04   8   7   6   5   4   3   2   1

Interpretation of the printing code: The rightmost number of the first series of numbers is the year of the book's printing; the rightmost number of the second series of numbers is the number of the book's printing. For example, a printing code of 04-1 shows that the first printing occurred in 2004.

Printed in the United States of America

Publisher: Marie Butler-Knight
Product Manager: Phil Kitchel
Senior Managing Editor: Jennifer Chisholm
Acquisitions Editors: Mikal E. Belicove, Paul Dinas
Senior Development Editor: Tom Stevens
Senior Production Editor: Billy Fields
Technical Editor: The Editors of *Psychology Today*

Copy Editor: Michael Dietsch
Cover Designer: Ann Marie Deets
Book Designer: Trina Wurst
Creative Director: Robin Lasek
Indexer: Heather McNeil
Layout: Angela Calvert
Proofreading: Donna Martin

This book is dedicated to our mentors: Albert Ellis, Ph.D. (M.B.), and Ilda Ficher, Ph.D. (A.G.), whose influence throughout our careers has been invaluable; and to our daughter and newest colleague, Joanne Broder Sumerson, Ph.D.

Contents

Foreword

Great sex is a sanctuary in our high-stress world. It's one of life's greatest pleasures, enriching us in every way and reminding us of what we cherish in ourselves and our partners. That's one of the reasons why the pursuit of truly ecstatic sex is so compelling.

However, as important as it is, sexual ecstasy can be elusive. What's the key to having satisfying sex? The critical factor is having the right attitude. Two people who approach their sex lives honestly and with an eye towards improvement are poised to experience sexual ecstasy together. It can be just that simple.

The authors of this book understand that attitude is as important as erotic technique in achieving great sex. Indeed, sexual ecstasy is built just as much on empathy and shared domestic chores as on extended foreplay and successful manipulation of the G spot. So, while *Secrets of Sexual Ecstasy* is a comprehensive road map to your most intimate physical terrain, it never loses sight of the sexual sentinel located above the neck.

That's why this book bears the imprimatur of *Psychology Today*, the only publication dedicated to harnessing behavioral science in service of our most intimate relationships. In the following pages, Michael Broder and Arlene Goldman use cutting-edge research to facilitate our journey to the best sex there is. The authors, a husband and wife team, are uniquely qualified to discuss current research in the field of sexual health, without losing sight of the men and women who will benefit from it.

In their combined 50 years of clinical practice, Goldman and Broder have helped couples with excellent sex lives who just wanted to ratchet it up to ecstasy, as well as couples who need to reawaken their sex life in the wake of kids or jobs or other distractions. You'll meet some of these couples throughout this book—you may even recognize yourself in them. And you'll share their journey to a stronger union through better sex.

Secrets of Sexual Ecstasy is the ultimate guide to our ever-changing, ever-deepening sexual landscape. Deftly exploring the powerful methods and techniques available to all couples, it enables us to reach the heights of true sexual fulfillment now and for the rest of our lives.

Kaja Perina
Editor in chief, *Psychology Today*

Introduction

You and your partner have everything you need to experience sexual ecstasy to the max if you both desire it and are willing to work and play together to create it. This book will show you just how to get to that wonderful place called sexual ecstasy. And if you haven't been able to experience it by the time you've finished this book, you'll know exactly why and what you can do about it.

No one definition of sexual ecstasy can apply to everyone, since sexual ecstasy is, in reality, as unique as your fingerprint. The purpose of this book is to help you define what ecstasy is *for you* in your present relationship, and then to help you and your partner experience it as often as you want to.

Sexual ecstasy is whatever you would describe as an ecstatic level of sexual fulfillment. It's very unlikely that any two people think about or experience sexual ecstasy in exactly the same way, and most people probably experience it slightly differently each time. It can mean one thing when you're dating, another when you're living together or when you're married, and something completely different later in your relationship. It usually evolves into new and better things over the course of your relationship and throughout your life. You can experience it one way Tuesday and have a completely different but equally ecstatic experience on Saturday. Sexual ecstasy is also about remaining open and letting your experience of it change, evolve, and expand.

This book is dedicated to helping you discover or develop a unique vision of sexual ecstasy as it applies to you in your relationship. We present you with our model—an approach that includes the five ingredients of sexual ecstasy. When and to what degree you and your partner make these ingredients a staple of your lovemaking together—and we'll show you just how to do it—the most ecstatic sex you can experience together will be the result!

We give you a smorgasbord of choices to reveal opportunities and options for expanding your definition and experiencing your sensuality and sexuality on as many different levels and in as many different ways as you and your partner choose. And we don't stop there. We provide exercises, strategies, suggestions, and resources that you and your partner can use to begin to explore one another's desires, discover what each of you finds most pleasurable, and tap into your secret fantasies for a never-ending supply of novel ideas that can keep sex sizzling throughout your relationship together.

In this book, we take a holistic approach to sexual ecstasy. We encourage and show you how to blend the psychological, physical, and relationship aspects of sex together to expand your experience of it and to find a meaning of sexual ecstasy that is better able to accommodate and adapt to any changes that you and your partner are likely to experience over the course of your relationship. We believe that sex can be the ultimate communication between partners, the ultimate experience of your connection to one another. So, in helping you to learn about your definition of sexual ecstasy, we emphasize your relationship with your partner in total—not just the physical aspects—as well as your relationship with yourself.

Many other books use a cookbook-style approach to sex, revealing new positions and performance techniques. While we also explore and provide you with a good share of these options to enhance your lovemaking, our focus is more on the psychology of creating the atmosphere, the attitude, and the connection with your partner and yourself that can help make sexual ecstasy happen for you, over and over again and for many years to come. True sexual ecstasy is less about performance and technique and much more about what goes on in your mind; how you feel about yourself, your partner, and your relationship; and how deeply you and your partner are able to connect.

Our model for reaching sexual ecstasy is based on years of experience, research, and clinical practice. We have drawn on our experience as psychologists in helping thousands of couples deal with their relationships and sexual issues more effectively and to develop an approach that helps couples establish a deeper connection that's highly conducive to sexual ecstasy. We're also married to each other, so much of what we offer to you we know not only as clinicians, but also as husband and wife.

We have tirelessly researched the latest studies and interviewed the leading sex experts in the country to provide you with the most state-of-the art information currently available. (You will meet many of these leading sex experts throughout this book and read what they have to say on a variety of topics.) Most importantly, we have used our model successfully time after time to help couples incorporate these five ingredients for sexual ecstasy into their lovemaking. Many have told us that, as a result, wonderful experiences they had never before imagined became possible!

Unlike other approaches that might tell you what to do and how to do it, our approach helps couples find the answers, information, and resources hidden inside themselves and each other in order to discover, experience, and explore their sexuality together. That's what we mean when we say that right now you and your partner have everything you need to enjoy sexual ecstasy to the max. If you both desire it and are willing to work and play together to let it happen, this book will show you how to get there!

How This Book Is Organized

Our model for sexual ecstasy calls for couples to spend time creating an environment that's conducive to sexual ecstasy. We believe that if you allow yourself to fully experience stimulating sensations and know just how to turn each other on, you are well on your way. So, in **Part 1, "Building Your Foundation for Sexual Ecstasy,"** we give you the experts' definitions of sexual ecstasy and then encourage you to develop your own. We then reveal the five ingredients of sexual ecstasy and provide information, suggestions, and exercises that can help you and your partner incorporate them in order to prepare yourselves for the glorious adventure you're about to undertake. We help you to evaluate where you are now and where you want to be, and then provide suggestions on how to get there. We show you how to develop the attitude for ecstatic sex, let sexual ecstasy happen (instead of trying to make it happen), psych yourself up for ecstasy, get in touch with your own body, explore your fantasies, use romance to set the mood, and open up a dialog with your partner that's so important in helping you learn how to pleasure each other.

In **Part 2, "Achieving Sexual Ecstasy,"** we shed our inhibitions and explore innovative ways to enhance lovemaking. Here you learn how to engage in sex with a more playful attitude, accentuate your love nest to appeal to more of your senses, heat things up with seduction and flirtation, explore sensual and sexual touch through massage and oral sex, experiment with different positions for inter-course, try new approaches to maximizing your orgasm, and much more.

If sexual ecstasy is still eluding you, the chapters in **Part 3, "Overcoming Your Barriers to Sexual Ecstasy,"** can help. Here, we explore relationship issues, such as anger and time crunches, that can get in the way of sexual ecstasy; sexual dysfunctions and other physical barriers that might be hindering you; and life changes that commonly occur throughout a long-term relationship that some-times need to be addressed. And, if you can't remove a particular barrier after reading these chapters, we provide references to plenty of other resources that can help. Although many readers might not need the information in Part 3, it's here if and when you do need it.

How to Use This Book

Our approach to sexual ecstasy is not a linear, step-by-step approach, and the ingredients we recommend do not all *need* to be present all the time for you to experience sexual ecstasy, so you don't need to read this book from cover-to-cover to reap its rewards. You can explore it in many different ways. If you would like to read it from start to finish, that's certainly an option that can keep you from missing some valuable tidbits. However, you can also choose to skip around; for example, if you're interested in learning about fantasies, jump to Chapter 6 or skip to Chapter 7 for suggestions on strengthening your bond with your partner.

You can choose to take a more systematic approach by first identifying what's working well sexually for you and your partner and what's not working so well, and then exploring the chapters that you think will benefit you the most. Chapter 3 provides 50 statements that might or might not apply to your relationship. Just mark the ones that apply and then read our suggestions for strengthening each of those factors in your relationship. We also point to specific chapters in the book where you can find additional information and suggestions.

You can use this book alone or with your partner as an erotic way to explore and enjoy your sexuality. Sometimes just thinking about sex in creative ways and fantasizing about your next sexual encounter can stimulate desire. Consider reading parts of the book to one another in bed and discussing some of the topics. Read the book slowly and try all of the exercises and suggestions that apply to you, so you can really absorb the material, not only on the level of knowledge, but viscerally, as well. Integrate it with your values and your future visions and with all other aspects of your relationship that you find to be sacred. And come back to the book again and again to read it with eyes made fresh by your ever-evolving vision of sexual ecstasy!

As you flip through this book, you will notice several different sidebars that are packed with inspiring quotes, plain English definitions, case studies, web resources, and expert advice. Here's what you'll see:

Q&A

What do these contain?
Here you can find questions from real people along with answers, both from us and some of the leading experts in the field.

PsychSpeak

Whenever we introduce a term that might be unfamiliar to our readers and we don't define it in context, we provide a plain English definition in these PsychSpeak sidebars. The term appears in *italic* in the text and **bold** in here.

GET PSYCHED

Look for the Get Psyched icon for inspirational quotes and bits of advice from experts and people who have something of relevance to add to the subject.

WEB TALK: If something valuable related to our discussion can be found on the Web, we point it out in these Web Talk sidebars and encourage you to expand your exploration beyond this book.

url.

you're not alone

If you're experiencing a particular problem, you're not alone—there's a good chance that others have had similar experiences. Here, we describe real case studies, which can inspire hope and often point to the solution.

Welcome to *Secrets of Sexual Ecstasy*

Let us take this opportunity to welcome you to this journey. This book can help you tap into your own sources of inner wisdom to define, explore, and discover your unique vision of sexual ecstasy and learn how to experience the highest level possible with your partner. We're delighted to be part of your process of growth, both individually and as a couple as you set out on this wonderful adventure to discover sexual ecstasy!

Acknowledgments Our heartfelt thanks go out to some of the many people who worked on this book to make it a reality: Mikal Belicove, Sondra Brownell, Julie Cowell, Michael Dietsch, Billy Fields, Phil Kitchel, Lybi Ma, Hara Marano, Kaja Perina, and Tom Stevens.

Our warmest appreciation to our colleagues who have shared their time with us and whose voices are heard throughout this book:

Stanley E. Althof, Ph.D., clinical psychologist and sexologist, professor of psychology in the Department of Urology at Case Western, past-president of Society for Sex Therapy and Research, coeditor of *Handbook of Clinical Sexuality for Mental Health Professionals*, and co-director of the Center for Marital and Sexual Health in Beechwood, Ohio.

Lonnie Barbach, Ph.D., psychologist and sex therapist, clinical faculty of the University of California Medical School; author of many popular books on sex and relationships, including *For Yourself: The Fulfillment of Female Sexuality, 50 Ways to Please Your Lover: While You Please Yourself,* and *The Erotic Edge,* among others. She practices in Mill Valley, California.

Ava Cadell, Ph.D., sexologist and author of *The Pocket Idiot's Guide to Oral Sex.*

Albert Ellis, Ph.D., psychologist and originator of Rational Emotive Behavior Therapy (REBT), the original cognitive behavior therapy. Dr. Ellis is the founder of the Albert Ellis Institute in New York City. In 1958, he wrote the ground-breaking book *Sex Without Guilt* (which was recently brought back for a second edition, *Sex Without Guilt In the 21st Century*). In a survey of his peers done by APA, Dr. Ellis was recognized as the second-most influential psychotherapist of all time (Sigmund Freud was the third). He has written a total of 75 books and over 800 articles. He was also the first president of the SSSS (Society for the Scientific Study of Sexuality).

Helen Fisher, Ph.D., is an anthropologist and research professor at the Center for Human Evolutionary Studies, Department of Anthropology at Rutgers University. She is author of *Why We Love* and *Anatomy of Love*.

Ilda Ficher, Ph.D., psychologist and sex therapist; professor emeritus, Institute for Graduate Clinical Psychology; and founder of one of the first sex therapy centers in Philadelphia, Pennsylvania at The Van Hammitt Clinic, Hahanmann University. She has a private practice in Philadelphia, Pennsylvania.

Cynthia Jayne, Ph.D., clinical psychologist and sex therapist; Kinsey Institute Dissertation Award for Research in Sex, Gender, and Reproduction.

Arnold Lazarus, Ph.D., psychologist and originator of Multimodal Therapy, and author of numerous books, including *Marital Myths* and *The One Minute Shrink*. He is professor emeritus at Rutgers University. In a survey of his peers done by APA, Dr. Lazarus was recognized as the fifth-most influential psychotherapist of all time.

Sandra Leiblum, Ph.D., psychologist, sex therapist, and researcher; professor of psychiatry and director of the Center for Sexual Health and Marital Health at the University of Medicine and Dentistry, Robert Wood Johnson Medical School in Piscataway, New Jersey; first president of the International Society for the Study of Women's Sexual Health; past-president of the Society for Sex Therapy and Research; co-editor or author of 9 professional books in the area of sexuality including *Principals and Practice of Sex Therapy* and the popular book *Getting the Sex You Want: A Woman's Guide to Becoming Proud, Passionate, and Pleased in Bed*.

Stephen B. Levine, M.D., psychiatrist, sex and relationship therapist, and clinical professor of psychiatry at Case School of Medicine in Cleveland, Ohio; past-president of the Society for Sex Therapy and Research; author of *Sexuality in Mid-Life*; editor of *Handbook of Clinical Sexuality for Mental Health Professionals*; and co-director of the Center for Marital and Sexual Health in Beechwood, Ohio.

Pat Love, Ed.D., marital therapist, co-founder of the Austin Family Institute, and author of *Hot Monogamy* and *The Truth About Love.* She is on the faculty of the Imago Institute for Relationship Therapy; she practices in Austin, Texas.

Wendy Maltz, M.S.W., L.C.S.W.; sex therapist and co-author of *Private Thoughts;* author of *Sexual Healing Journey;* and editor of several books on sexual poetry, including *Passionate Hearts: The Poetry of Sexual Love.* Maltz is co-director of Maltz Counseling Associates in Eugene, Oregon.

Barry McCarthy, Ph.D., is a clinical psychologist specializing in marriage and sex therapy. He is a professor of psychology at American University and co-author of seven popular books (many with his wife), including *Getting It Right the First Time, Sexual Awareness, Rekindling Desire* and *Coping with Premature Ejaculation.* He practices at the Washington Psychological Center in Washington, D.C.

Michael Metz, Ph.D., psychologist, marital and sex therapist, affiliated with the University of Minnesota's Department of Family Social Services, creator of the Styles of Conflict Inventory (a clinical assessment instrument for evaluating conflict patterns in couples), co-author of *Coping with Premature Ejaculation.* He practices at Meta Associates in Minneapolis-St. Paul, Minnesota.

Andrew Milberg, Tantric instructor.

Carol Munter, psychoanalyst and certified eating disorders specialist, co-director of the National Center for Eating Disorders, co-author of *When Women Stop Hating Their Bodies.* Munter started the first anti-dieting group in 1970. She practices in New York City.

Gina Ogden, Ph.D., marriage and family therapist, certified sex therapist and associate professor of sexology at the Institute for Advanced Study of Human Sexology in San Francisco, California. She is the author of *Women Who Love Sex* and co-author of *How Women Can Say Yes to Pleasure and No to Unsafe Sex.* She practices in Cambridge, Massachusetts.

David Schnarch, Ph.D., clinical psychologist and certified sex therapist; director of the Marriage and Family Health Center in Evergreen, Colorado; author of *Passionate Marriage, Resurrecting Sex,* and *Constructing the Sexual Crucible;* creator of the Crucible approach to marital therapy.

Julian Slowinski, Psy.D., psychologist and senior clinical psychologist, Pennsylvania Hospital; certified sex therapist; and co-author of *The Sexual Male: Problems and Solutions.* He practices in Philadelphia, Pennsylvania.

William Stayton, Th.D., Ph.D., professor and director of the Human Sexuality Program at Widener University; past-president of SIECUS (Sexuality Information and Education Council of the United States); past-president of AASECT (American Association of Sex Educators, Counselors, and Therapists); vice-president of Planned Parenthood of Southeastern, Pennsylvania. He practices in Wayne, Pennsylvania.

Marianne Tebbens, M.S., eating disorders specialist. She practices in Radnor and Philadelphia, Pennsylvania.

Michele Weiner-Davis, M.S.W., marital therapist and coach; author of six popular books including *The Sex-Starved Marriage, Divorce Busting,* and *The Divorce Remedy;* and director of The Divorce Busting Center in Woodstock, Illinois.

Beverly Whipple, Ph.D., R.N., F.A.A.N., professor emerita, Rutgers University; vice-president of the World Association for Sexology (2001-2005); director of the International Society for the Study of Women's Sexual Health (2002-2004); past-president of the Society for the Scientific Study of Sexuality (SSSS); past-president of AASECT (American Association of Sex Educators, Counselors, and Therapists); sex researcher; vice-president of the World Association for Sexology; director of the International Society for the Study of Women's Sexual Health; past-president of the Scientific Study of Sexuality; and co-author of *How Women Can Say Yes to Pleasure and No To Unsafe Sex* and *The G-Spot and Other Discoveries About Human Sexuality.*

Carole Zawid, Ph.D., R.N., C.S., sexologist, clinical nurse specialist, and author of *Sexual Health: A Nurse's Guide*. She practices in Absecon, New Jersey.

Marvin Zuckerman, Ph.D., psychologist; professor emeritus, Department of Psychology, University of Delaware; creator of the first sensation seeking scale and the first to coin the term "high sensation seeking"; author of *Behavioral Expressions and Biosocial Bases of Sensation Seeking*. His research over the last 40 years has been investigating the sensation-seeking trait and the behaviors associated with it.

Part 1

Building Your Foundation for Sexual Ecstasy

Achieving sexual ecstasy can be effortless, as long as you and your partner foster an environment that's conducive for experiencing it and can then let it happen. By giving yourself permission to experience pleasurable sensations in the moment, by connecting to your partner, and by learning to openly express your desires, turn-ons, and pleasures and by asking for what you want, you will be well on your way to making sexual ecstasy a scintillating new facet of your relationship. In this part, you learn how to begin building your foundation using the skills, knowledge, and resources that you and your partner already have at this moment—this book and each other!

Great Sex Begins with the Right Attitude

Our culture sizzles with sex. TV shows and movies bombard us with sexual themes and images. Magazine racks are packed with pornography. Romance novels, sex manuals, and other sexually oriented publications crowd the shelves at bookstores. And the Internet can pump a steady flow of digitized pornography, sex chat, advice (good and bad), and whatever else your desires dictate right into your home or office with the click of a mouse.

You might think that this sexually charged atmosphere would transform us all into highly aroused, sexually fulfilled individuals. Unfortunately, and quite often, the sexual information that bombards our brains often has the opposite effect. It can fill us with false expectations, inspire shame and guilt, and even frequently seduce us into trading real sex with our partner for virtual sex with a machine. It can muddle our thinking and block the natural flow of thoughts and feelings our minds require to become aroused.

This chapter gives you the real scoop about sex. It dispels common myths, challenges sexually repressive beliefs, and provides the tools you need to form realistic sexual expectations. Here you learn how to liberate your mind and identify and remove any obstacles that might be getting in the way of you and your partner's sexual ecstasy.

Sexual Attitudes: Different Times, Different Cultures

Sexual attitudes are learned. They're passed on to you by your parents, branded on your brain by teachers and preachers, carved into your heart by friends and lovers, and broadcast to you by the media. Throughout life, and on an ongoing basis, these forces act as cultural representatives to help continually mold your *attitudes* about sex.

PsychSpeak

An **attitude** is an organized and enduring set of beliefs and feelings toward an object, person, or situation. Attitudes predispose people to the way they behave towards something or someone.

When you begin to consider changing your attitudes about sex, it helps to realize that sexual attitudes have always differed greatly between cultures, and attitudes within a culture change dramatically over time. Just look at some of the huge swings in the evolution of sexual attitudes throughout recorded history:

Fifth century B.C.E. The ancient Greeks and Romans know how to party. Sexually permissive, they celebrate human sexuality through their festivals, poetry, and art.

Fourth to third centuries B.C.E. "Sexologists" working independently in parts of China and India set out to write the first sex manuals to help people maximize their sexual pleasure within their belief systems. In India, one of the most famous sex manuals of all time, the *Kama Sutra*, presents sex as a way to attain greater spiritual fulfillment. (This book is still popular today.)

2000 to 1500 B.C.E. The party's over for Western culture. The teachings of Abraham, the founding father of the three great Western religions—Judaism, Christianity, and Islam—begin to condemn certain sexual practices and strictly limit others. These rules and beliefs still have a strong influence on many people's sexual attitudes.

1839–1901 It's the Victorian era, and any sex, other than sex between a husband and wife in highly proscribed settings, is considered dirty or evil. A prevailing attitude is that sex actually hampers higher achievement.

Early 1900s Sigmund Freud and many of his contemporaries consider sex in terms of *psychopathology* and mental illness. Many of the sexual behaviors viewed today as normal were considered patholo-gical or sick.

> **PsychSpeak**
>
> **Psychopathology** is the study of mental and behavioral disorders.

1940s–50s Pioneering sex researcher Alfred Kinsey takes the topic of sex out of the realm of opinion and morality to study human sexuality objectively and empirically. His research inspires the prevailing view that whatever is experienced voluntarily by consenting adults is pretty much okay, thus beginning the quest to strip away the layers of guilt and shame that tend to dampen sexual pleasure. This plants the seeds for the sexual revolution.

1960s Fueled by the birth control pill, the virtual absence of incurable venereal diseases, and research by Masters and Johnson, the sexual revolution ignites and rages well into the 1980s. No longer is sex seen by most as morally rep-rehensible or pathological. It is now widely considered a healthy form of pleasure and self-expression.

1980s The party's over, again. With the outbreak of sexually transmitted diseases no longer curable by medication, the sexual revolution grinds to a halt. The risks begin to far outweigh the potential pleasures of free sex. Understandably, many people reign in their desires.

1990s to now Education and better treatments for STDS help alleviate some fears of these dreaded diseases. Viagra and other prescription medications become available for treating male erectile dysfunction, and medications are in the works for female sexual dysfunctions. The world sees an explosion of sex information, advice, and erotica. The Internet provides easy (and often free) access to unlimited resources and helps normalize behavior that previously was considered taboo.

Cultures often take decades or even centuries to change their sexual attitudes and redefine what they consider normal. Yet in our practice, we have seen individuals, through commitment and hard work, change their attitudes in a matter of days or weeks. Couples, ready to bail out of their sexually unfulfilling marriages, have often turned around their sex lives completely and achieved a level of satisfaction that was previously beyond their dreams.

WEB TALK: For a more complete history of human sexuality, check out:

www.bigeye.com/sexeducation/history.html

Safer Sex, Better Sex

A new sexual revolution is in the works, but this revolution isn't about more sex with more people. This revolution is about more and better lovemaking in a long-term relationship with a committed partner. Studies consistently and overwhelmingly show that couples who live together (including married couples who have been together a long time) find their sex lives much more satisfying than single people do. The purpose of the new sexual revolution is to help those in long-term sexual relationships fully experience the intensity of sexual ecstasy with their partners. Today, most experts in the field of human sexuality—and you will meet many prominent experts in this book—share this vision and are committed to helping couples achieve the highest degree of sexual satisfaction possible.

GET PSYCHED

The way, my dear, you think of me will give me sexual ecstasy.
–Anonymous

We believe that having sexual ecstasy within your marriage or other long-term sexual relationship is much more about your attitude—toward your partner and yourself and sex in general—than it is about position, technique, or anything else. Of course, we will teach you all the ingredients for attaining sexual ecstasy, but our primary goal here is to help you and your partner use all of your inner resources to launch your lovemaking to the pinnacle of pleasure.

Simplifying Sexual Attitudes

Generally speaking, people have sex for two reasons: to procreate or to experience pleasure. It's as simple as that. Sadly, though, sexuality often becomes convoluted. For some people, it becomes a source of conflict. For others, it becomes a tool for manipulating a lover. It can even become a source of pain. To further complicate matters, sex can trigger every imaginable emotion—from joy to anger, from confidence to humiliation, from love to hate. It can generate anxiety and depression. Many people even use their sexuality to define their self-image or assess the value of their entire relationship. These are all obstacles to our most prevalent purpose, which is pleasurable sex. And if any of these obstacles is in the way, no new position, innovative technique, or fancy contraption alone will provide you with a pleasurable and satisfying sex life.

Albert Ellis, Ph.D., who has practiced sex therapy for more than 60 years, explored the detrimental effects of one of the main obstacles to sexual ecstasy in his groundbreaking book, *Sex Without Guilt*, back in 1958. When we asked him recently how he would define sexual ecstasy, he gave us the simplest definition yet heard: "It is sex that you define as way more than simply pleasant or pleasurable, but ecstatic." According to Ellis, whatever you define as ecstasy and truly believe is ecstasy you will experience as ecstasy. The only caveat he offers is that sex be practiced by consenting adults. With the exception of that simple and almost universal restriction, there are no "shoulds," no right or wrong, and no reason to feel guilty or upset with your partner about what you do or do not do together. His advice is for you and your partner to experiment until you find what works best for you, enjoy it, and then keep experimenting. This attitude seems simple, yet in our experience with counseling thousands, we rarely meet individuals or couples who can totally prevent guilt, shame, anger, judgment, or their own misdirected agendas from complicating and spoiling a potentially satisfying sexual relationship.

Ellis as well as other experts (therapists, educators, and researchers) identify several obstacles to sexual ecstasy. One of the more prevalent is setting a goal for your degree of sexual pleasure. For instance, a man might set a goal of making his lover experience orgasm. He then becomes upset with himself or with his lover when they "fail." Or a couple might set a goal of having sex three times a week and then become disappointed when they manage it once a week. In addition to being absurd, goal-oriented sex is self-defeating and can cause a great deal of anxiety and grief.

Later in this chapter, in the section "Your Sexual Attitude," we help you identify your own attitudes toward sex so you can begin working to remove any obstacles that might be preventing you from experiencing sexual ecstasy.

you're not alone

Jill (a school teacher) and Tom (a banker) met in college and are now in their late 20s. Both had come from traditional, religious homes, and they reported having a good sex life prior to marriage. When they began discussing the level of satisfaction each felt in terms of their current sexual relationship, they concurred that their sex life wasn't great anymore.

Tom felt Jill didn't love him and was not interested in having sex with him. Tom had had oral sex in previous relationships, he liked it, and he fantasized about it. Jill had never experienced oral sex in any of her prior sexual relationships, and when Tom would bring it up, she adamantly refused to even discuss it. Through therapy, Jill explored possible reasons why she had negative thoughts about oral sex and discovered that her conservative upbringing had led her to consider it filthy and sinful. Moreover, Jill had two concerns: first, that she might choke and, second, that she might not be good at it and Tom would leave her. Some reassurance from Tom along with instructional information on ways to perform oral sex without the possibility of choking was all that was needed to resolve these issues.

Redefining "Sex"

Another common obstacle to sexual ecstasy is the definition of sex itself. Many people limit their understanding of sex to mean "sexual intercourse." A couple might share an intimate dinner, walk hand-in-hand along the banks of a romantic canal, make out in the hot tub under a full moon, go to bed without having sexual intercourse, and then wake up the next morning thinking that they *didn't have sex last night.*

However, as any Sex 101 teacher will tell you, sex encompasses much more than intercourse. Your sexuality is part of who you are, how you feel about yourself as a man or woman: *Do you feel sexy?* It is part of what you think and feel about sex: *Do you radiate a sense of sexual attraction to and for your partner?* It's about how you and your partner choose to express your sexuality, what you do, and how you do it: *What kinds of sexual activity do you engage in?* This covers everything from gazing into each other's eyes and holding hands to oral sex and intercourse. When we talk about your sex life, we refer to all of that. When we talk about having sex, we mean touching, kissing, and genital touching as well as intercourse, orgasm, and afterplay. Start thinking about your sexuality in terms of whatever turns you on and whatever turns on your partner, and you'll have a much more accurate and applicable understanding and vision of sex.

To broaden your personal understanding of sex and how it relates to you and your partner, explore your impression of yourself and your partner as sexual beings by answering the following questions:

- How do you feel about your body? Do you feel sexy?
- How do you feel about your partner's body? Does anything in particular about your partner's body turn you on or turn you off?
- How do you feel about your current sexual activity with your partner? Do you feel as though you're able to adequately please your partner? Do you feel as though your partner is capable of pleasing you?
- How do you feel about your partner outside the bedroom? Do you feel sexual energy between the two of you?

Again, refrain from overanalyzing yourself or your relationship. These questions and your answers to them are merely a way of helping you to increase your awareness of your own sexuality as it relates to you and your relationship.

you're not alone

B ill (in his mid 30s) and Susan (in her late 20s) had been married for five years. They had begun to suspect that maybe they were sexually incompatible. According to Bill, Susan was insatiable, a nymphomaniac. She wanted sex all the time, even on days when he worked 10 to 12 hours. He couldn't possibly satisfy Susan. Susan thought Bill was frigid and suspected that perhaps he just didn't find her attractive anymore. He seemed more interested in playing poker with his buddies than in having sex with her. By the time they sought therapy, both of them were pretty pessimistic about the future of their relationship.

The therapist first informed Bill and Susan that they might be experiencing a very common phenomenon called *desire discrepancy*. One person in the relationship desires sex way more than the other person. (In nearly every long-term relationship there is some level of desire discrepancy.) A substantial discrepancy can cause all sorts of problems, including anxiety, fear of abandonment, guilt, jealousy, and bitterness. Just hearing that what they were experiencing was normal was a great relief to both of them.

To determine whether Bill and Susan did have significantly different levels of sexual desire, the therapist asked each of them how often they wanted to have sex. Susan wanted it daily, whereas Bill wanted it once a week. The therapist pointed out that both of their desires were well within the normal range of between once a day and once a month. This comforted them even more and made their differences seem manageable—issues that they could negotiate.

Simply having the right information to work with can do wonders to bring a sexual relationship back from the brink.

Reassessing "Normal" and "Average"

When you hear that the average family in the United States has 1.5 children, you can begin to realize just how absurd and useless are the terms *normal* and *average* when applied to individuals. The term *average* is a generality that describes a broad range of whatever it is applied to: frequency of sex, duration of sex, penis size, and so on. The meaning of *normal* is even more relative and obscure. *Normal* can apply to anything within the range of acceptable human behavior as defined by a particular community at a particular time. *Normal* can mean anything that is within the range of what a therapist or doctor defines as not needing treatment.

Of course, we can't just ditch the terms *normal* and *average,* because they do provide *descriptive* generalizations. They become problematic, though, when people use them *prescriptively* to evaluate themselves, their partners, or their sex lives. To make matters worse, people commonly have exaggerated notions of what's "average" and "normal." A couple might seek counseling because they're not having enough sex, thinking it's normal to have sex at least three times a week. When they learn that the normal range lies between once a day and once a month, they're pleasantly shocked. It usually lets the air out of the anxiety balloon that's been hanging over them and enables them to give up the notion that their sex life is deficient. So, what else is normal? Here are a few examples:

- It is normal for men to have an orgasm during just about every sex act and for women to have orgasms sometimes.
- It is normal to think about other things or fantasize about being with other partners during sex rather than focusing on your partner in the present moment.
- It is normal for your arousal level to fluctuate greatly during any given sexual encounter.
- It is normal for a man to lose his erection at times for reasons that have nothing to do with how turned on he is by his partner.
- It is normal for a woman to stop lubricating for no apparent reason.
- It is normal for sexual intercourse to last between three and fifteen minutes.
- It is normal for sexual desire to wax and wane in a long-term relationship.

- It is normal to need more physical and psychological stimulation to arouse you when you get older than you did when you were younger.
- And here's the biggie: It is normal in a long-term relationship to think that your sex life is disappointing!

The trick here is to make the terms *normal* and *average* work *for* you instead of against you. Use them to scrub away unrealistic expectations.

Moving Beyond Normal

Who really wants a *normal* sex life, anyway? Normal is boring. It's "just good enough." In this book, we hope to move you beyond normal to ecstatic. We provide the information and techniques you need to experience sexuality in a higher range we call *healthy* sex with frequent peaks that bring you and your partner to the level of what you will experience as great sex and what we call *sexual ecstasy*.

With healthy sex, you and your partner feel good about yourselves and each other before, during, and after sexual activity. Sex is no longer a competition in which you need to outperform unrealistic ideals or conquer your lover. Sex becomes free of conflict within yourselves or between the two of you over what you want or what you do. And when conflicts do arise (and they will), you and your partner are committed to resolving them quickly so you can return to the joy of pleasuring each other. This will become your norm, and there will be no downside.

When sex is healthy, issues such as how often you do it, what positions you do it in, and the types of sexual activities you engage in are not sources of discomfort for either of you. They become precious opportunities to explore and express your love for one another in different and, most importantly, in pleasurable ways. When sex is healthy, you and your partner are focused on the primary and very simple reason for having sex—pleasure.

Understanding "Sexual Ecstasy"

The concept of "sexual ecstasy" is intentionally ambiguous. It means and should mean different things to different individuals and couples. However, it does suggest a very broad concept of the blinding joy a person feels when he or she has the ultimate sexual encounter. To get a feel for what most people consider "sexual ecstasy," we asked people what it means to them. Here is a sample of their responses:

- "When I totally lose track of time during sex."
- "The first time I ever made love to my husband."
- "When I feel bliss after we've made love."
- "Receiving great oral sex."
- "The feeling I get when I've truly satisfied my partner."
- "A rare occasion when for reasons I don't fully understand sex is just extremely pleasurable—way more so than usual."
- "When my mind and my body are in complete sync with my partner during sex."
- "Doing something novel or new that really works."
- "When I feel time stops and I want to stay in that moment forever with my husband and for a couple of days afterwards everything just seems right between us."
- "Sex when there's a little bit of risk involved."
- "Feeling loved and turned on at the same time."

Then we asked a number of the experts on human sexuality, in addition to Albert Ellis, for their definitions of sexual ecstasy. Here is a sampling:

It is sex that gives you far-out pleasurable sensations and beautiful images, and puts you in an almost trance-like state, which is virtually the highest form of consciousness where you transcend all of that which is present.

—Arnold Lazarus, Ph.D.; psychologist; author, *Marital Myths Revisited*

Sexual ecstasy in my mind is when two people have a spiritual meeting of the mind, body, and soul. I look at good sex as a matter of technique. Anyone can learn soft touch, hard touch, fast touch. The difference between good sex and great sex is this chemistry.

—Alex Robboy, M.S.W.; sex therapist; founder, howtohavegoodsex.com

In my professional experience, very often it's hard for couples to achieve sexual ecstasy because they have a mistaken view of what they're looking for. Rather than kinky positions or sexy lingerie, what seems to produce an ecstatic experience is a profound sense of peace. Most of us have no experience of peace while we're having sex.

—David Schnarch, Ph.D.; clinical psychologist; director, Marriage and Family Health Center in Evergreen, Colorado; author, *Passionate Marriage* and *Resurrecting Sex*

GET PSYCHED

"Sex is exciting only when it is a subtle and pervasive part of the relationship between men and women, varying in its form from adolescence to old age and it dies only with death, if it is properly nourished in life." –Pearl Buck

Two sexual beings joined by intimacy. To be sexual for some is a matter of relaxation, technique, variety, risk-taking, breaking routine—waking up your brain. But for others, it may mean a change of diet or lifestyle. There is a strong physical component, which has to do with hormones and neurotransmitters and has to do with our lifestyle, not just being intimate.

—Pat Love, Ed.D.; marital therapist; author, *Hot Monogamy*

Your Sexual Attitude

An important aspect of sexual ecstasy hinges on your ability to examine yourself and your relationship without blaming yourself or your partner. This is no small feat. Humans have a natural tendency when they spot trouble to look for a cause, point it out, and dwell on it—to blame themselves or their partners and feel worse about it. So let's do some honest (and admittedly painful) self-exploration to bypass this tendency. How many of the following statements do you agree with?

- Every sensible and intelligent person is comfortable about sex.
- All touching between my partner and me should lead to sexual intercourse.
- Good sex is always spontaneous.
- Great sex occurs only when we have simultaneous orgasms.
- Men have stronger sexual urges than women.
- If you love or are highly attracted to someone, you should want sex with that person all the time.
- In sex, performance counts most.

These are some of the most common myths about sex. And, by definition, they are all incorrect. Throughout the book, we offer you numerous ideas and strategies to dispel them so that they never again undermine your pleasure. At this point, simply realize that to the extent you harbor them, they are free to wreak havoc. Cutting them loose is a choice you are free to make, and one you will not regret.

WEB TALK: For accurate, reliable information about sex, explore the Sexuality Information and Education Council of the U.S. (SIECUS) website at: www.siecus.com

Assessing Your Relationship

Successful long-term relationships are about much more than sex. They require love, trust, mutual respect and understanding, clear and honest communication, sharing of values and visions, cooperation, dedication, commitment, a willingness to compromise, and a host of other emotional and interpersonal skills. If your relationship is missing some of these essentials, we will show you the benefits of addressing them with vigilance. After all, the

15

relationship problems you bring into the bedroom can climb in between your sheets and wedge themselves between you and your partner like a 600-pound gorilla.

If you and your partner are experiencing serious disagreements about issues other than sex, and you seem to have reached an impasse, seek professional counseling. An astute therapist can help you identify and deal with issues one at a time, so they don't become overwhelming, and can help you work out acceptable compromises. As a bonus, the process of working through problems with your partner can help you hone your communication skills, foster mutual respect, strengthen your dedication and commitment, help you understand each other, and bring your individual visions closer. This can have an amazingly positive effect on your sex life.

What You Can Do

The following are some exercises you can try as you begin your journey towards sexual ecstasy. If your partner is receptive, have him or her complete the exercises alone or with you. If not, do the exercises alone; but keep in mind that as the book progresses, you will get many ideas about how to bring your partner on board.

☐ Identify the sexual myths that are getting in the way of your sexual pleasure. What are some of the likely sources of these myths? How can you remove these myths and obstacles from your sex life?

☐ Reflect on how your upbringing may be connected to certain attitudes and beliefs you may have today about sex. Ask yourself a simple question: Do these beliefs and attitudes support me/us or not? If the answer is no, then your task is to let go of those that don't.

☐ In private, write down your own personal definition of sexual ecstasy. Ask your partner to do the same, in private. Share what you have written. If your views of sexual ecstasy differ, begin to discuss ways in which you can reconcile any differences.

☐ Identify at least one other source or type of information that could help you to resolve questions that you have regarding sex and your sexual potential.

☐ If possible, identify at least one non–sex-related issue in your relationship that could possibly be hindering sexual pleasure.

Letting It Happen Versus Making It Happen

Today's society is goal-oriented. People set career goals, financial goals, self-improvement goals, you name it. So, it's tempting to set goals for sex—perhaps a goal to have sex at least three times a week, or to experience simultaneous orgasms. However, sexual satisfaction is the one area of your life that does *not* benefit from this goal setting. In fact, trying too hard can even undermine sexual pleasure.

Achieving sexual ecstasy does require effort, but the effort involved will focus you on pleasure, getting comfortable with your sexuality, and feeling connected to your partner, not on performance goals. Pleasure can't be forced, but we will show you how to enhance and expand it.

Sexual ecstasy is quite simple and is well within the reach of you and your partner—assuming both of you want it and are willing to work on it together. This chapter shows you how to let it happen by assembling the basic ingredients for sexual satisfaction at its best and identifying the personal and relationship areas that need enhancement. Here, you learn a new approach to sexuality that can help make your mind and body more receptive to the scintillating pleasures that you and your partner are about to experience. This new approach is the essence of breaking through from good sex to great sex!

The Right Ambience

The key to letting sexual ecstasy happen is to create and foster an atmosphere in which you and your partner become receptive to your own and to each other's pleasures. In such an environment, you feel pleasure without reservation, free yourself from worries about the past or present, become more in tune with your senses, connect intimately to your partner, and learn how to use your desires and fantasies to generate that healthy sex drive we call *lust*.

These are the five ingredients for sexual ecstasy:

- Giving yourself permission to experience pleasure
- Fully experiencing the present moment
- Connecting to and with your partner
- Experiencing sensual pleasures, inside and outside your bedroom
- Using your turn-ons to generate lust

PsychSpeak

Lust is your sex drive, which is produced by your body's response to a stimulus and your mind's attitude about it. Lust varies for all of us over time and from one person to another.

The sections that follow explore each ingredient in greater detail. As you proceed, keep in mind that all of these ingredients are not *required* and they can be present in varying degrees. The more of the ingredients you can incorporate and the higher degree to which you can incorporate each, the more fulfilling your lovemaking will be.

Giving Yourself Permission You probably permit yourself to experience a wide range of personal pleasures—a tasty dinner, a relaxing jog, a hot bath, a good book, whatever it is you enjoy. When it comes to sex, though, you might feel a tinge of guilt or shame. You might feel selfish for wanting sex too often or self-conscious because of a pleasurable fantasy about something you consider outside social norms. Often the guilt might be so strong that it stops you from becoming aware of what makes you feel good.

Giving yourself permission means freeing yourself of guilt, self-consciousness, and self-judgment, accepting your body, and giving it permission to feel pleasure. It means letting yourself think pleasurable thoughts, no matter what anyone else might believe about those thoughts, and letting yourself experiment with different things that make you feel sexual pleasure.

Here as well as in other chapters, we will help you identify any sexual inhibitions that might be acting as obstacles to your experience of sexual ecstasy. If you recognize that you'd be better off without certain inhibitions, take these steps toward giving yourself permission:

> ### GET PSYCHED
>
> "Sex is a natural function. You can't make it happen, but you can teach people to let it happen."
> –Dr. William Masters, pioneer sex researcher

1. Identify the thought or act that turns you on. Include anything that comes between the way you are and the way you would like to be, the way you feel and the way you would like to feel.

2. List any and all obstacles that stand between you and the pleasure you identified. Ask yourself what useful purpose it serves in your life and in your relationship.

3. Remove the obstacles. Take as many steps as necessary to overcome your inhibitions and try something different. We will continue to address the most common (and sometimes tenacious) obstacles and show you just how you can remove them so they no longer interfere with your pleasure. Commit yourself to becoming free of any obstacles that might be preventing you from giving yourself permission.

Experiencing the Moment Think of a time when you were so engaged in something that nothing else even occurred to you. You were not thinking about whether you were hungry, what you were going to do later, or what happened five minutes ago or will happen next. When you are completely connected to

21

the present moment, time stops; your anxieties and stresses dissipate; and you may even feel the soft glow of a joyful awakening. This is because for that moment you were able to let go of past hurts, disappointments, regrets, and any haunting concerns about the future.

Chapter 4 will discuss several strategies for putting yourself in this frame of mind more often, but here is a simple exercise you can try right now: Close your eyes and spend one minute concentrating on absolutely nothing but your breathing. Don't breathe any differently, just be aware of your breath going in and going out. Of course, you can use this very basic meditative technique for as long as you like, but after you've done it for a minute, notice how you feel. If you can stay in the moment, chances are you will experience a feeling of calm. When you bring this same type of "present moment" focus to sexual activity, you're likely to experience those great emotions and sensations of sexual connection more intensely.

Connecting to Your Partner Sexual pleasure at its best results from connecting to and with your partner in a way that lets you feel safe and secure. Think of a moment when your partner was the center of your universe. This could be the very first time you became attracted to each other, the first time you made love, or a time when you decided to make a long-term commitment to each other. Perhaps nothing came between you, and you were at peace in the presence of one another. You felt pure love and excitement, untainted by extraneous thoughts or emotions.

Now try to feel *empathy* for your partner. Tune in to the way your partner feels and feels about things—both physically and emotionally, inside and outside the bedroom. The understanding that comes from the empathy you feel opens the channels of

PsychSpeak

Empathy is understanding how another person feels. In the bedroom, this can mean knowing what excites and arouses your partner—and what doesn't. Outside the bedroom, empathy is knowing what your partner's experience is or feelings are at any given moment about something specific.

communication, enabling you and your partner to talk to one another more freely. Partners who can openly communicate their feelings, emotions, desires, and preferences almost always have better sex than those who don't.

As David Schnarch, Ph.D., clinical psychologist and author of *Resurrecting Sex: Solving Sexual Problems & Revolutionizing Your Relationship,* explains, "The essence of great sex lies not in mastering specific sexual skills or reducing sexual performance anxiety or having regular orgasms, but in the ability to allow oneself to deeply know and be deeply known by one's partner. People often have difficulty with long-term sexual relationships because they repress their fears of not being accepted or acceptable, of losing what they love, and of exposing everything within them that is vulnerable and helpless." Intimacy requires courage to become more open, and empathy to enable your partner to feel safe enough to open up to you.

Enhance your *intimacy* with your partner right now by taking the small risk of talking about something you may have felt silly about or uncomfortable discussing previously—for example, something you secretly worry about (only you know what it is), a dream or vision you haven't shared, or even something your partner doesn't know that he or she does to make you feel pleasure. Keep it light, at least until you read Chapter 7 in which you will learn techniques for establishing the intimacy and trust necessary to communicate effectively about more difficult issues.

PsychSpeak

Intimacy is a feeling of closeness and acceptance that enables two people to freely communicate without the fear of being judged or ridiculed.

Being silly and playful together is another form of intimacy. Sex, after all, can be a form of adult play. Couples who play and laugh together in ways other than sex may find that sex becomes better as well. Couples who build on this almost always find that their connection both in and out of the bedroom improves dramatically. Don't take your sex life so seriously that you turn it into a chore, a bargaining chip, a source of anxiety, or a power trip. Keep it fun.

you're not alone

Barbara and Tim, a couple in their 40s who have been married for 20 years, had some problems at the beginning of their relationship. Tim had been married before, but his wife left him for another man. Tim had rapid ejaculations at first, but they worked it out. Barbara had a problem pregnancy and was unable to have intercourse for six months. And Tim's daughter from his previous marriage was quite a handful. Throughout it all, they stayed together and worked through their problems.

When asked about their sex life, Barbara and Tim smiled lovingly at each other. They say that sexual ecstasy is something they experience often. Explaining why their sex life is so good, Barbara said, "Well, we see sex as fun. We're flexible. We're creative and we don't take ourselves too seriously." Tim chimed in, "Yes, especially as we've gotten older, we both let go of anxiety and the pressure to perform. We know it's not going to be great every time, but we both care about each other and care about pleasing each other. So if something doesn't work, it's really no big deal." Barbara added, smiling, "Also, you kind of learn to compromise a lot and we just don't get angry at each other very often. That seems to make things easier in bed."

A Sensuous Experience Think about what makes your body feel wonderful—perhaps a great massage, a whirlpool bath, the taste of chocolate, the aroma of a favorite fragrance, the sight of a beautiful painting, the sound of your favorite song, or the way your partner feels when you cuddle up. Think of these sensory pleasures as your nongenital stimulants. The key to this exercise is for you and your partner to identify what heightens each of your senses. By knowing what stimulates you and your partner's senses, you can begin to focus on maximizing these sensory stimulants and introduce new ones into your lovemaking.

Avoid making the common mistake of assuming that your partner likes what you like. For example, you might both truly enjoy touch, but one of you likes to be touched softly (almost like being tickled) whereas the other enjoys a harder or firmer touch. A great way to enhance the sensual

GET PSYCHED

"I recently convinced my husband to use aftershave every time we make love, and I love it. I find it a real turn on. I've found that the little things can make a big difference for me."
—*Rachael, age 36*

24

part of your lovemaking is to exchange massages—with the receiver giving detailed yet loving instructions as to how he or she wants to be touched. This develops physical empathy, which is crucial for maximizing pleasure during lovemaking. We will talk more about this in later chapters, and many exercises throughout the book will help you enhance your sensual connection.

Doing What Turns You On One of the challenges of achieving sexual ecstasy is to discover what each of you really wants sexually, what makes you feel lustful, and then to communicate those desires to each other in some way. The term *lust* carries unjustifiably negative connotations. People mistakenly view it as a sinful, self-indulgent emotion. We prefer to think of lust as healthy sexual desire—a desire that arouses you and helps you to appreciate yourself as a sexual being. In this more positive light, lust becomes a very important ingredient in achieving sexual ecstasy for you and between you and your partner. In several chapters, we provide you many strategies and exercises to help you and your partner explore and communicate your sexual turn-ons.

> **GET PSYCHED**
>
> "Sex is such a powerful tie that binds two people, that we have to know, care about, and honor our spouse's feelings about the sexuality we share together." –Michele Weiner-Davis, M.S.W., marital therapist and author of The Sex-Starved Marriage

Now, Let It Happen

Let's take this one step further. The most important secret of sexual ecstasy is that you cannot force great sex or ecstasy or make it happen. You have to *allow* it to happen by incorporating as many of the five ingredients as possible and then letting the ecstatic feelings overtake you. That's right. You and your partner can begin to enjoy sexual ecstasy immediately. Once the ingredients are in place, the less you try to *make* ecstasy happen, the more it will evolve.

Think of a time when you got into bed and tried to make yourself sleep because you needed to awaken early the next day. Were you successful? Probably not. The same can be said of sexual ecstasy. If you try to have great orgasms, to be in the mood a certain number of times per week, or to make each sexual encounter better, longer, or deeper than the last, the pressure to perform itself can be the very thing that stands in the way of getting what you seek. And even if you did meet your expectations sometimes, your lovemaking could become less about play and more about pressure.

GET PSYCHED

In 1992, the National Opinion Research Center interviewed 3,432 scientifically selected men and women and found that people married or living together experienced their sex lives as the most physically and emotionally satisfying.

Focus on being in the moment without expectations. If you must have a goal, make it pleasure, not performance. Practically any willing couple can have *pleasure* in just about every sexual encounter. *Performance* is different: The body can't be willed to deliver an erection or to lubricate on cue, nor can you expect every sexual experience to be ecstatic. But if you let go of your expectations, you'll find some form of pleasure just about every time you seek it.

Great Sex Begins with Good Sex and the Right Relationship

Our approach to sexual ecstasy assumes that you are in a good relationship with some degree of sexual satisfaction. If this is not the case, you might want to skip ahead to Part 3 to identify and address any potential issues that might be blocking the way. Then, come back to this point to learn the difference between long- and short-term relationships and explore the various reasons why your sexual relationship with your partner might have lost a little of its sizzle and spark.

Why the Initial Passion Passed Think back to when you and your partner first met. Recall how you interacted and felt toward one another. Try to replay the feelings and excitement that your partner's presence evoked. Achieving ecstasy was probably a fairly effortless task. You might even say that you and your partner had the right chemistry. So, what happened?

26

According to sexual anthropologist Helen Fisher, Ph.D., gradual changes in brain chemistry over the course of a relationship commonly, and quite naturally, lead to diminished passion. Fisher and her colleagues studied individuals in the initial "falling in love" phase and found that their brains were saturated with the chemical dopamine, a neurotransmitter. This chemical, the researchers believed, produced that rush of energy and infatuation common in the early stages of love. This explains the effortless feelings of sexual ecstasy you might have experienced in the very beginning of a relationship. Early in a relationship, you don't usually need an approach for achieving sexual ecstasy, but as your relationship evolves, our model provides you with conscious steps for bringing ecstasy back into your relationship.

WEB TALK: To find out more about the physiology of both romance and long-term relationships, check out Helen Fisher's website at:

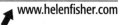 **www.helenfisher.com**

Fisher believes that three different systems in the brain affect the way you experience love. Each system appears to be connected to different brain chemicals. Levels of these chemicals can change, thus influencing the type of love you're feeling:

- Lust (sexual desire) is associated with the chemical testosterone.
- Attraction (which she defines as romantic or obsessive love) is associated with the neurotransmitter dopamine.
- Attachment (sense of security and bonding in a long-term relationship) is associated with the chemicals oxytocin and vasopressin.

As your relationship evolves (and you age), your chemistry naturally changes; testosterone and dopamine levels tend to dip while oxytocin levels (in the woman) and vasopressin levels (in the man) might increase. The net result for some relationships is attachment at the expense of lust and attraction. This might seem like one of

GET PSYCHED

Dr. Sue Carter and her colleagues in their work with prairie voles found that oxytocin seems to be the neurotransmitter that enhances pair bonding and monogamy in the species.

life's cruel jokes, but it is actually one of nature's well-crafted plans. Lust and attraction bring two creatures together, and attachment keeps them together through the long and difficult process of building a deep, interpersonal relationship and (if they choose) raising offspring.

Although diminished levels of sexual desire are very common in long-term sexual relationships, it is important to realize that more couples in long-term relationships report a higher level of sexual satisfaction than single people or couples in short-term sexual relationships. The point here is that although you might feel less sexually satisfied now, your sexual relationship with your partner has the potential to become much more conducive to sexual ecstasy on an ongoing basis.

Can I have those wonderful feelings of being in love once I'm in a long-term relationship?

"Of course you can have that romantic feeling again. You just have to trick the brain a little. The reason is that if you're in a long-term relationship with another human being, you probably have high levels of attachment chemicals in you that are suppressing the kinds of chemicals that give you that elation of romance. So you have to work at it. To recapture the romantic feeling, you need to trigger those 'romance' chemicals; and a good way to do that is to engage in new activities with your partner. Novelty is associated with elevated levels of brain chemicals that are linked with elation, arousal, euphoria, and romantic love. So, if you do novel things with your partner on a regular basis, you can begin to once again stimulate some of that brain chemistry.

"One of the reasons that people really can fall back in love on a vacation is because so much is novel. And thus it's exciting. But it's not just about taking vacations. Go to a different kind of restaurant once a week. Wear different clothes at dinner. Go to the theater. If you live in the city and hear a parade, dash out and watch it for a little while. Do something unexpected, something exciting, and also, something a little bit risky. I don't mean skydiving. I mean a walk in the woods—taking a new direction where you're not quite sure where it will lead."
—*Helen Fisher, Ph.D., author of* Why We Love

Short-Term Versus Long-Term Relationships Yes, initial passion can be delicious. But if you stick around long enough, you may discover that it's possible to achieve a higher level of sexual pleasure; your sexuality becomes fueled not only by natural desires but also by the strong feelings that develop between the two of you over the course of your relationship. People who seem to go from one short-term relationship to another are usually to some extent addicted to initial passion. When initial passion begins to diminish, it can feel quite natural to assume that the relationship has fizzled out at that point, and many decide it's time to bolt. Virtually every couple experiences this decrease in initial passion to some degree; that's why it's referred to as *initial* passion.

This waning of excitement can occur after only a few weeks or months, or after a couple has moved in together or married. It's not uncommon for panic to kick in because of the tendency to assume that sexual desire is gone forever. In reality, the waning of initial passion is a common sign that it's time for the couple to focus conscious attention on parts of their relationship that were once automatic—like sexual excitement.

Everyone's greatest fantasy is to have a partner who will continually trigger that feeling of passion. The truth is, no one can make you feel anything that you did not already have the capacity to feel. In other words, the feelings of love, infatuation, passion, or lust that you attribute to someone else are produced *within* you. Your partner simply triggers them. The challenge for each couple is to decide whether the relationship is worth pursuing once it requires effort. If you and your partner recognize that you are beginning another phase of your relationship and make the mutual commitment to stay together, then by our definition you are in a *long-term relationship*.

Q&A

What is the difference between love and infatuation?

Infatuation can be extremely intense. But infatuation decreases as you get to know that person better. On the other hand, love usually increases as you get to know the other person better. Love is part of your connection to a specific person, while infatuation pertains to the climate of romance. Infatuation is tantamount to falling in love with love. Long-term relationships often elude those who confuse infatuation with love, because they don't stick around and allow love to grow when infatuation wanes.

Transitioning to a Long-Term Relationship Successfully transitioning from a short-term relationship to a long-term relationship is usually easier if a couple knows what to expect. William Stayton, Th.D., Ph.D., and professor and director of the Human Sexuality Program at Widener University, explains that over time, relationships become less about nurturing one another and more about maintaining the relationship. According to Professor Stayton, "When people meet, they usually give 100 percent to nurturance and almost nothing to maintenance. As their relationship progresses, the balance shifts. During dating or an engagement period, nurturance might be 80 percent and maintenance 20 percent. When the couple actually move in together or get married, the maintenance goes up, the nurturance goes down, and all too often what happens is that they get so caught up making a living, taking care of the home, raising children, and so on, that's required to keep everything going, they get to where it's 100 percent maintenance and 0 percent nurturance."

To rekindle the excitement, Stayton recommends that couples who are busy maintaining their lives together focus on nurturing, as well. Couples can become

GET PSYCHED

"If you give up longing for the high of falling in love you can really love being in a committed relationship, and sex while different can be so much better, but you have to stop looking for what you had." *–Pat Love, Ed.D., marital therapist and author of* Hot Monogamy more attentive to one another's needs on a day-to-day basis and make their sexuality a more central part of their relationship rather than "an addendum to a busy day." Stayton advises that couples set aside time for sex at different times to give their sexual relationship a sense of importance.

you're not alone

Keeping a Marriage Fresh

Linda and Bill have been married for 25 years, with two grown children, and still enjoy each other very much sexually. I asked them how they keep their passion alive. Bill said, "We stay closely in touch with each other's feelings and moods. If I feel distant I'll tell Linda and we'll talk about it." Linda added, "At first it felt risky to talk about my feelings, but now I can't imagine it any other way. We have a definite need to be near and close to each other because we each find it nourishing. Being open, we have developed a level of trust that certainly wasn't there at the beginning."

Both Linda and Bill assured me that theirs isn't a storybook romance either. Bill admitted, "We don't have sex as often as we once did, but we are just as affectionate. If one of us isn't into it, we won't let it be a problem. Neither of us feels rejected or too sensitive about it. It took us a long time but we feel no shame with each other and we constantly experiment. We rarely let anger hold over to the next day and we don't attempt sex when we're angry." According to Linda, "We've been through some tough periods and without that communication we wouldn't have made it this far. But now I can't imagine anything we couldn't handle."

Some of the other discoveries that Linda and Bill found helpful include beginning their foreplay before entering the bedroom, when possible. (Sometimes you can prolong the anticipation of sex for hours beforehand, by flirting with each other, talking sexy, dancing, or doing anything else that puts you in the mood.) They also sincerely compliment each other's bodies—both verbally and by doing a lot of touching—and have often gone to motels for the sole purpose of lovemaking when it was difficult to relax with the kids at home. Linda and Bill demonstrate a dynamic that almost any couple can achieve if they are willing to focus on pleasure and attend to using communication to keep sex in their long-term relationship fresh.

If you are in a relationship in which the initial passion is starting to fade, and you're weighing your options to decide whether or not you want to stay together, here are some things to consider:

- Expect change. Remember, it's normal for sexual passion to wax and wane. Sex may not be as spontaneous, but that is okay. Diminished passion alone is not necessarily a reason to bolt. Things will get better if you both want them to and you work on your issues together.

- Try adding some variety to your sex life. This is a time to experiment—and enjoy it! Start by making a small change to your lovemaking, add music or a candle, change the room or time of day you usually make love.

- Talk, talk, talk about your feelings, about each other, about what you like and don't like sexually, and about your sexual fantasies and how you might like to play them out in novel ways.

- Keep your eyes on the prize. Long-term relationships can experience some ups and downs. But if the two of you are willing to do what it takes, the rewards can be enormous.

GET PSYCHED

Marvin Zuckerman, Ph.D. professor emeritus, Department of Psychology, University of Delaware and author of *Behavioral Expressions and Biosocial Bases of Sensation Seeking* and creator of the first sensation-seeking scale, describes sensation seeking as a biologically determined personality trait that describes the tendency to seek new, novel, and intense sensations and experiences. As with all personality traits, individuals can be high, low, or somewhere in the middle. High-sensation seekers crave more novelty and variation in sexual activity. High-sensation seekers may dive right into the pool. Low-sensation seekers may need to slowly wade in the shallow end.

Abandoning Your Comfortable State of Discomfort

A comfortable state of discomfort is otherwise known as a rut. As you know, it's possible to hit a rut in virtually any area of your life. Your job can feel monotonous, the same foods can become flavorless, and chitchat over the same old topics can become quite boring. So it's easy to see how a sexual relationship that was once spontaneous, passionate, and fulfilling can start to feel like just another domestic chore.

Instead of doing something as drastic as abandoning the relationship, consider abandoning your rut. Leave your sexual comfort zone behind and realize that, even in a good relationship, sex might require some conscious effort. By now you understand it is a myth that sex can stay on automatic pilot and still remain hot. Go beyond what has become routine. Acknowledge that it is not only okay but crucial to tell each other what you need and desire sexually.

> **GET PSYCHED**
>
> Don't be afraid to experiment and explore. Your sexuality can be a wonderful journey. Your notion of sexual ecstasy will change—not just in the long term but day to day, as well.

What You Can Do

We give you many exercises, strategies, and techniques in later chapters to enhance your capacity for sexual ecstasy. Our approach involves simple steps, but remember that *simple* doesn't necessarily mean *easy*. Keeping that in mind, here are a few steps you and your partner can take, both individually and together, to begin your quest towards sexual ecstasy:

- ☐ List at least six novel things you might like in your next sexual encounter with your partner—for example, a scented candle, a different position, a different room, music.

- ☐ Read through your list and identify one thing you could introduce into your lovemaking, on your own, that you're not too reluctant to try.

- ☐ If you feel comfortable sharing your likes with your partner, have your partner list some of his or her likes. Then exchange lists.

- ☐ If you and your partner exchanged lists, identify one item from each of your lists that you would be willing to include in your next lovemaking session and follow through with them.

- ☐ Set aside time to talk to your partner about what each of you considers the best sex you've ever had with each other. Learn ways to include elements to revitalize that excitement now.

- [ ] List the things that heighten each of your six senses: touch, taste, smell, sight, hearing, and the feeling of body movement. If you are doing this with your partner, use the list your partner made as a valuable frame of reference when pleasuring him or her.
- [ ] Set aside some time to be with your partner in a nonsexual way. Lie naked holding each other, without talking. Without any goals or expectations, experience what you feel in your body, and what your partner's body feels like to you.
- [ ] Stand together with your partner, face to face, for 30 seconds. Focus on your breathing and on being fully engaged in the present moment. Next, focus on your partner. Notice three things about your partner that you would normally overlook: the color of his eyes, her scent, or even what he is wearing. Then embrace—staying connected in the present moment.

Taking an Inventory of Your Sex Life

Before embarking on your journey to sexual ecstasy, it's a good idea to know where you are sexually and as a couple, as well as where you want to be. In this chapter, we invite you and your partner to take an inventory of your sex life to identify areas that you have mastered, areas that need a little work, and areas that require a major overhaul, and also the skills and resources you already have that can help you in your quest. Moreover, what you learn from your inventory can assist you and your partner in creating a shared vision of what sexual ecstasy means for each of you, so you can have a destination in mind before you start.

Following the inventory, we provide you the information you need to assess your responses, and we point the way to chapters where you can find additional information, suggestions, and strategies that can help you proceed from your unique point of departure to your unique destination.

A Sexual Satisfaction Inventory

The sexual satisfaction inventory that follows provides a way for you and your partner to gather information about the condition of your sexual relationship as it is right now. We strongly recommend that you and your partner each take the inventory separately and in private, so you can each feel comfortable responding honestly, and then meet later to discuss your answers if that is your choice.

What one of you might think is working in the relationship, the other might think needs work. Copy the inventory or simply write the numbers 1 to 50 on a sheet of paper, and place a check mark next to the number of each statement that applies to you or your relationship. There's no score, so don't worry about passing, failing, outscoring, or underscoring your partner!

The section that follows the inventory explains the significance of each response (whether you thought a statement applied or did not apply to you or your relationship), provides some tips for dealing with any issues related to each item that you might think need some work, and refers you to chapters in this book where you can find additional information and suggestions relating to the particular topic or issue. Grab a pen or pencil, and let's get started!

- ☐ 1. I think of myself as sexy.
- ☐ 2. My orgasms are not as satisfying as they used to be.
- ☐ 3. I have fantasies I'd love to play out with my partner but don't dare ask.
- ☐ 4. I put myself down sometimes because of the way I look.
- ☐ 5. When we do anything sexual that's out of the ordinary, I feel guilty.
- ☐ 6. I often get distracted during sex with thoughts unrelated to sex.
- ☐ 7. I worry that I am not satisfying my partner.
- ☐ 8. I'm less interested in sex than I used to be.
- ☐ 9. My partner never initiates sex.
- ☐ 10. I wish my sex life were more exciting.
- ☐ 11. I certainly enjoy sex, but my partner wants it much more often than I do.
- ☐ 12. I always close my eyes during sex.
- ☐ 13. I don't feel comfortable asking my partner for what I want sexually.

☐ 14. I am not as attracted sexually to my partner as I used to be.

☐ 15. We're just not as romantic as we could be.

☐ 16. I've never been able to find my G spot.

☐ 17. My partner doesn't seem to like oral sex at all.

☐ 18. Our sex is usually spontaneous.

☐ 19. My sex life has enough novelty and variety for me.

☐ 20. I often fantasize about having sex with other people while having sex with my partner.

☐ 21. Sexual play normally leads to intercourse.

☐ 22. I don't know enough about what turns me on to be able to tell my partner.

☐ 23. I feel guilty when I find anyone other than my partner to be sexually attractive.

☐ 24. I love to talk during sex. My partner doesn't.

☐ 25. Ever since our child was born, sex has not been the same.

☐ 26. Sometimes I feel as though I *love* but I'm not *in love* with my partner.

☐ 27. Sex is my favorite way of connecting with my partner.

☐ 28. Sex is a great way to release tension.

☐ 29. I know just how to satisfy my partner sexually.

☐ 30. I often feel a spiritual connection during or after sex.

☐ 31. I often lose my erection/don't lubricate, during intercourse.

☐ 32. I know when my partner is interested in sex.

☐ 33. I love to be touched all over by my partner.

☐ 34. I love music and scented candles during sex.

☐ 35. I have definitely experienced sexual ecstasy.

☐ 36. I don't think I'm functioning well sexually.

☐ 37. I feel inhibited when I really try to let go sexually.

☐ 38. I am completely comfortable with my partner seeing me nude with the lights on.

☐ 39. My partner and I generally want the same amount of sex.

☐ 40. My partner always does for me what I enjoy the most during sex.

☐ 41. Sex sometimes bores me.

☐ 42. I am uncomfortable with some of my own sexual thoughts and fantasies.

☐ 43. Sometimes I'd like to initiate sex, but I don't.

☐ 44. We love to try new things sexually.

☐ 45. We are often way too busy to have sex.

☐ 46. My partner or I ejaculate way too quickly.

☐ 47. If I am angry with my partner, I will refuse sex.

☐ 48. I feel emotionally close to my partner during sex.

☐ 49. There are times when no matter what I do, I cannot get turned on.

☐ 50. My partner and I have a shared vision of what sexual ecstasy is.

Evaluating Your Inventory

Now, let's take a look at your answers and what they might mean. Remember, we're not interested in tallying the number of statements that each of you marked as applying to you or your partner or the relationship between the two of you. What's important is your response to each statement and what it reveals about a particular aspect of your sexuality and your sexual relationship, what sorts of suggestions can help you and your partner strengthen and enhance particular aspects of your relationship, and where you can look in this book for additional information, strategies, and suggestions.

1. I think of myself as sexy.

   Sexiness comes not from how you look but how you feel about yourself. If you feel sexy, then you're off to a great start. If something about your body bothers you, pay special attention to the exercises in Chapter 5. Do you feel that you're too old to be sexy? Chapter 14 addresses this. Does the word "sexy" seem to carry negative connotations to you? Then look to Chapter 4.

2. My orgasms are not as satisfying as they used to be.

   No one factor determines the "quality" of orgasms, so explore any and all possible reasons. Chapter 2 can help you form realistic expectations. Chapter 11 is entirely about maximizing orgasm; try some of the strategies and guidance that we give you there. If you still haven't found a solution, go to Chapter 14 to learn about possible causes and available solutions.

3. I have fantasies I'd love to play out with my partner but don't dare ask.

   In a vast majority of long-term relationships, you have much more to lose by not sharing a fantasy or communicating your desires than by choosing to share them. Chapter 6 provides a very extensive discussion of fantasy, and Chapter 8 talks about communicating your ecstatic desires. If you're comfortable with your fantasies, head to Chapter 9 to learn how to generate more ideas and begin not only sharing them but also playing them out.

4. I put myself down sometimes because of the way I look.

   In terms of sexual ecstasy, how you look is far less important than how you *feel about* the way you look. If this is an issue for you, Chapters 4 and 5 can help you achieve the kind of self-acceptance you might be looking for.

5. When we do anything sexual that's out of the ordinary, I feel guilty.

Giving yourself permission is a *crucial* component of sexual ecstasy. By giving yourself permission, we mean permission to do what turns you and your partner on in a consensual way and to let yourself be pleasured free of any self-consciousness. When guilt comes into play, it's usually because of some old belief or idea that's probably not valid anymore. You owe no loyalty to beliefs that produce guilt. Chapter 4 will help you to put this into perspective.

6. I often get distracted during sex with thoughts unrelated to sex.

   Focusing on the moment is one of the ingredients of sexual ecstasy. It enables you to give sensation and pleasure your full attention. Perhaps what you really need is more lead-in time to sexual activity—a period of time during which you relax more with your partner and let the focus be on just the two of you. If you keep your eyes closed during sex, try opening them. Also try talking to your partner or playing music—something that will distract you from your own distractions. You can find more tips on how to do this in Chapter 4.

7. I worry that I am not satisfying my partner.

   Until you ask your partner whether he or she is satisfied sexually, you probably don't know for sure, so ask your partner and then share your perceptions and feelings as well. Don't be afraid to do this. The issue of how to satisfy each other is something the two of you can talk about, and Chapter 8 will help you to open and maximize that dialogue.

8. I'm less interested in sex than I used to be.

   If you have noticed a gradual decrease in desire over the duration of your relationship, you might simply be experiencing the natural tapering off of initial passion. If that's the case, Chapter 2 can help you understand what's going on. Relationship issues or the stresses of everyday life might be a factor, in which case we send you first to Chapters 7 and 8 and then possibly to Chapter 13. Chapter 12 discusses specific sexual dysfunctions that can cause a lessening of desire. Or it might be a function of the aging process, as we discuss in Chapter 14.

9. My partner never initiates sex.

   If your partner never initiates sex, and you really want him or her to, it's important for you to talk to your partner about it. We provide strategies for opening a dialogue in Chapter 8. It's also possible that your partner does not initiate sex because you want to have sex a lot more than he or she does; if so, look to Chapter 13 where we discuss sexual desire discrepancy.

10. I wish my sex life were more exciting.

    Because novelty can do so much to enhance sexual satisfaction, many chapters in this book provide suggestions for discovering new ways of making love and relating romantically and sexually. Consider working on your fantasies, as explained in Chapter 6 and on communicating them, as explained in Chapter 8. Add more sensuality into your sex life by focusing on sensation, as explained in Chapters 9 and 10. Learn how to make more connection through breathing and eye contact in Chapter 11.

11. I certainly enjoy sex, but my partner wants it much more often than I do.

    Rarely do any two partners want exactly the same amount of sex in exactly the same way. This is an extremely common situation called sexual desire discrepancy, and we address it in Chapter 13. Talk about what sex means to both of you and how you can connect in ways that are satisfying for both of you, sexually and nonsexually. Refer to Chapters 7 and 8, as well.

12. I always close my eyes during sex.

    This is perfectly okay, but many couples find that burning a candle or turning on a lamp and keeping their eyes open, at least for part of the sexual activity, helps them feel more connected to their partners and more in the moment. Learning to breathe together can also provide an added enhancement. See Chapters 9, 10, and 11 for details and additional suggestions.

13. I don't feel comfortable asking my partner for what I want sexually.

    Few things can help improve sexual satisfaction more than communicating your desires and pleasures with your partner. If you're not giving yourself permission to want something, see Chapter 2. If you're thinking that your partner might not be receptive, see Chapter 8. Open a sexual dialogue with your partner by initiating it yourself. You might find that your partner leads the way and makes it a lot easier for you.

14. I am not as attracted sexually to my partner as I used to be.

    If the reason you feel less attracted to your partner is related to issues in your relationship, such as anger or loss of control, look to Chapter 13. Chapter 7 can help you establish a more romantic connection that often leads to sexual desire, and Chapter 14 can help you address any physiological changes, typically related to age, that might be leading to decreased desire.

15. We're just not as romantic as we could be.

    Many people need to feel a more romantic connection before they can begin to feel sexual desire toward their partners on a given day. Our suggestions in Chapter 7 can help you learn ways of becoming more romantically connected. Chapter 13 provides suggestions for how to reprioritize your life to give romance and sex the time they deserve.

16. I've never been able to find my G spot.

    Finding the G spot is not really that important, but it's perfectly okay to be curious about it. Refer to Chapter 10 for a discussion of the G spot and instructions on how to locate it. Keep in mind that not all women have an easily identifiable G spot and we're not even sure every woman actually has one at all, and even if you do find it, there's no promise that it will be the button that leads to ecstasy. Be open to exploring your whole body, as suggested in Chapters 5 and 10, to find as many of your body's pleasurable erotic spots as you can, and then see Chapter 8 to learn more about communicating them to your partner. Chapters 11 and 12 also have some information that you might find useful.

17. My partner doesn't seem to like oral sex at all.

    Oral sex, like anything else sexual, is a preference. If you want to explore oral sex, but your partner feels uncomfortable about it, find out specifically what makes your partner feel uncomfortable, and then refer to Chapter 10 for ways to approach oral sex that might help your partner become more receptive to it. If your partner still is reluctant, discuss other ways you can enhance your sex life together.

18. Our sex is usually spontaneous.

    As long as you and your partner are having satisfying sex, whether you plan for it or it spontaneously happens, it's okay. At the beginning of a relationship when it's just you and your partner and lots of free time, you can afford the luxury of spontaneous sex. When life gets a little busier and more complicated, however, spontaneity usually becomes more elusive. The suggestions in Chapter 13 can help you and your partner make time for sexual ecstasy.

19. My sex life has enough novelty and variety for me.

    Even if it does, why close yourself down to even more and better ideas? Use this book and your discussions with your partner to begin expanding your horizons. Let your fantasies lead to other fantasies, as suggested in Chapters 6, 10, and 11. Communicate your desires and what you find pleasurable, as we explain in Chapter 8. Try anything that you might be comfortable with that you haven't tried before.

20. I often fantasize about having sex with other people while having sex with my partner.

This is a very common fantasy. However, if it is a problem for you because you feel guilty or disconnected from your partner, there are several things you can do. Following the suggestions in Chapter 7 might help you feel a more romantic connection with your partner. Learning to discuss what you want sexually from one another, as explained in Chapter 8, might also help. You can also try making your fantasies a more integral part of your lovemaking, as suggested in Chapter 6.

21. Sexual play normally leads to intercourse.

This is fine, if it is not an issue for either of you, but if one of you likes to play sexually without always having it lead to intercourse, it can begin to limit affection and sexual expression. When this becomes a problem, it sometimes points to a sexual desire discrepancy, which we discuss in Chapter 13 or to inhibited sexual desire, covered in Chapter 12. Sometimes agreeing to take a brief hiatus from intercourse while remaining physically affectionate and engaging in other stimulating sexual activities can help.

22. I don't know enough about what turns me on to be able to tell my partner.

The suggestions we provide in Chapters 4, 5, and 10 can help you discover what arouses your mind and body. Follow the exercises in Chapter 6 to tap into your fantasies for information about what turns you on. Chapter 8 can help you teach your partner what you've learned.

23. I feel guilty when I find anyone other than my partner to be sexually attractive.

    Mental exclusivity is a myth. It's a very rare person who does not find some other members of the opposite sex to be attractive. Any guilt you feel may be the result of a very unfair demand that you are placing on yourself—that thoughts you have should just go away simply because you think you shouldn't have them. To read a little more about this phenomenon, look at Chapter 4, and remember that these thoughts are quite normal, so enjoy them.

24. I love to talk during sex. My partner doesn't.

    Talking or not talking during sex is a matter of preference. If you would like to explore this, start by talking to your partner outside the bedroom. Tell your partner that you find it pleasurable to talk during sex. Describe what it does for you. Sometimes just asking for things without explaining why can make it difficult for the other person to comprehend or be receptive to what you're asking. The suggestions in Chapter 8 can help you learn how to open the channels of communication and help you to work out a compromise.

25. Ever since our child was born, sex has not been the same.

    Pregnancy, birth, breastfeeding, and child rearing can all usher in significant changes to a relationship, both physiologically and psychologically. We address all of these issues in Chapter 14. Chapter 7 can help keep you more in tune with your romantic connection, Chapter 8 can assist in keeping the lines of communication open, and Chapter 13 can show you how to deal with time-crunch and space-crunch issues.

26. Sometimes I feel as though I *love* but am not *in love* with my partner.

    As partners become more comfortable with one another in a long-term relationship, the initial passion they felt earlier in the relationship might be replaced by a deeper and more meaningful form of love. Chapters 2 and 7 can help you understand and appreciate the differences in a long-term relationship. If you simply want to spice things up, you can find suggestions in nearly every chapter of this book on ways to do just that.

27. Sex is my favorite way of connecting with my partner.

Feeling a connection with your partner through love-making is very healthy. It can be problematic, however, if your partner feels differently and the two of you are in conflict with that. If you and your partner face issues along those lines, consider some of the strategies we offer in Chapters 7 and 8.

28. Sex is a great way to release tension.

For some people, sex is primarily a physical stress reliever, and that's fine as long as it works for you and your partner. But sex can be much more. Reaching sexual ecstasy involves learning to experience sex in other ways—as a connection to your partner. So throughout the book, we talk about ways of engaging in sex and attitudes about sex that can help you achieve a more expansive experience of it. You can try new things and add new facets to your lovemaking without losing a thing—sex can still release tension, but perhaps it can do that in better, more fulfilling ways.

29. I know just how to satisfy my partner sexually.

Whether or not you agree with this statement, it's a good idea to ask your partner to be sure. If your partner doesn't know what he or she wants romantically or sexually and wants to find out, we recommend Chapters 5 and 7. If your partner already knows and is looking for suggestions on communicating them to you, Chapter 8 can help both of you open up to each other.

30. I often feel a spiritual connection during or after sex.

People who can do this, who can expand their sexual experience into the spiritual realm, really do get quite a bonus. We provide suggestions in Chapter 11 that can help you and your partner become more intimately connected during sex and more aware of your connection to things beyond yourselves and beyond your sexual lovemaking. Exploring this potential together can be very fulfilling on many levels.

31. I often lose my erection/don't lubricate during intercourse.

   It is very common for a man to experience a temporary inability to obtain or maintain his erection or for a woman to feel less aroused and not have adequate lubrication for intercourse. If this persists, you might be experiencing a sexual dysfunction, such as erectile dysfunction (for men) or sexual arousal disorder (for women). Chapter 12 explores possible causes and remedies. If you suspect that unresolved issues in the relationship are at work, refer to Chapter 13. If you need more in the romantic realm to become aroused, look to Chapter 7.

32. I know when my partner is interested in sex.

   Whether or not you agree with this statement, it's a good idea to ask your partner to be sure. You could be acting on assumptions that might not be completely accurate. If that's the case, you might be missing some opportunities for sex or trying to initiate sex when your partner really just wants to be affectionate. Some signals might be verbal, and others might be nonverbal. We talk about this in Chapter 8 as well as in other chapters of the book.

33. I love to be touched all over by my partner.

   If you don't know how you like to be touched, take some time to explore your own body through the exercises in Chapter 5 or through sensate focus massage, with your partner, in Chapter 10. To teach your partner what you prefer, sensually and sexually, and learn what he or she prefers, see Chapter 7 and Chapter 10.

34. I love music and scented candles during sex.

   The intensity of visual stimulation and genital sensation can often eclipse the more subtle sensual sensations of sounds, smells, and tastes, but these sensations can have a profound influence on the quality of your sexual ecstasy. If you and your partner can discover ways to incorporate these sensations into your lovemaking, you will be way ahead of most people who don't even consider these things. Chapters 9 and 10 provide plenty of suggestions to get you started.

35. I have definitely experienced sexual ecstasy.

   Explore that experience and look at what was present that made these sexual encounters so satisfying for you. Sexual ecstasy is not a destination, and your experience of it can change over time. Remain vigilant to changes you and your partner experience, and refer back to the appropriate sections of this book to learn how to maximize the evolution of your sexual experiences together.

36. I don't think I'm functioning well sexually.

   If you agreed with this statement, what seems to be the problem? If you suspect that it is a physical one, refer to Chapter 12. If you think relationship issues are getting in the way, see Chapter 13. If aging is a factor, refer to Chapter 14. Whatever the problem is, solutions are always available, and you will find many in this book.

37. I feel inhibited when I really try to let go sexually.

   If you agree with this statement, ask yourself what you really need permission to do and what might be holding you back. Read about permission in Chapter 4 and use some of the suggestions that we give to help you feel more comfortable exploring all aspects of your sexuality. If you're worried that the children or neighbors will hear, we talk about that and other time- and space-crunches in Chapter 13.

38. I am completely comfortable with my partner seeing me nude with the lights on.

    If you feel self-conscious at all, the question is, "What makes you uncomfortable?" If it has to do with feelings about your own body, follow the suggestions in Chapter 5 to learn more about your body and learn how to appreciate its sensuality. If you're feeling inhibited sexually, perhaps you need to look to Chapter 4 to learn more about how to give yourself permission to be sexual. If you're thinking that your partner will be critical of you or your body, you might want to have a serious talk with your partner about it.

39. My partner and I generally want the same amount of sex.

    If this is true, you are a rare, lucky couple, particularly if you have been together for a while. If this has become an area of conflict in your relationship, look for ways of dealing with desire discrepancy in Chapter 13. Chapters 9, 10, and 11 explore ways of enhancing sexual pleasure for both of you. Romance and affection can also fill some of the need for sex, so don't miss Chapter 7.

40. My partner always does for me what I enjoy the most during sex.

    Communicating sexual needs is an area that many people find to be difficult, especially since we get no training in it. However, it's really a matter of showing and telling your partner, as we discuss mainly in Chapters 8 and 10. If you think your partner is lacking in motivation, find out what he or she wants, or wants more of, in the relationship, both sexually and nonsexually, as suggested in Chapter 7.

41. Sex sometimes bores me.

    If you're in a long-term relationship, you can expect to have a certain number of sexual encounters that are not great or even good. If sex usually is boring, ask yourself what might be missing from it. Look at the five ingredients of sexual ecstasy to see where you and your partner can add to it together. The key to removing sexual boredom from a relationship is to add novelty. You can do this by adding more spice from any one of the five ingredients we discuss in Chapter 2.

42. I am uncomfortable with some of my own sexual thoughts and fantasies.

No matter what your fantasy might be, as long as it is kept on a fantasy level, the only harm it can do is to produce guilt that can distract from your sexual satisfaction. Take the strategies we discuss in Chapters 4 and 6 to allow yourself the freedom to fantasize.

43. Sometimes I'd like to initiate sex, but I don't.

If you don't initiate sex and would like to, try thinking about what might be stopping you. If you feel inhibited by your own thoughts, explore any old beliefs you might be having, as explained in Chapter 4. Consider talking with your partner about it. He or she might feel that having to initiate sex *all the time* is a burden. Explain how erotic you think it might feel to you. If your partner does reject you when you try to initiate sex, talk about it in a non-angry way. Look to Chapter 8 for ways to discuss this productively.

44. We love to try new things sexually.

This is the key to keeping sex fresh and novel. If you're satisfied with your lovemaking in its current form, that's okay, but you can often get more out of it by exploring other options and opportunities. If you don't try new things and your sex life seems to be in a rut, work together to turn that around. In Chapters 8 and 9 and throughout this book, we encourage you to explore, discover, and communicate your pleasures. Adding a little something special to the time you spend together—reading to each other, listening to music, being sexual at different times of day, talking, and keeping your relationship interesting outside as well as inside the bedroom—are all things that can help.

45. We are often way too busy to have sex.

    This is a very common concern of modern couples in which both partners may hold down jobs outside of the home as well as maintain a home and family. But sex is too important to let life's stresses and strains get in the way, so skip to Chapter 13 to learn how to give yourselves the necessary space and time to experience sexual ecstasy.

46. My partner or I ejaculate way too quickly.

    Premature ejaculation is the most common of male sexual dysfunctions. A number of treatments and exercises are available that can help. In addition to getting in touch with your own sensations and body that we encourage throughout this book, specific suggestions can be found in Chapter 10, where we discuss Kegel exercises, and in Chapter 12, which addresses that specific sexual dysfunction.

47. If I am angry with my partner, I will refuse sex.

    Very few people feel sexual when they are angry. But the key here is to see whether you're either chronically angry or using your anger to avoid sex. Look at the issues that underlie whatever it is you are angry about. We provide suggestions for dealing with anger in several chapters, specifically in Chapter 13, where we call anger the world's "leading anti-aphrodisiac."

48. I feel emotionally close to my partner during sex.

    If you agree with this statement, you are experiencing the partner connection, which is one of the most important secrets of sexual ecstasy. If not, look at what seems to be standing in the way. Are you so focused on your own sensations that you feel no connection? Do you feel distant from your partner prior to sex? Are you having sex just because your partner wants it? Discuss this with your partner and explore ways to connect both inside and outside the bedroom. Chapters 7, 8, and 13 provide plenty of suggestions.

49. There are times when no matter what I do, I cannot get turned on.

   Lack of desire for sex and an inability to become aroused before or during sexual activity is a very common issue, particularly in long-term relationships and as you become older. If the problem is health- or age-related, check out our suggestions in Chapter 14. If something is going on in your life right now that is distracting from your pleasure, Chapter 4 can help bring you more into the moment. If you can't get turned on by your partner but you can get turned on by yourself or when you think about other people, then look to Chapter 12 for information about inhibited sexual desire and Chapter 13 for the relationship aspect of the problem.

50. My partner and I have a shared vision of what sexual ecstasy is.

   If this is truly the case, you have a great thing going. Take that vision as far as you can as often as you want to, and enjoy it as much as you can. If that's not the case, however, we provide many very doable strategies throughout this book that can get you to this point. And once you're there, you will never go back!

Look at what's good in your relationship and see whether you can expand on it. If you're not sure what you need, try lots of things. Don't be disappointed if some things don't work. We are all different. Some people love to fantasize, for example, whereas others love touch much more. For others, romance is the key to ecstasy. This book will help you find out what works for you and your partner and allows you to create the ingredients for sexual ecstasy together.

What You Can Do

Your inventories can help you and your partner determine some of the issues you need to work on, clarify the type of sexual relationship you really want to have together, and find ways of building the sort of relationship that you both desire. Using your inventory and this book, here are a few things you can do right now to further your journey towards sexual ecstasy:

☐ Compare your inventory with your partner's. Discuss any of your issues. This is not an all-or-nothing approach. Any one thing you can improve will bring you that much closer to sexual ecstasy. Err in the direction of talking more. The more you talk, the more intimate you're going to be with one another. Talk about where you are now versus where you want to be with respect to your responses.

☐ If you're having a difficult time deciding whether to discuss an item with your partner, ask yourself what is the worse thing that could possibly happen if you chose to bring it up? Chances are that it's not anything really dire, and the rewards that you will likely reap probably far outweigh any discomfort you might feel about opening a dialogue.

☐ Use the inventory as a guide for exploring your options and reviewing chapters or sections of the book that you find particularly beneficial for you in your current situation. Even if you read them before, read them again; you might have more questions or a different perspective. Follow any suggestions we give you and explore other resources we mention—books, audio programs, or websites.

☐ Save your inventories for future reference and come back to this chapter every so often to witness real positive changes to your sex life as you incorporate the various ingredients of sexual ecstasy. Remain vigilant so you can remain proactive in achieving ever deeper, ever higher levels of sexual ecstasy!

How Sexual Ecstasy Starts with Your Mind

The mind is neither good nor evil, neither kind nor cruel. It is a powerful force that is equally skilled at producing delight and disgust, pleasure and pain, desire and loathing. With an instrument as powerful as your mind at work in your sex life, it is essential that you be aware of its power and understand that your mind controls how you perceive and feel about *everything*—your partner's appearance, your own body, the fragrances you smell, and the sexual activity itself.

One of the secrets of sexual ecstasy is that you can learn to change and use your thoughts and feelings to increase your satisfaction of your sexual experiences. You can begin right now by learning and practicing the approaches described in this chapter for helping to dispel meddlesome thoughts, block distractions, heighten sensations, and experience pleasure in the present moment.

Your Mind: The Real Pleasure Center

The body's response to sexual arousal leaves many with the false impression that sexual pleasure and desire are created only in the genitals. The penis becomes erect, the vagina becomes lubricated, and it feels so good "down there," so people often jump to the false conclusion that this is the only erogenous zone. In fact your brain, your mind, is primarily responsible for how you experience sexual pleasure. Of course, your sensory organs and nervous system need to deliver the required sensory data to the brain, but the brain interprets the data and gives it a positive or negative spin. Moreover, the brain's signals instruct the genitals on how to respond. A hot fantasy, unaccompanied by any physical stimulation, can cause the penis to become erect, the vagina to become lubricated, and can, in some cases, even initiate orgasm.

GET PSYCHED

The mind is in its own place, and in itself can make a Heaven of Hell, a Hell of Heaven. –John Milton, 1608–1674

The Most Important Sex Organ—Your Brain When you are involved in any sexual activity, alone or with your partner, your brain is at least as active as your body. In addition to telling your body how to move and processing all of the sensory data that's pouring in, your brain is interpreting the data in the light of any attitudes you have, good or bad. In addition, your mind can be involved in all sorts of activity that either increase or decrease the amount of sexual pleasure you experience. It is either helping your body by focusing on pleasurable sensations or thoughts or interrupting your pleasure with distractions or negative self-talk or spectatoring about your adequacy as a lover, your body, your partner's level of arousal, or even whether you have reached sexual ecstasy yet. It might be fantasizing about a romantic holiday at the beach, focusing attention on the softness of your lover's body, or worrying about whether your lover is really into this.

To understand the powerful effect the brain has on how one interprets sexual experiences, take a look at the following example: Five women experience cunnilingus exactly the same way with precisely the same technique and intensity. Throughout the experience, one woman focuses on her genitals thinking, "This is dirty, filthy, and disgusting." The second woman might be merely self-conscious, thinking, "Is this really supposed to turn me on?

Am I now obliged to give him oral sex?" The third woman might begin wondering whether the experience is quite as good as it was with her previous lover. The fourth woman finds her mind somewhere else, wondering if she remembered to turn off the stove. The fifth woman is lying back, feeling her sexual desire growing, becoming more and more aroused, believing that what she is experiencing is pure pleasure, and thus letting the experience fully and completely turn her on. She is about to let ecstasy happen. All five women have the same physical experience, but only the fifth has a mindset that is open to experiencing sexual ecstasy.

> **PsychSpeak**
>
> **Self-talk** consists of the internal thoughts and dialogue, positive or negative, that play in your mind. **Spectatoring** is the process of evaluating yourself and your performance during sexual activity, usually negatively. It can pull your focus from the moment and decrease desire. It might even lead to sexual dysfunction.

To the extent that you are experiencing sexual ecstasy, you are in the moment, surrendering to your feelings and the sensations you're feeling at that moment. Perhaps you are fantasizing or having pleasurable thoughts about your partner. But whatever your thoughts are, they are fully connected to your experience of the moment. So remember that mindset is far more important than performance or technique.

Giving Yourself Permission Each and every person has a unique value system that affects his or her thoughts and behaviors. Most people choose not to steal, for example, because it's against the law as well as contrary to their value system. Values and beliefs are essential for determining how you choose to live your life. Some of your values, however, change simply because you outgrow them.

The first step is to understand how your brain creates these values. Many of your values probably came from parents, religious training, teachers, and peers when you were young. You might store them in your mind, without questioning or qualifying them and then make them your absolute truth. This is called *introjecting*. If, over time, you don't examine or evaluate what you may have considered an absolute truth in order to bring it in line with your current reality, the belief or value you introjected might begin to hinder your enjoyment. You may not even realize this is happening. For example, a woman might grow up believing that women who desire sex are loose. Even though she is now an adult and married, to the extent that she carries this idea around, she might never initiate sex. Or, she might think that oral sex is immoral, so she won't ask her partner for it, even though this would give her a great deal of pleasure. Old and unworkable values act as stop signs, shutting down or at least slowing down certain pleasurable thoughts and inhibiting you from pursuing pleasure.

PsychSpeak

To **introject** is to completely adopt a belief or value in its entirety without examining or questioning it. For example, many people (such as fundamentalists) introject their religious beliefs, and of course, sexual values are commonly introjected by people from all walks of life.

Once you understand how these values are formed, you can begin to identify them and then choose to remove or modify any that no longer apply to you. Does the belief or value in question still carry validity for your life? Does it serve you? If not, make an internal policy change—within yourself. Your choices rule! You need not play by anyone else's rules anymore! When it comes to sex, you and your partner call the shots. Free your relationship from everyone else's shoulds and should-nots. These rarely serve any purpose other than to diminish your sexual pleasure and increase your own feelings of self-doubt. If you have a belief or value that you're uncertain of or that conflicts with your pleasure, ask yourself these questions: "If I heard this belief or value for the first time today, would I believe it? Would I want to teach my child this value?" Your answers are usually enough to know whether the belief or value in question is your friend or enemy. Dr. Albert Ellis, originator of Rational Emotive Behavior Therapy offers this simple bottom line: Keep the ones that serve you, and let go of the rest. You owe them nothing!

Psyching Yourself for Ecstasy Sex is about sensations—it's about how the mind records sensations, interprets them, and uses them to generate desire and pleasure. Problems arise when associations caused by prior painful or uncomfortable sexual activity pop up or the mind becomes cluttered with extraneous thoughts, especially pleasure killers like these: "This used to feel so much better." "I wonder if I'll have an orgasm this time." "Do we really have time for this?" Or, maybe your partner turns you down for sex and you tell yourself it's because you're not a good lover. When you have sex later on, you start critiquing your technique and lose your erection, this only "confirms" for you that you're a lousy lover.

you're not alone

The Power of an Attitude Change

Jen (a dental hygienist in her mid 30s) and Scott (a medical technician in his early 30s) had been married for eight years and were beginning to feel as though they were drifting apart. Scott still thought Jen was pretty and they had no major disagreements or serious marital issues, but for Scott, the spark was gone. He knew he was still capable of desire, because he noticed he could be highly aroused while fantasizing during masturbation, but Jen just didn't do it for him anymore. He didn't tell that to Jen, but Jen felt it through his avoidance of her. Gradually, Jen had begun to fee less attractive and somewhat guilty that she was unable to turn Scott on.

Scott expressed his concerns to Matt, his closest friend, who had known the couple since before they were married. Scott told Matt that he was thinking of leaving Jen. Matt listened with disappointment and sadness. Scott and Jen were his best friends. When Scott was finished expressing his feelings, Matt told Scott in no uncertain terms that Scott would be making a huge mistake if he decided to leave Jen. He told Scott that Jen was one of the sexiest women on the planet, and he ticked off a long list of her positive qualities—her love and devotion to Scott, her patience in putting up with his sloppiness, her killer sense of humor, and so on. He reminded Scott of how lovingly Jen cared for him after his motorcycle accident and that she was always there to help Scott's aging parents.

Scott took Matt's words to heart, and they played over and over in his mind. Soon Scott began to focus on Jen's curves, on the way she moved, on her laugh, her smile, and all the little things she did for him every day. His desire was rekindled, and he became more physically affectionate toward Jen. Jen began to feel sexier and her self-confidence grew. It began to show in the way she dressed and the way she acted toward Scott. This made her even sexier in Scott's eyes.

You can often muffle the negative self-talk and spectatoring during sex, by learning to interrupt or ignore the negative thoughts:

- Be aware you're doing it.
- Challenge the self-imposed thoughts that are standing in your way.
- Either dispute the thought by asking, "If I heard that for the first time today would I believe it?" Or just say "Stop" to yourself and to the negative statements.
- Focus on your partner, on a fantasy, or on a sensation you're experiencing. In other words, crowd out the negativity in your mind with positive thoughts and self-talk.
- Talk with your partner to share any fears or anxieties you have, as well as a loving feeling, or some erotic talk.

These techniques will work if you remember to practice them and remember that any new habit takes some time to form. So remember to use them again and again until they become second nature.

One of the most beneficial attitude shifts we help couples make is accepting the idea that good sex involves effort and work. When we tell a couple that they need to work at their sexual relationship or we give them assignments to do at home (which when it comes to sex we prefer to call *homeplay* rather than *homework*), they often display a look that says, "Ugh, another thing on my to-do list." But then we explain that all sexual relationships demand some effort (also known as *work* or *energy*). In the beginning, you might not perceive it as "work," because you *want* to do it. You want to dress sexy, comb your hair, smell nice, act considerate and polite,

WEB TALK: For help with removing shoulds, anxieties, anger, and negative self-talk from your mind, check out the Albert Ellis Institute's website at: www.rebt.org

GET PSYCHED

"I think that to maintain a long-term erotic feeling requires work, meaning intentionality, and I do believe that all couples can have it if they aspire to it and are determined to go as far as they need to go to get it." —*Pat Love, Ed.D., marital therapist and author of* Hot Monogamy *and* The Truth About Love compromise, touch, share, and so on. All of that requires energy, but you love doing it. When you're married or living together, however, all those wonderful little details that acted as foreplay can become chores, and the household chores may take a priority to time spent together. To rekindle the desire it helps to think of your sexual relationship as a priority, as well as play—the way you did when you first met. It doesn't need to be serious or perfect or lead you to sexual ecstasy every time. It just seems to flow better if you can adapt an attitude of fun, connection, and pleasure.

One way to become more attentive to your relationship is to remain focused on the five Ps: practice, priority, pleasure, play, and partner. The goal is to maximize pleasure, not performance. Think of "work" more in the sense of *intent* and *energy* so it doesn't seem so much like drudgery. Practice to improve your lovemaking.

Being in the Present Moment

The crystal intensity of a moment can often elude you, because the experience becomes clouded with distractions and extraneous thoughts. You walk down the street blind to your surroundings, thinking about yesterday's meeting or tonight's dinner plans. You gobble up lunch while reading a magazine, barely tasting your food. Your mind even wanders when you're making love, to remembrances of things past, future worries, or thoughts of what your partner is thinking.

You fully experience the moment when you give yourself permission to experience it *as it is right now.* Or you experience the moment when you're so *passionately engrossed* in an activity that you blot out any distractions. Orgasm is a time such as this, for most people. Practice experiencing the moment. Give yourself permission to

> **GET PSYCHED**
>
> Eckhart Tolle, author of *The Power of Now,* believes that when people are completely in the present moment, they don't experience anxiety or depression. If something is troubling you, you either decide to let it go in the moment or you take some action to address the issue.

listen, *really listen*, eyes closed, to your favorite music without letting extraneous thoughts creep in. You begin not only to hear the music but also to feel its vibrations and sense its movement and purpose. The music might call up emotions that make you laugh or cry. Some people can even *taste* the music or *see* it! Other people experience this sense of complete focus when playing tennis or dancing. If you stop to look at or tell your feet what to do, you lose your focus, your rhythm, and, in the case of tennis, the ball. When you're making love, keep your focus.

Start living in the present by becoming more aware of when you lose your focus in the moment. Are you totally in the present moment now, reading this book, or are you concentrating on holding down the cover of the book to keep people from seeing what you're reading? Are you wondering how great sex will feel when you're done with the book? When you're at work, do you focus on work or do you worry about how much time you still have to put in? At lunch, do you eat or watch the clock? Once you become more aware of your tendency to dwell on the past or future, you can begin to work on being more in the present moment throughout the day. Here are some suggestions:

- Leave your worries of home at home. Leave your work at work.
- When you do something pleasant, such as taking a walk, focus on the sensory details, not on thoughts. Listen to the leaves, feel the ground, taste the air, look around.
- Put on your favorite music, sit back in a comfortable chair or lie on your bed, and let the music flow over and through you.

Don't assume that every experience will be positive; you could feel bored, uncomfortable, or anxious. That's okay—it's all part of that moment.

To live more in the moment with your partner, try to feel the sexual energy that exists between you throughout the day. Take the time to let go of thoughts about the future or the past. And then, look into each other's eyes. Touch one another, not necessarily in a sexual way. Get close and smell your partner's scent. Notice the way your partner interacts with you and with others, how your partner moves, the sound of his or her laugh. Examine the contours of your partner's body. Before you had your first date, you probably checked these things out: Why not now?

you're not alone

Mark and Diane were having trouble getting pregnant. They had been trying for five or six months. Every time Diane had her period, she became angry with Mark and with herself. Then Mark lost his erections when they tried to make love. This increased Diane's anger and bitterness and Mark's frustration and anxiety. At the suggestion of Diane's gynecologist they finally sought counseling. The therapist listened to their story and made one simple recommendation. He suggested that perhaps the pressure to get pregnant was causing problems for both of them individually and as a couple. He asked them to stop trying to get pregnant for at least three months. No temperature taking, no ovulation kits, no timing of sex. They agreed to take the pregnancy issue off the table.

Almost immediately, Diane stopped becoming so angry around her period, Mark started getting erections, and unexpectedly Diane became pregnant, before the three months were up. The problem had been that Diane was anxious that she would never be able to have children, and she had a false expectation that once you started trying to get pregnant, you became pregnant within a few months. Simply by taking the pressure off their sex life, the couple was able to revive it.

Sexual Desire 101

Few experts would dispute the fact that sexual drive is created in the brain and involves both our thoughts and our physiology, but researchers are just beginning to understand the components of it and the process behind it. Experts know that levels of sexual desire vary from person to person; that sexual desire tends to decrease over the course of a relationship; that it decreases with age; and that it fluctuates throughout the day (and even during sexual activity). Also available are several findings and theories about what causes sexual desire, why the levels of sexual desire change, and why they vary from person to person.

We explored one such finding in Chapter 2, when we looked at the work of Dr. Helen Fisher, whose research focused on the brain chemistry behind sexual desire. We mention the study here to point out that certain chemicals, including dopamine, can surge in the short term due to novelty and other factors and may also contribute to an increased production of testosterone. Testosterone, which fluctuates daily, establishes our base level of desire; it is the hormone that fuels sex drive and is considered the gasoline of sex. You need some to get you going, but once you're running ... you get the idea. Testosterone also decreases with age, especially for midlife women (and many women during the menstrual cycle). However, it *does not prevent* you from having sexual desire or experiencing a sexually satisfying life. If you can become aroused by any form of sex-related material, you have the brain chemistry and physiology you need to become aroused with your partner. You just need to work on your mind, the psychological aspect, and on your interpersonal relationship (*intimacy*). (Later in the book we deal with the chemical and biological obstacles.)

Stephen B. Levine, M.D., clinical professor of psychiatry at Case School of Medicine in Cleveland, Ohio; author of *Sexuality in Midlife;* and codirector, the Center for Marital and Sexual Health in Beechwood, Ohio, describes desire as having three aspects: sex drive, motivation, and wish. Levine defines *sex drive* as the biological component, which deals with brain chemistry and physiology. *Motivation* is the psychological component, which is influenced by a person's mental state (for example, sorrow or joy), interpersonal state (how a couple is getting along), social content (friends and community), relationship duration, and so on. *Wish* is how you might want to express your sexuality and choose to express it or not express it because of your own values or society's rules—for example, you might want to have an affair at the office, but you're married. Levine points out that in long-term relationships, sex drive and motivation tend to taper off, while wish increases. When these three components are not in sync it can lead to dissatisfaction with one's sexual relationship.

Recent studies on sexual desire are beginning to reveal that the stages most people experience when involved in a sexual encounter are not linear. Sexologists once believed that you needed desire to create arousal that led to orgasm and then resolution. This model was applied to both men and women. But new studies and writings, especially in the area of female sexual response, suggest otherwise. Rosemary Basson, M.D., M.R.C.P., clinical professor of psychiatry and obstetrics/gynecology at the University of British Columbia in Vancouver, Canada, presents a circular model in which drive, motivation, arousal, climax, and orgasm lead to and build on one another. In many cases, a woman does not feel desire until she is physically involved in the act of making love. This becomes even more common for menopausal or postmenopausal women. Other times a woman might feel sexually neutral, but be motivated by a need for intimacy. If, in fact, a woman's biological sex drive is more variable than a man's, motivation becomes even more important for a woman. And sexual motivation for a woman relies heavily on her feelings about her relationship and her partner. The old adage that "Women need love to make love and men make love to have love" is in play.

We provide a very basic and practical definition of sexual desire: *Sexual desire is a total of all factors that work together to lead us toward and away from sexual behavior.* This includes brain chemistry, physiological and emotional components, psychological issues, social factors, and every other human factor that affects the way an individual perceives and feels about sexuality. Sexual desire is as individual as each human being who feels it, and each person has the choice and power to increase the level of sexual desire in his or her life.

Dispelling Myths About Sexual Desire Our culture's myth mill packs many people's brains with false assumptions and exaggerated expectations concerning sexual desire. It makes people think that they should all be highly aroused men and women in their early 20s, ready, willing, and able to have mind-blowing sex with their equally ready, willing, able, and gorgeous partners. Here's the truth behind some of the more common and detrimental of these myths:

- **Myth:** Sexual desire and great sex just happen.

    Fact: Maybe this is true when your relationship is starting out, but in long-term relationships, desire and great sex often require the right mindset and some serious joint effort.

- **Myth:** Every loving couple has the same level of desire.

    Fact: Desire levels differ within and between partners and during different stages of a relationship.

- **Myth:** Men are always ready to have sex.

    Fact: Sexual desire commonly diminishes in men, as in women, with stress, lack of sleep, and the natural aging process. As men and women age, they might require more psychological and physical stimulation.

- **Myth:** Good sex should be natural and spontaneous.

    Fact: Sex might *seem* spontaneous early in a relationship, but the preparation for a date can take a lot of time and effort. Plus, the mere expectation of what's going to happen, the mystery of it, can increase desire.

- **Myth:** "If you really loved me, you would have sexual desire for me."

    Fact: Sexual desire (passion) and intimacy (love) are different. You can love a person deeply without feeling sexually attracted to the person.

According to author Michele Weiner-Davis, the common myth that sexual desire needs to be present before initiating sex leads to many lost opportunities for experiencing sexual pleasure. Weiner-Davis cites Dr. Rosemary Basson's research showing that women in long-term monogamous relationships often become aroused *during* sexual activity, but Weiner-Davis is fairly convinced that the same is true for at least 50 percent of men. According to Weiner-Davis, the myth causes two problems. First, it makes people think that they need to wait for desire before they initiate sexual activity. And second, it makes many people feel anxious over not being as turned-on as their partners. The fact is that people have different levels of desire. Weiner-Davis recommends taking a more relaxed approach and "encouraging yourself to be responsive to your partner's initiations, even if you initially feel rather neutral. Many people who begin to take this approach report that for the first time in a long time they're *discovering the siren within*."

Weiner-Davis finds that the "Just Do It" philosophy is especially useful for couples who "recall a time earlier in their marriage when things were much better, and generally it's often in the beginning stages of the marriage." Barring any major physical changes and even accepting the fact that hormonal changes can affect desire, couples who experienced the passion before are typically able to reignite their passions. "If things had been better, they can become better, and not just for your more highly-sexed spouse, but for you as well. Feeling sexy, feeling vibrant makes people feel alive. I really help people to see their own benefits in becoming more sexual."

We asked relationship expert and author of *The Sex-Starved Marriage*, Michele Weiner-Davis, the following question: *In your experience, what is the biggest misconception about sexual desire?*

"The biggest misconception that leads to problems in the bedroom is the myth that sexual desire and good sex just happen. That is a fallacy. Desire is a decision. I really teach couples the importance of adopting the Nike philosophy— "Just do it!" I wish I had had a dollar for each time someone in my practice said to me, 'Michele, I wasn't in the mood to make love when we started. It was the last thing on my mind, but once we got going I really, really enjoyed myself.' I would be a very wealthy woman."

The Truth About Sexual Desire Most couples involved in a long-term relationship hit some speed bumps along the way in terms of their sexual desire. One person wants sex too much, the other wants it too little, or they're both just too tired or complacent to really care. If they are not too pessimistic or apathetic, one or the other or both eventually will begin to wonder what happened. What changed?

Several factors might lead you to wonder what changed. The most obvious factor is that things *did* change—dopamine levels taper off, novelty decreases, stress increases, and so on. Your existence just isn't the same as it once was—some parts are better, some are worse. That's reality.

Another reality is that when you're younger and you first become involved romantically, your sex drive and your partner's are fairly equal. Any differences in testosterone and dopamine levels are eclipsed by the anticipation of being together and the overwhelming novelty of everything you do together. Early in a relationship, a person with a biologically low sex drive can become very desirous of someone with a biologically high sex drive and not perceive any noticeable difference. They get married, the novelty wears off, the child arrives, and then the difference in sexual desire may rear its ugly head. We estimate that this happens in 99 percent of relationships. The good news: How you and your partner deal with this may lead to no sex *or the best sex you ever had.*

Another major factor that decreases desire in a long-term relationship is that you can no longer easily avoid confrontation and unsightly situations. In a short-term relationship, you don't have a bunch of negative baggage from the past, and you generally have a much more cavalier attitude in handling differences of opinion, taste, or desire. If you feel sick, you don't go out. If you're too tired to be entertaining, you call and cancel the date. You approach the relationship with an easy, relaxed attitude that lets you enjoy one another. When you move in together, however, you get the whole package—sickness and health, riches or poverty, and so on.

Now that you know what changed, how do you get it back? The bad news is that you don't. Accept the fact that you and your partner have different levels of sexual desire; those differences are normal. Accept your differences in taste; everybody likes something different. Stop trying to recapture things as you remember they were (they probably weren't as good as you remember them, anyway). And then focus on experiencing sexual pleasure in the present moment.

Barriers to Sexual Desire As your relationship ages and evolves, the various components that contribute to your sexual desire suffer some serious jolts, especially when you or your partner or both of you experience a significant life change. You might not even realize that the life change wreaked havoc on your sexual desire until one or both of you becomes dissatisfied enough to point it out.

One of the biggest life changes is something we already discussed—the transition from a short-term into a long-term relationship. Another big desire-killer is the stress that's inherent in having and raising children. Both parents are working, carpooling two or three kids around, maintaining and cleaning a house, doing laundry .... At the end of the day, they collapse in bed, immediately fall asleep, wake up the next morning, and do it all again. People living out such realities frequently, and understandably, choose sleep over sex. Sex becomes an item to check off the list. Any life change can cause stress that places similar pressure on the relationship—a career change, change in financial status, a family illness, or the death of a loved one.

A change in self-image can also lessen your sexual desire. Anything from gaining 5 to 10 pounds to losing a job or taking on a new role as a mom or dad can trigger you into thinking that you're less sexy or less desirable. This can negatively affect your sexual desire directly, but also indirectly, if your partner sees it as a problem or you *think* your partner sees it as a problem.

To overcome these barriers to sexual desire, the most effective approach is to deal with the changes as they occur, rather than waiting until they push your sexual desire below an acceptable level. If you have a life change or experience that coincides with a decrease in sexual appetite or ability to have fun together, address the issue and work it out. Unresolved issues, even those that are not sex-related, can derail your sex life. Don't just apologize and assume the issue is resolved; if either of you still feels the slightest discomfort over it, work it out. The process of solving problems and resolving issues together not only removes the block, but can also raise your level of intimacy greatly.

GET PSYCHED

"Novelty, you can't say enough about it. The only new thing I would add to the mix, is the whole issue of anxiety as sexual stimulant. Too often we think that anxiety is an inhibition. Clearly, if a person has free floating anxiety, general anxiety disorder about a particular kind of sexual behavior, it is a turn-off kind of anxiety. On the other hand, there are turn-on kinds of anxieties and that could be generated by doing something forbidden, doing something public, doing something that kind of extends your scope of what you would have considered normal and natural. Playing around with S&M, bondage, or fantasy scripts. I think that adding a little edge to sex can really kind of be a turn-on."
—*Sandra Leiblum, Ph.D., director of the Center for Sexual Health and Marital Health at the Robert Wood Johnson Medical School and co-author of* Getting the Sex You Want, A Woman's Guide to Becoming Proud, Passionate and Pleased in Bed

Creating and Enhancing Sexual Desire

Enough about what might be inhibiting desire. Let's turn our thoughts to another secret of sexual ecstasy that reveals three simple ways in which you can maximize desire: introducing novelty into your love-making, building anticipation, and pursuing the sensations that you find pleasurable.

Experts almost universally agree that introducing novelty into your relationship is essential. Routine is boring. If you eat the same meal, at the same time, every day even if it's your favorite, it is going to lose its flavor or at least you'll lose your ability to fully taste it. If you have sex the same way at the same time in the same place in the same position and with the same thoughts, the routine can begin to dull your senses.

Imagine what turns you on sexually. Imagine with all of your senses. Take in even the smallest detail.

Once you have some novel ideas, work on *increasing your anticipation* of your next encounter and *decreasing your expectation*. Look forward to meeting your partner at the end of the day or waking up next to your partner in the morning. Imagine how your partner looks, smells, sounds, feels, moves. Think of all the positive feelings you have for your partner, the little quirks that only you notice and appreciate, the tiniest things that turn you on.

Novelty and anticipation can do wonders for your sexual desire. Add to that the pursuit of pleasurable and sensual sensations, and arousal is almost sure to occur. Ask for what you want or bring it into your lovemaking on your own. If there is a turn-on your partner can do for you (and might be receptive to trying), ask. Or ask in subtle ways by telling your partner what feels good. If your partner is unreceptive or you can attend to something that turns you on, attend to the detail yourself; for example, you can play music that turns you on, burn candles, change the sheets, or even declutter the bedroom. Doing these little things can function as foreplay and help you create a romantic and stimulating ambience that inspires sexual desire.

What You Can Do

The focus in this chapter is on you and what you can do by and for yourself with your own mind to psych yourself up for sexual ecstasy. Here are a few things you can do right now to create and enhance sexual desire in yourself:

☐ Identify the desire-killing myths that you and you alone are holding onto about sexual desire. Reflect on these myths or discuss them with your partner. What do you get from holding onto them? What would it take to let go of them?

☐ Consciously stop at different times during the day when you're involved in activities other than sex and notice how your mind habitually wanders away from what you're doing in the moment. Bring it back and allow yourself to focus fully on your experience of the moment.

☐ The next time you are involved in any pleasurable activity, sexual or not, try shifting your mind's attention to the different senses. Close your eyes and listen, smell the surrounding scents. Focus on everything around you that is touching your body—your clothing, your watch, the chair you're sitting in, everything. If you are moving, take note of how the movement feels to your body.

☐ The next time you and your partner are having sex, pay special attention to anything going on in your mind that may be taking you out of the moment. (You don't necessarily need to tell your partner you're doing this.) Then, consciously try to let it go. Remain tuned-in to your breathing and your partner's breathing and aware of the sensations you're feeling without putting yourself down or judging yourself. What thoughts make you exit that moment?

☐ List the things that increase or decrease the amount of sexual desire you feel. These can be things about your partner, about yourself, thoughts that turn you on or off, the setting, and so on. Include at least one turn-on each time you and your partner are together sexually this month. And work on removing one thing that turns you off.

☐ Do something novel with your partner this week. The only requirement is that it be something you have never done together. Go to a new restaurant or store, hike somewhere you have never been, or try a new sexual position.

☐ Think back to a time when you were intensely aroused in the presence of your partner. Describe the scene, focusing on all of the surrounding details, plus all the sensations and thoughts that you had inside. And it always helps to think about what first attracted you to your partner—any positive sexual experiences you might have had. It's even better if you can feel the feeling in your body and your emotions connected to those memories.

Getting in Touch with Your Sexual Self

Your brain might be in complete control of how intensely you feel desire and pleasure, but your body is no slouch. Before, during, and after sexual activity, your body absorbs all of the sensations and sends them to the brain for processing. Your eyes observe the sights; your ears take in the sounds; your nose records the aromas; your tongue tastes the flavors and feels the textures; and your skin absorbs the sensations of everything that presses up against it.

But your body's function as a sensory sponge is only half of the role it plays. Your senses tell you what your body *feels* during sexual activity. How you *feel about* your body and about sexual activity is the other half of the role your body plays. If you believe that your body is deliciously sensuous, you're probably going to approach sex with much more prowess than if you feel dumpy or unattractive.

This chapter addresses both aspects of your body and its role in delivering sexual ecstasy: how your body feels and how you feel about your body. Here you learn how to boost your body image (or at least stop worrying about it), give your body permission to feel pleasure, and become a little more in-tune with what your skin feels and what it likes. Accepting yourself and your own sensations can help you to be more receptive to pleasure and more open with your partner.

Building a Better Body Image

Our culture is obsessed with body image. Bodies and sexuality are used in the media to sell everything from Coke to cars. The implication is if you look right, the world will be your oyster. Unfortunately, men and women both buy into the message that this is how she and, more recently, he should look. In addition to generating a multimillion-dollar diet industry, this has generated an epidemic of eating disorders starting in young children and lasting a lifetime for some. A discussion of why this is occurring is far beyond the scope of this book, but how this obsession with body image affects many people's ability to experience sexual ecstasy does need to be addressed. To the extent you are dissatisfied with your body or your partner's body, you will experience obstacles to sexual ecstasy.

Obsessing over changing what you might perceive as imperfections in your own body is often a futile attempt that only leads to misery, and you certainly cannot change the appearance of your partner's body. What is in your power to change is your attitude about your body and your partner's body. How you look or how your partner looks is not nearly as important as how each of you feels about your own body, and how each of you feels about each other's body.

One reason it matters so much that you accept your and your partner's bodies is that it improves your satisfaction with your sexual relationship. Research shows this. In 2000, Diann M. Ackard and colleagues surveyed almost 4000 women about body image and their own levels of sexual satisfaction. The results showed that women who were more satisfied with their body image had more sexual activity and more frequent orgasms, initiated sex more often, were more comfortable undressing and having sex with the lights on, were less inhibited in trying new sexual behaviors, and felt more confident that they were pleasing their partners sexually than those who were dissatisfied with their body image. They also reported being less self-conscious, placing less importance on physical attractiveness, and being generally more satisfied with their lives. In 2003, Jennifer Berman and her colleagues performed a study in which they found that women who had a positive genital body image reported less sexual distress, less depression, and more sexual desire.

Q&A

Why don't guys worry so much about their weight and appearance?
According to Marianne Tebbens, M.S. eating disorders specialist, body image issues are not solely in the domain of the female population. More and more men are becoming self-conscious of their body image, as well. As the media parades its action hero hunks and beefcake studs across the screen and plasters their pictures on the pages of magazines, men are reporting many of the same insecurities about their bodies that women do.

Weighing in on Weight Issues For many people, weight becomes the main issue that blemishes their body image—they think they have too much weight or (less often) too little. Or they think their stomach isn't flat enough or firm enough. In their book *When Women Stop Hating Their Bodies,* Jane Hirschmann and Carol Munter give their readers a very simple exercise to do and we suggest you do it now: Imagine that today there is something in the air, that no matter what you do you will not lose or gain a single ounce for the rest of your life. What would you do? What wouldn't you do? How would you live your life differently? Would your behavior in bed change? Would your attitude towards yourself change? Would your attitude towards your partner change? Now take a minute to consider what you've learned. Are you prohibiting yourself from fully enjoying an entire smorgasbord of sexual delights because of your attitudes toward your body?

Q&A

How does a woman's feelings about her body affect her sexuality?

"For women especially, body image is an important determinant in how desirable they feel. A gradual weight gain of five or ten pounds that goes unnoticed by her partner can become a woman's center ground, because of her sensitivity to the smallest changes in body weight and body shape. I think this kind of self-consciousness obviously interferes with sexually letting go, with experimentation, and with availability to the extent that the woman handicaps herself with distractions of how she looks rather than how she feels. As therapists we try to reassure them that no one cares as much as they do, no one notices it."
—*Dr. Sandra Leiblum, author of* Getting the Sex You Want

Pumping Up Your Body Image Whether you're a man or a woman, comparing your body to that of a Hollywood model is like comparing your investment portfolio to the portfolio of Bill Gates. Chances are you're never going to measure up to that well-crafted image, so give it up! That's a little tougher to do than it is to say, but we're here to show you ways that you can do it.

If you're not fully satisfied with your body, try this: List what you like and dislike about your body. Place an asterisk next to the attributes that you are ready, willing, and able to change, and cross out any aspects that are beyond your control or beyond the effort and resources you are willing to invest. You might want your body to look more like the Julia Roberts or Tom Cruise model, but realistically consider what you're starting with and ask whether you're willing to invest the discipline and energy it would take to achieve that ideal. If so, honor that choice and maybe hire yourself a trainer. If not, let it go, because ultimately it will only lead to feelings of failure, disappointment, and misery.

Marianne Tebbens, M.S., mental health counselor and eating disorders specialist, suggests that you work on seeing yourself as others see you. Others generally do not examine each part of your body in fine detail; they glance at it or scan it for a few seconds. Tebbens suggests this scanning exercise to help people stop focusing and obsessing on specific parts of their bodies: Look into the mirror without staring at any one part of your body. Scan your body from head to toe and back up. Move away from the mirror. Do this for no more than 10 seconds at one standing. This exercise can help train your mind to see yourself more realistically, as others see you.

WEB TALK: To learn more about how to feel good without losing a pound, visit: 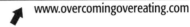 www.overcomingovereating.com

We asked Sandra Leiblum, Ph.D., psychologist, sex therapist, and author of *Getting the Sex You Want: A Woman's Guide to Becoming Proud, Passionate and Pleased in Bed,* for suggestions on how to overcome body image issues that get in the way of sexual ecstasy. Dr. Leiblum recommends that you *reframe* your body image by thinking not in terms of how your body might *look* but in how it might *feel*: "Close your eyes. Focus on how you feel. Allow yourself to look at a woman who's kind of voluptuous. Imagine how soft her skin feels, what it would feel like to be nestled between her breasts. Imagine how comforting and sexy that skin might feel. Imagine what it would be like to make love with someone who is heavier, softer." Instead of worrying about how your partner might think you *look*, imagine how wonderful your partner might think you *feel*.

Once you have created a reasonable acceptance of your own body, the next step is to let go of negative thoughts about your partner's body. Draw up a list of likes and dislikes, but this time, cross out all of your dislikes and commit yourself to doing whatever it takes to permanently erase them from your brain; Marianne Tebbens's scanning technique can help you avoid focusing on them. Remember, it's not in your power to change a single one of them. Use Dr. Leiblum's exercise to fantasize about your partner, working all the things left on your list into the fantasy, and embellishing all the wonderful attributes about your partner's body and how it feels moving against you. Keep in mind that how you view your partner's body can dramatically affect the intensity of pleasure that you feel when you make love. In other words, it's in your own self-interest to work on forming the most positive body image possible of your lover!

Feeling More Alluring You probably know people who emanate sexuality; perhaps they establish eye contact more, exhibit self-confidence, or tease with gentle jokes. You might not even consider the person physically attractive, but they come across as sexy. Ninety percent of your sexuality is in your mind and how you feel about yourself as a sexual being. Make yourself feel sexier. Dress in something that helps you feel more sensuous or naughty—it does not need to look provocative, although it can. This can be skimpy underwear, a silky shirt or blouse that feels good against your skin, a pair of pants that hugs your thighs, or whatever talks sexy to you. Pamper yourself with a soothing bubble bath, a fresh haircut, a massage, or a manicure. Feeling sexy about yourself is something that's well within anybody's reach; sometimes the feeling just needs to be awakened.

you're not alone

Pam and Don are a couple in their 30s who came into therapy. One major complaint was his loss of interest in sex since his wife gained 30 pounds. In exploring their relationship it appeared that Don found Pam less attractive and talked about her weight usually after he felt criticized by her for not helping around the house.

In speaking with Don alone he admitted that when they were sexual together things were fine and he found her very pleasing; when they had a lot of positive interaction he saw her as appealing. Work with them involved Don hearing Pam's concerns and the couple working together positively, which allowed Don to be more loving and attracted to Pam. His desire returned, and their sex life improved. We did notice several times that when conflict arose he would focus on her weight. Once this pattern was corrected, the couple engaged in more enjoyable sexual activity. Don was able to compliment Pam on the things he truly liked about her and the things about her he found attractive.

As a side effect of their connection, Pam decided to go on a diet and lost a considerable amount of weight. She felt that Don was supportive of her in this process. The fact that she initiated the diet was something Don believed helped him to be even more attracted to her because he felt that she was hearing his needs. In fact, his desire increased before she even lost a pound.

Dispelling the Size Myths The inordinate focus many people give to genitalia leads to concerns about one's own adequacies in those areas. Sometimes a man might wonder how the size of his penis compares to his wife's previous lovers'. A woman might think her normal-sized breasts are a little too small to make her desirable to her husband. In terms of sexual pleasure, size usually doesn't matter. We have found that a vast majority of couples who express concern about breast or penis size really have other issues causing these concerns, such as jealousy or fear of rejection, ego issues, or feelings of inadequacy in other aspects of their lives.

So, let's clear this up once and for all. The average size penis is five to seven inches erect and three inches flaccid. Smaller flaccid penises tend to expand more when they become erect. The vagina is a muscle, which accommodates to the size of the penis. There is a very small percentage (perhaps one tenth of 1 percent) of men whose penis size (whether too large or too small) is truly problematic when pleasuring their partners. Most of the nerve endings in the vagina are in the outer 2 inches, so with rare exception there is a fit. Women are sometimes concerned about their breast size, but again, the size of a woman's breasts does not affect their sensitivity or arousal and only becomes an issue if perceived to be one.

Size isn't what matters. It is only your attitude about size that can make a difference. Focus instead on the connection with your partner, and never lose sight of the fact that being critical of yourself during sexual activity is not an erotic or arousing thought.

> **GET PSYCHED**
>
> Jennifer Berman, M.D., urologist, and Laura Berman, Ph.D., sex educator and therapist, call exercise the *natural Viagra*.

Putting Your Body in Motion Exercise and physical activity are usually beneficial no matter what your reason for doing them. Walking, jogging, playing tennis, or riding a bike can get your blood pumping, your muscles working, and your entire body oxygenated. It can even stimulate your brain and make it more alert. And all these benefits can carry over to the bedroom, improving sexual stimulation and pleasure. Some men who suffer from erectile dysfunction find that aerobic exercise can help significantly by increasing blood flow to the penis. C. G. Bacon and colleagues in *Annals* *of Internal Medicine* reported that in a study of men over 50, an inactive life style was a risk factor for developing erectile dysfunction.

A study done at Duke University in the 1950s found that the frequency of sexual intercourse was a significant predictor of longevity for men while enjoyment of intercourse was a predictor of longevity for women. Thus, quantity is generally more important for men and quality is more important for women. Of course, this does not prove whether healthier people have more sex or people who have more sex are healthier. Still it does provide us with yet one more possible incentive to have sex.

you're not alone

Susan is a married woman in her late 30s. She came in because she was feeling sexually inhibited. Although her husband very much wanted her to have an orgasm, she had been holding back.

As we talked, one of the major issues that arose was that Susan felt uncomfortable freely expressing her feelings during sex. She was very concerned about being overheard. She was particularly fearful that her neighbors would overhear her sounds. She really didn't understand why she was that fearful and admitted that she heard her neighbors above her and she was not critical of them. In fact, she thought they were having a good time.

Once Susan became aware that she was operating under old, no-longer-valid values that were stopping her from getting what she wanted, she was willing to experiment with a new way of being. What we suggested was that she consciously exaggerate any feelings she had, especially sounds. She made them louder and longer and exaggerated her body movements. At first she felt awkward, and she and her husband laughed a lot that first time; but after a couple of weeks her sounds and movements seemed to fit in her body, and then she found the elusive orgasm she was searching for.

Loving Your Body

Your body has its own unique substance, texture, and contours, its own distinctive aroma. It can master the most intricate of movements and feel the subtlest touch. It can perceive the near-silent whisper of your lover's voice and respond by covering your skin with tiny goose bumps. It can tune itself to the rhythm of your lover's body and entwine with your lover in a tight embrace. Your body is the ultimate unit of pleasure. Celebrate its sexuality!

The Largest Sex Organ—Your Skin Your entire body is designed to sense, to feel. Think about the last time you experienced a relaxing massage or a long, hot shower. It probably felt pretty good, especially if the moment was tranquil and you were open to fully experiencing the sensations. If you give yourself permission to feel good, your body will respond. And if you give your *entire* body permission to feel good during sexual activity, your *entire* body will feel good.

Be aware that your own body, every square inch of surface area, is ready and able to experience pleasure. The next time you take a relaxed bath or shower, try to feel the different sensations all over your body. Slowly wash each part of your body, being aware of how it feels—the texture and pressure of your touch. If you use skin lotion, the next time you put some on, shift your focus to the pressure on your skin and the feel of the oil. Imagine how it might feel to have your lover or a sexy, mysterious stranger rub it on you. Bring what you learn about your own body and how it senses pleasure to your next lovemaking session. Use your skin to communicate with your partner.

Celebrating Your Sexual Self For most of us, and more so for men, the visual and genital stimulations involved in sexual activity can often eclipse other potentially pleasurable sexual sensations, even to the point of making us unaware of their presence. This is unfortunate, because it causes us to miss out on a large part of what feels good and overlook opportunities to introduce other stimulating sensations into our sexual activities.

To enable your body and mind to fully experience pleasurable moments, sexual or not, work on becoming more aware of different sensations. If you go out to eat, take a few seconds to shift your focus to the music playing in the background, the surrounding chatter, or the various aromas wafting through the air. Try closing your eyes for 10 seconds. Smell your food, feel its texture in your mouth, focus on the distinct flavors you taste as the food passes over different areas of your tongue.

The next time you and your partner plan a romantic interlude, try to introduce some other sensory stimulant into the mix. Try a new perfume or cologne. Set a bouquet of flowers next to the bed. Play some soft, relaxing music in the background. Or simply shift your focus to something that is already present—the taste of your lover's tongue, the texture of your partner's skin, the heat emanating from your bodies.

GET PSYCHED

Make friends with your sexy body. Once a day, stand in front of a mirror in various stages of undress, or nude, and take a few minutes to appreciate its beauty and power.

Tuning In to Sexual Pleasure Through Self-Pleasuring

Masturbation is often referred to derogatorily as "playing with yourself," as if playing with yourself is shameful. But without its negative connotations, the phrase is actually a pretty accurate description of what masturbation is; it is the act of *playing* with your body, seeing how it feels if you do this or that to this or that part, getting a sense of how it might feel to have your partner touch you, and all the time learning what feels good to you and what sort of focus and thinking really turns you on. Masturbation is a way for you to communicate with your body and learn what it likes, so you can teach your partner more effectively what your body likes.

For most men and some women, masturbation is their first natural sexual activity. It is the way they discover their erotic feelings, learn about their genitals, and begin to fantasize about being with a partner. Masturbation is a way to learn about one's body and sexual preferences in private with little risk and great pleasurable benefits. It is a way of exploring and identifying one's sexual desires. When we ask people what turns them on sexually, they typically have a tough time coming up with an answer. But when we ask, "What turns you on when you masturbate?" they can answer that question quite readily. Masturbation helps you discover your turn-ons.

Exploring the Benefits of Self-Pleasuring Not everyone masturbates, nor do you need to masturbate in order to achieve sexual ecstasy. Some men and women prefer not to do it. Some stop doing it once they have a significant other. That's your choice. You might, however, want to consider adding it as another way of learning about and experiencing your own sexuality. It is one of the most underrated of sexual activities and one of the least discussed, but a large and growing majority of people, both men and women, find it pleasurable. Some even find it to be their most stimulating sexual experience, because they can do it in a relaxed environment without worrying about performing or pleasuring their partners.

Albert Ellis, Ph.D., author of *Sex Without Guilt In the 21st Century*, points to another important benefit of masturbation. According to Ellis, masturbation can help alleviate anxiety in relationships in which one person's sexual desire is stronger than that of the partner. The person with the stronger desire can use masturbation to satisfy any desire out of his or her partner's range. Masturbation offers some additional benefits:

- It can be useful in helping some men to learn how to slow down or interrupt their ejaculation.
- It can be used by women who need to learn how to be orgasmic.
- It can help you take more responsibility for your own sexual pleasure. Not only in pleasing yourself during masturbation but in knowing what turns you on, so you can use your turnons to achieve sexual ecstasy during lovemaking with your partner.

Although masturbation carries with it many benefits, people do need to be careful about how they approach it and what role they choose to give it in their lives. According to Stephen B. Levine, M.D., clinical professor of psychiatry at Case School of Medicine in Cleveland, men need to become a little more aware of any "rhythmicity" they might be setting in private in terms of their sexual desire. Levine believes "that men tend to masturbate at a certain rate and want to have sex at a certain rate." This can become a problem if the man begins to expect the rate he established in private to be the rate at which he and his partner engage in sexual activity.

Masturbation can also become problematic if you develop an obsession about it, masturbate compulsively, or begin to use masturbation to replace sexual relations with a partner. Masturbation can also cause difficulties if a person interprets the fact that his or her partner masturbates as a sign that the partner no longer desires him or her. (Sometimes masturbation can be shared with partners to help both of them learn what feels good to each other.) However, when masturbation is used in moderation, it can significantly enhance one's overall sexual satisfaction.

Learning Through Self-Pleasuring In the context of this book, masturbation and other self-pleasuring sexual activities are treated as opportunities to learn more about your body and about physical touch and other sensations that you find pleasant, arousing, and satisfying.

If you are not yet comfortable touching your genitals, you can begin by first looking at your genital anatomy. Here is an exercise you can try: Take a mirror and look at your body to explore the different parts of your genital anatomy. By touching your genital area in a nonsexual way, you can begin to desensitize yourself to any uncomfortable feelings you might have about touching yourself.

If you choose to explore the different sensations you feel when touching yourself, take some time to prepare for your self-pleasuring activity as you might prepare for a lover. Perhaps you can take a bath or shower, put on some music, light candles, or set out a sex toy or soft fabric, such as velvet or silk. Then you can touch yourself to see how your body responds to different kinds of touch. You can also try oils or lotions (for women, make sure any lotions are water-soluble).

Men and women have different experiences masturbating. Most men don't need to be told what to do. The problem is that they do it the same way every time and miss out on opportunities not only to feel better but to learn more about what makes them feel good.

Changing your routine to experience it in a new way is not so automatic. Often, you need to consciously consider new ways. If you always masturbate with one hand, try with the other. Change position while masturbating. Change the kind or speed of stroke. Touch different parts of the penis. Touch more than the penis—touch your testicles, the perineum, your legs, your nipples. Slow down and focus on pleasure, not orgasm. If you feel yourself nearing ejaculation, stop, let the intensity decrease, and then start again.

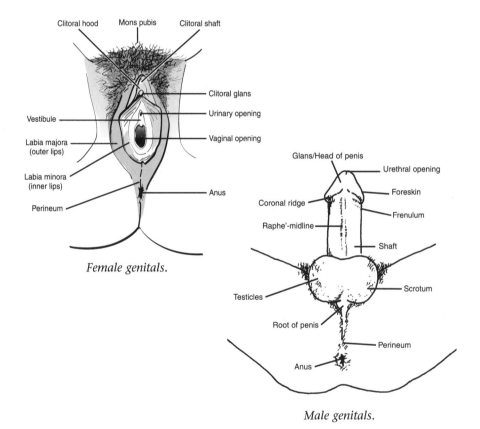

Female genitals.

Male genitals.

Unlike men, who are generally accustomed to touching their penis, women often need to become more comfortable with their body in general and genitals in specific. They need to see and explore the uniqueness of their own physical makeup, and explore the various sensations they feel over and throughout their entire bodies, including the genitals. Touch different parts of your vulva—the clitoris (with the most nerve endings), the inner and outer labia, and the vagina. Touch your legs, your nipples, your belly. Slow down and focus on pleasure not orgasm. Try different touches, circular movements, back-and-forth, up-and-down, different pressures. If you feel yourself nearing the point of orgasm, stop, let the intensity decrease, and then start again. Never lose sight of the most important part of this: Focus on pleasure.

What You Can Do

Knowing and celebrating your body's sensuality and sexuality can do wonders for your sex life. Start exploring and enjoying your body today!

- ☐ List your favorite sensory stimuli: a work of art, a scene out the window, the smell of a particular flower, the feel of a special fabric against your body, the taste of chocolate or cheese .... Try to experience many of your pleasant sensory stimulants together.

- ☐ When performing some routine activity involving your body, do it in a different way or frame of mind. If you're putting on lipstick, look in the mirror and imagine yourself seducing your partner. When you undress, pretend you are doing a striptease in front of your lover.

- ☐ Do something to completely pleasure your body, something it really enjoys. It doesn't need to be sexual, but it can be.

- ☐ When bathing, massaging your partner, or masturbating, change something: slow things down, use a vibrator, light a candle, play music.

- ☐ Add a new sensation to your sexual lovemaking. Start with a small change: change the lighting, tickle each other with lamb's wool or a feather duster, use lotion or oil for a massage, use aromas or scented candles, include food or edible lotions in your lovemaking.

The Role of Fantasy

We all fantasize. As children, we imagine ourselves blasting off on the first spaceship to Mars, being elected president, or playing lead guitar in a rock-and-roll band. As adults, we daydream about retiring early, winning the lottery, or vacationing in Bora Bora. We might acknowledge that our fantasies are in another galaxy far from the real world, but we give ourselves license to explore, to play, to escape to a better place. After all, it never hurts to dream, and sometimes dreams come true. But even if they don't, they inspire us to improve our realities.

When it comes to sexual fantasies, however, we too often feel guilty or ashamed for allowing our mind's eye to wander. For example, we might hear a voice from the past ordering us to banish impure thoughts, or a repressed culture dictating what's normal and what's not. Unfortunately, some of us completely shut down our fantasy factories and resign ourselves to a lifetime of uninspired, unimaginative sex.

This chapter encourages you to reignite your fantasy flames for the benefit of both you and your partner. Here you learn the upside of sexual fantasies, how to use them to identify and understand your secret desires, how to embellish your existing fantasies, and how to utilize fantasy as a technique to effectively infuse your lovemaking with spark and sizzle.

Understanding Sexual Fantasy

Fantasies often are intense scenes or sensory impressions that either pop into your brain like uninvited guests or you choose to play over and over in your mind like a favorite movie. They might be inspired by incidents you experienced or witnessed, by friends or passersby you find attractive, by magazine photos or romance novels, or by a host of other input that stimulates your sexual and sensual appetite and feeds your imagination. They can be as innocently pleasurable as an intimate massage or as repulsive as rape.

However, it is important to realize that fantasies are thoughts, not actions. They are your possessions, which you can choose to lock away in your mind or share with your partner. You can choose whether you act them out, how to act them out, and with whom you act them out. Never forget that you are in control.

As long as your fantasies remain in your mind, they have little downside. They cannot get you into trouble with the law, harm you or anyone else, or serve as a valid reason for guilt or shame. (One of the most useless and misery-provoking exercises is to feel guilty about having a thought.) On the other hand, the potential benefits of fantasies are countless. Here are a few of the benefits of fantasies:

- Fantasies are usually pleasurable.
- Fantasies enable you to airbrush out the imperfections. You can trim pounds off your thighs, remove wrinkles, improve your socioeconomic status, and even maximize your natural endowments.
- Fantasies provide a risk-free environment for sexual experimentation. You can do things and have things done to you that you would never consider doing in reality.
- Fantasies can help identify what's missing for you from your sex life or what could enhance your lovemaking. (Be careful not to blame yourself or your partner if you see something as "missing.")

- Fantasies give you more control over your own pleasure, thus taking some of the pressure off of your partner. Fantasies during sexual intercourse can increase your arousal and give you the extra boost you might need to achieve orgasm or a higher level of satisfaction.

- Fantasies can help you add novelty to your lovemaking and make it more pleasurable for both you and your partner.

- Fantasies enable you to rehearse sexual behavior, no matter how risky it might be, in a safe, secure environment. You can act promiscuous without the risk of disease or complications of an unwanted pregnancy, have an affair without committing adultery, and even break the law without being arrested.

- Fantasies can greatly enhance your masturbation experience.

GET PSYCHED

"Sexual fantasy is the mental juice, or the vibrator of the mind. It is a wonderful, natural phenomenon, and I believe it's universal and very similar to dreaming. I call it a 'sibling to a dream,' and it helps both men and women in terms of sexual responsiveness and interest. It is a wonderful resource when it's functioning well and doesn't have any negative side effects." —*Wendy Maltz, L.C.S.W., sex therapist and author of* Private Thoughts, Exploring the Power of Women's Sexual Fantasies

Fantasies as Fingerprints Just as no two people have the same fingerprints, so do no two people have the same fantasies or combination of fantasies. A powerful CEO might fantasize that he's at the mercy of his dominatrix secretary. A conservative businesswoman might fantasize about making love to a gypsy. A person might even have conflicting fantasies—one fantasy of being timid and inhibited and being coerced into sex, and another fantasy of doing a striptease in a crowded bar.

People fantasize while driving to work in the morning, shopping for groceries, in the middle of passionate sex, or while taking a coffee break. The fantasy can be a vivid, complex scene that plays like a movie during masturbation, or it can be as understated as the memory of a morning kiss or an arousing scent that wafts past your mind. Some people have a single fantasy that they've had all their lives, whereas others have hundreds of very detailed fantasies, and still others do not fantasize at all. (We'll work on that issue later in this chapter.)

Debunking Fantasy Myths Our culture has generated several popular myths about sexual fantasy that give this very positive sexual tool a somewhat negative reputation. To liberate your mind and help you enlighten others, let's address and debunk the most common myths about fantasy:

GET PSYCHED

Many people are reticent to share their fantasies with their partners out of fear that the partner will feel jealous or inadequate or will view the fantasy as sick or abnormal. Although you might need to be careful about sharing your private fantasies (only you know what is prudent to do in your unique relationship), some partners discover, much to their delight, that they actually have the same or similar fantasies. Frequently, one partner in the relationship will find the other partner's fantasies quite arousing or complementary to their own.

- **Myth:** People fantasize because they're not getting sex.

  Fact: Studies show that people who have the most active sex lives have the most active fantasy lives, as well.

- **Myth:** If you fantasize it, you must want to do it.

  Fact: People commonly have fantasies about things they would never do because the act would be unlawful, harmful, overly risky, impossible, or beyond their personal limits and values, or because they simply do not want to act it out.

- **Myth:** Women rarely, if ever, fantasize.

  Fact: Nearly all women fantasize, although they might not classify what they're doing as sexual fantasy, because their fantasies can be less graphic, more sensory.

Male and Female Fantasies

Although women and men both fantasize, the focus of their fantasies differs greatly. Men tend to be more visual and their fantasies more extensive, more specific to the sexual act, more focused on genitalia, and less focused on the relationship, their partner, intimacy, or romance. No knows for sure why this is so. Some speculate that the cause is biological—men must seek out partners to procreate, or simply because men have higher levels of testosterone. Others point to the availability and acceptability of the sexual media that targets the male audience. And still others chalk it up to the fact that cultures commonly discourage men from focusing on or expressing feelings about other aspects of their sexuality that might turn them on, such as a strong emotional bond or a woman's scent. But what we do know is that men think and fantasize about sex more than women. In 1992, Edward Laumann and his colleagues found that over half the men they surveyed thought about sex one or more times a day, while that was true for less than twenty percent of the women. They also found that those who fantasized most about sex were those who sought out the most sex with their partners.

Although men and women typically focus on different sensory stimuli during lovemaking, their fantasy lives share a great deal. Men and women both commonly fantasize in daydreams, while masturbating, and while making love with their partners. Both sexes are also turned on by similar themes: sex with a stranger or in a group, forcing sex on someone or having it forced on them, making love in different places such as a car or on a beach, or watching themselves or others having sex.

GET PSYCHED

B. J. Ellis and L. E. Symons, in the *Journal of Sex Research,* summarized their review of the literature on sex differences with respect to sexual fantasies as, "male sexual fantasies tend to be more ambiguous, frequently visual, specifically sexual, promiscuous, and active. Female sexual fantasies tend to be more contextual, emotive, intimate, and passive."

Types of Fantasies According to Wendy Maltz, some women tend to "discount their fantasies because they're not as specific as male sexual fantasies ...." In her study, Maltz interviewed 100 women ages 19 to 66 and asked them to describe their fantasies.

Maltz found that female sexual fantasies could be broken down into two categories: *sensory type* and *scripted*. Sensory-type fantasies focus on sensations, images, or pictures. Maltz reports that a number of women in her study mentioned "Denzel Washington's lips or Patrick Swayze's biceps" or a horse charging up a hill. Scripted fantasies are scenarios that play out more like plots in a book or movie. Maltz identified female scripted fantasies as representing six role types: Pretty Maiden, Wild Woman, Beloved, Dominatrix, Victim, and Voyeur.

Whenever I share a fantasy or act it out, the fantasy loses its erotic appeal. Would I be better off keeping it private and not trying to act it out?

"The decision of whether to share or act out a fantasy is up to you. The simple process of sharing a fantasy can diminish its erotic appeal, but many people find that sharing fantasies is erotic in itself, and it can also help educate your partner on what you might like. You can always revise a fantasy to focus on some other aspect of it that turns you on or to embellish it, making it even more erotic. In some cases, sharing your fantasy or acting it out makes it seem less erotic simply because the reality of it just wasn't as good as you had fantasized it to be. If that's the case, you might be able to "rewrite" the fantasy and try it some other way, or you might just need to practice; for example, if you acted out a fantasy about having sex in a different position, and it seemed awkward, you might need to practice three or four times to master it."
—*Cynthia Jayne, Ph.D., clinical psychologist and sexologist*

Although Maltz's study focuses on female sexual fantasies, her categories apply to male sexual fantasies, as well. As a general rule, male sexual fantasies are more scripted, whereas female sexual fantasies lean more toward the sensory type. Trends do change, however. Maltz is finding that female fantasies of younger women are beginning to become more scripted, due perhaps to the increase in the amount of information available in the last 20–30 years, such as articles in *Cosmopolitan* that tell women just what to do and how to do it.

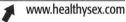

WEB TALK: Wendy Maltz provides some excellent information for exploring your sexuality at:

www.healthysex.com

Male Fantasies Reading descriptions of male fantasies can benefit both partners. The man might come away less inhibited and carrying a few movie trailers for his own fantasies, while the woman picks up a few tips on what her man might find erotic. The following fantasies collected from a variety of men can help inspire your own:

- I imagine myself looking out my bedroom window, peering through the neighbor's window. My neighbors are undressing each other slowly and deliberately. I watch as the husband unbuttons his wife's blouse and removes it, as he undoes her bra, as he drops her skirt, revealing her luscious body.

- I picture myself seducing my unapproachable co-worker, getting closer and closer to her with each passing glance. As she's making copies, I sneak into the copy room and silently close and lock the door. I lift her skirt, bend her over the copy machine, and we proceed to have sex. Afterward, we continue to have a normal work relationship as if nothing had happened, but we exchange knowing looks and realize that she can play the dominant role at any time.

- I dream that my wife hires a sexy maid to clean the house once a week knowing that I think she's hot and perceiving that the maid has a thing for me. One day, she schedules the maid to clean the house knowing that I'll be there alone. The maid arrives in one of those skimpy French-maid outfits and leads me to the bedroom where she begins to force herself on me. My wife returns home and feigns being stunned. She becomes aroused and joins in the *ménage à trois*.

- I envision my wife giving me oral sex. One evening, while we're driving to dinner, she scoots up close against me, reaches over, slowly unzips my pants, reaches in, and strokes my penis. Instant rush. She then leans down, takes me in her mouth, and slowly sucks till I explode.

- I imagine myself going down to my condo's swimming pool to take a dip just before it closes. Nobody's there, so I strip down and dive in naked. My sexy neighbor who rarely even glances at me shows up, drapes her towel over one of the chairs, and, with her back to me, seductively removes her suit. She turns to face me, slowly approaches the side of the pool, dives in, and swims over to me. We proceed to have wet, wild, passionate sex. When done, we both swim away as if nothing had happened.

- I picture myself sitting on a beach watching the world pass by when I see a group of bikini-clad, college coeds off in the distance walking toward me. As they get closer, they begin running toward me. They pin me to the ground, strip me, spank me, and humiliate me in front of passersby, and force me to join in a wild orgy.

Female Fantasies Reading descriptions of female sexual fantasies can help make a woman feel more comfortable with her fantasies and teach a man a thing or two about slowing down and paying attention to the sensual elements his lover desires. These fantasies, collected from various women illustrate the point:

- I imagine myself on vacation in St. Martin. Walking down the street, I meet a gorgeous Frenchman. He takes a strand of ivy off the wall, puts it around my neck, and draws me toward him. We walk down the street and sit at a bistro enjoying the wine and a sensuous meal. Then he takes me back to his bedroom where we make wild intense love for three days. Afterward he wants me to meet his friends.

But I realize it's time to leave. He walks me back to the street where we met, we kiss goodbye. I know I've had the best of him.

- I picture myself at the end of a long day, hot, tired, and achy. I stretch out on my bed naked on cool silk sheets surrounded by the soft light of scented candles. My sexy, sensitive neighbor enters with a bottle of silky massage oil and gently massages my tired muscles from my shoulders to my ankles to the soles of my feet. We proceed to make slow, comfortable, romantic love until sunrise.

- I like to daydream that my partner and I have a fabulous night out. The food is fabulous, the restaurant's ambience is scintillating, and we talk as we haven't talked since our college days. We go home and slip naked into the pool for a quick dip and gently stroke each other as we swim past one another. When we get out of the pool the air feels warm and comforting and I wrap my towel around me tight and toasty.

- Any time I need help to get aroused, I imagine our honeymoon, making love on the beach at night, how everything seemed perfect, and in the middle of it I always come.

- I fantasize about being at a party when another woman approaches my husband and me. She asks if a woman has ever made love to me. I say, "No." She takes my hand and asks us to join her in another room. She undresses me as my husband watches, and she starts touching me all over.

- I imagine myself strapped to my bed and blindfolded. I hear movement but cannot make out the sounds. I feel the soft intensity of feathers sliding up and down my arms and along the insides of my thighs, tickling me mercilessly. I struggle to free myself as the sensation travels up, along my stomach, circling my breasts, and traveling down to my genitals.

- One of my favorite fantasies is to have sex at an exclusive restaurant with my lover. I'm wearing the little black dress, no panties. I sit across from him gazing into his blue-gray eyes, but as we talk, we scoot closer together. I feel something under the table … a little firm pressure on my upper thighs. My skirt begins sliding up higher on my thighs. I feel his finger slide slowly up along the inside of my legs and then gently brushing his hand on me, feeling my wetness.

- I have a fantasy in which I'm a nurse in white stockings and high heels giving a male patient an enema. I reach up to the cabinet; the tops of my stockings show and I know he is getting aroused. I come back to him and shave his pubic area for surgery. I know it's sweet torture for him.

WEB TALK: Check out the following website for additional details about fantasies and to read more actual fantasies written by others:

↑ www.howtohavegoodsex.com

Using Fantasies to Achieve Ecstasy

Your fantasy itself can often be enough to help you and your partner achieve sexual ecstasy. You needn't explore it for hidden meaning or use it to analyze your relationship or to modify your techniques. The fantasy alone can help you feel sexy and confident. It might arouse you during the initial stages of a sexual encounter or act as the boost you need to achieve orgasm. Simply by embellishing your fantasies, as explained later in this chapter, you can maximize their effectiveness.

Then again, some self-reflection on what a fantasy means to you can often reveal facets of your lovemaking that you can build upon. For instance, a fantasy about group sex might reveal a desire for more physical contact and stimulation. Group sex might not be safe, prudent, or in tune with your lifestyle. However, by reflecting on the fantasy without judging it, you might be able to think up ways to establish greater physical contact or introduce sex toys into your bedroom.

Making the Most of Female Fantasies Because women typically involve more senses in their sexual fantasies, female sexual
fantasies commonly reveal sensual details that the woman finds
stimulating. To maximize the power of your fantasies, ask yourself
the following questions: What scents are in your fantasy? What
sounds do you hear? How does the bed feel—silky and cool, soft
and warm, like a sunny beach? Do you taste anything? Are you
looking into your lover's eyes? Zoom in on the details and if you
find something specific that turns you on, try to work it in to
your lovemaking or give it more focus. Here are some examples:

- A woman fantasized about having sex with a gargoyle. Upon
  exploring the fantasy, the woman noticed that the gargoyle
  was groaning deeply during the encounter. She encouraged
  her lover to try moaning during lovemaking and found it
  intensely arousing.

- Many women and men remove the visual element of sex
  simply by flipping off the lights. If you fantasize about gazing into your lover's eyes or watching people have sex, you
  might need more visual stimulation. The soft light of a candle on a nightstand is often sufficient.

- Some women find particular scents very arousing and others
  repulsive. Focus on any pleasant aromas that might waft
  through your fantasies and try to re-create them where you
  make love. Massage oils, scented candles, perfumes, colognes,
  and fresh-cut flowers can do wonders for lovemaking.

- A fantasy about being naked in public might reveal a secret
  desire to act out as an exhibitionist. Perhaps doing a striptease for your partner (or even visiting a nude beach) would
  be enough to satisfy your desire.

- Focus on the sounds you hear in your fantasies. Can you
  hear a train passing by? Is music playing in the background?
  Is there a particular song that turns you on? If you fantasize
  being on a beach, perhaps a relaxation tape that plays the
  sounds of waves could be the aphrodisiac you are seeking.

Keep in mind that all women are different and that you have your own unique fantasies and sets of fantasies. Your fantasies might have a strong visual element. If they do, focus on the visual—the way your partner dresses, the appearance of the room, the color of the sheets, and so on.

Making the Most of Male Fantasies Given that most male fantasies focus on the visual, on genitalia, and on the sex act itself, it's logical to examine those aspects of male sexual fantasies when trying to discover factors that might make the sex act more pleasurable for a man. Unlike female fantasies that commonly reveal a desire for increased sensory stimulation, male sexual fantasies often reveal a desire for increased visual and physical stimulation. Following are some examples:

- A man fantasized that he was having sex with his wife when she was a little girl. When he expressed the fantasy to his wife, she was repulsed and began to suspect that he was a pedophile. She finally came to understand that the fantasy was not a reflection of her husband's desire to behave in a particular way; it was simply a thought that turned him on. She shaved her pubic hair and role-played with her husband, using the fantasy to increase their sexual pleasure.

- Men commonly fantasize about lingerie models, but it's usually unrealistic to try to live the fantasy with an actual lingerie model. However, you might be able to role-play it with your partner in a lingerie outfit that you find most appealing.

- If you like to watch couples making love to one another, in your fantasy what is it you like, specifically? Is it the undressing itself or the fact that the lovers are standing and facing one another? Is there something about what the man is wearing that turns you on? Something about what the woman is wearing? Something about where they are? Is there some element you can incorporate or give greater focus to in your own lovemaking?

- Other sensory stimuli turn on men as well as women. Scents, sounds, music, and tastes can all contribute to arousal. Sometimes sensory impressions call up vivid memories of the past that can add even more to the intensity of your fantasy.

Fantasizing During Sex

Fantasizing during sexual activity is perfectly normal and acceptable, as long as you don't put yourself down for it. Studies show that approximately 50 percent of women and 75 percent of men fantasize while engaging in sexual activity with their partners, most frequently at the beginning to increase their arousal and at the end to achieve orgasm. Fantasy is a way of taking responsibility for your own orgasm and assisting your partner. Moderate fantasizing during partner sex rarely leads to problems unless guilt or jealousy creeps in to spoil it.

There are good reasons to share and also to not share some of your sexual fantasies with your partner. If your partner is the jealous type or feels insecure, it might be better to consider keeping your fantasies private. Later in this book, you will learn what factors to consider when deciding, but for now, it's better to err on the side of caution. Most people do not become upset when their partner fantasizes about making love to a complete stranger, such as a movie star, but a jealous partner is more likely to become upset with fantasies about a friend, neighbor, a family member, an ex, or some unusual practice he or she doesn't understand.

GET PSYCHED

Think back to the best sex experience you've had in your life. Close your eyes and relive it. Imagine having that level of sexual satisfaction with your current partner. Relive the scene in your mind with your current partner. What's similar? What's different? Which details do you find most arousing?

Taking Fantasy Breaks

If you don't fantasize or don't fantasize very often, start taking fantasy breaks during the day—two to three breaks of one to five minutes each. Close your eyes, and allow one of your favorite fantasies to unfold. Make it a habit, and you'll find that your fantasy breaks can help you feel much more sexual throughout the day.

If you're having trouble getting started, you can often expand your capacity for mental eroticism by shifting focus to any erotic thoughts that you might have during the day. Do you stop them? How? Why? Do you feel guilty for giving your sexual thoughts license to play out? If so, this can immediately shut down your fantasy. Ask yourself if there is any valid reason why you should feel guilty over having pleasurable thoughts. When you find that there is none, you know that your next step is to release the guilt and savor the pleasure.

For those who have trouble coming up with ideas, try focusing on some aspect of your partner that you find particularly attractive: a body part, vocal quality, scent, skin texture, hair, whatever, and expand from there. Or, read some erotica. There is a wide selection of erotica from which to choose, ranging from soft porn to hard-core stuff, for both men and women. If you're embarrassed to purchase these items at the store, seek them out by mail or on the Internet. Try visualizing yourself in the stories, or even write your own erotic adventure. Start with a tiny detail, such as a person you find attractive, a song that stimulates you, or a specific event or activity, such as a dance, dinner out, watching a movie, or swimming. Then, of course, feel free to work up to making love.

Embellishing Your Fantasies

Once you have one or two fantasies clearly in your mind, you can begin to embellish them to intensify your feelings and fully exploit their power. Novelty is the key. If you fail to invest in a fantasy by changing it, adding to it, or taking it a little further, it can quickly transform itself from a dynamic sensual escapade into a boring rerun. Try the following techniques to re-invigorate your fantasies:

- Write them down without worrying about spelling, grammar, punctuation, or storyline. Just write. Free writing is an act of invention. You might just find that your fantasy embellishes itself and leads you on an erotic journey.

- Work your partner into the fantasy to take it one step closer to reality. How would it play out in reality? What did you need to change to make it work?

- Try placing yourself in different roles or viewing the fantasy from different angles. If you're passive, imagine yourself as assertive. If you're watching, imagine yourself as involved in the act with someone else watching. But, don't dwell on what doesn't work. Simply move on to something else. You will know very clearly when you are on target.

- Examine the scene using all of your senses, one at a time. What do you hear, touch, smell, taste, see, and feel?

Remember, this is pleasure, not performance. In the world of fantasy, you never need to prove anything. You are the absolute ruler of your fantasy domain!

Fantasies on the Fringe

Fringe sex is sex outside the box—any type of sexual behavior that tests the boundaries of what our culture considers normal. This includes bondage and discipline (B&D), sadomasochism (S&M), swinging, *ménages à trois, fetishes*, and many other variations that are beyond the scope of this book:

Bondage and discipline (B&D) is a sexual practice in which a person restrains or pretends to restrain or overpower his or her partner in some way. Bondage relates to restraint of some sort. Discipline refers to power control—domination and submission.

PsychSpeak

A **fetish** is an attraction to and need for an inanimate object or a part of the body that serves as the focus of sexual arousal.

Sadomasochism (S&M) refers to sexual practices in which a person inflicts mental or physical pain on another person (sadism) or is subjected to pain (masochism) for erotic purposes.

Swinging is an alternative lifestyle in which two couples or more agree to trade partners, allow each other to seek out other partners for sex, or have group sex together. It can include *ménages à trois.*

Ménages à trois occur when three people engage in sexual activity at the same time.

Because the fantasy world has infinitely less serious consequences than the real world, people obviously are less inhibited in fantasizing about all types of fringe sex than they would be in actually acting it out. That's fortunate for couples, because fantasies about sex on the fringe, whether or not they're acted out, can be extremely erotic.

Whether or not you fantasize about fringe sexuality or choose to act on those fantasies, these variations can add much novelty to your lovemaking, introduce role-playing, and stimulate very erotic discussions.

GET PSYCHED

A 1990 Kinsey report stated that 6–10 percent of Americans have actually engaged in or practiced sadomasochist (S&M) or bondage and discipline (B&D) sex. Of course, that estimate is much higher now, and the increase in media coverage is making it more mainstream. The topic is commonplace on the Internet and has even been featured in *Time* magazine. Several clubs around the country also invite people to explore the possibilities. But be careful, some S&M sex can be dangerous.

Disturbing or Compulsive Fantasies

Although sexual fantasy has little downside, fantasies can become problematic if they are disturbing or compulsive. A disturbing sexual fantasy is typically one that clashes with what the fantasist considers morally acceptable; the person finds the fantasy repulsive, and yet it might be the only way he or she can become aroused. A compulsive fantasy is any fantasy that takes over way more of a person's time or sex life than he or she wants it to—for example, when a person refuses sex with a partner to explore sexual content on the Internet or finds a fantasy very disturbing and can't find a way to change it or get it out of his or her mind.

Making Fantasies Less Disturbing Although fantasies have an overwhelmingly positive effect on most sexual relationships, guilt and shame can spoil the moment. For example, if you feel guilty fantasizing about your best friend's husband while making love to your husband, you're likely to feel a little less aroused. To prevent this from happening, remember that crucial ingredient of sexual ecstasy—self permission.

you're not alone

Susan and Tom, a professional couple in their mid 30s, had been married for five years and were getting along well. However, Susan had no interest in having sex with Tom, and Tom complained that Susan was unresponsive and was having sex only to please him. Tom was thinking of leaving the relationship, because he felt as though he was the cause of Susan's suffering. Unknown to Tom, Susan had private sexual fantasies about women, though she had no intention of exploring that lifestyle. Unfortunately, Susan's fantasies triggered her feelings of guilt and shame. So she shut down in the presence of Tom. Eventually, Susan reluctantly shared her fantasies with Tom who not only accepted and understood Susan but also found himself aroused by her fantasies. The fact that Tom knew, now, and accepted it relieved Susan immediately. Tom would ask Susan to describe what she did in the fantasy, which turned them both on. They then worked toward bringing Tom into the fantasy as part of a *ménage à trois*. Susan had thought she was *inorgasmic* (unable to achieve orgasm); she eventually became orgasmic and no longer needed to use her fantasy every time to achieve orgasm.

If a particular fantasy makes you feel ashamed or guilty, ask yourself the following questions: *What is it I'm really doing that is wrong?* Remember, this is a thought, not an act. You haven't *done* anything that warrants a judgment of right or wrong. *Why do I think it's wrong?* (As opposed to asking why society thinks it's wrong, why your mother thinks it's wrong, or why your parish priest or even your partner may think it's wrong.) *If I heard this dictum/belief or condemnation for the first time today, would I believe it?* These questions can serve as a powerful self-intervention to pull you out of a tailspin when guilt or shame try to ruin your fantasy or love life.

you're not alone

Tanya is very disturbed by her fantasy. She had been sexually abused by her father and was having a recurring fantasy that involved an older man seducing a little girl. She and her therapist worked on this issue, and the therapist used every technique she knew to address the issue and thoroughly explore the fantasy. The therapist would even interview characters from the fantasy to have them speak about their core desires, their unfulfilled needs, so that Tanya could see and analyze the connection to the past abuse that had occurred.

Tanya and her therapist also explored the fantasy from a sensory perspective and found that the seduction occurred very slowly—a little touch and then no touch, a little touch and then no touch—and so Tanya realized that the sexual fantasy had also served as a way of providing a stimulating rhythm and pace that she found arousing. Over time, she was able to integrate that into her lovemaking with her husband; he would approach her much more slowly and gradually.

Tanya's therapist also helped her bring the fantasy gradually to the point at which both actors in the fantasy were consenting adults. Tanya would replay the fantasy, each time making the girl older and the man younger until both participants were around 20 years old. Her fantasy retained the arousing effects of the slow, rhythmic seduction but she was able to eliminate the details that she found repulsive.

If you have a disturbing or compulsive fantasy that is out of control or getting in the way of sexual ecstasy with your partner, you can try reducing or eliminating the guilt and then gradually revise the fantasy to make it less disturbing. Most people can take control of such fantasies (typically with the help of a qualified therapist) by following this simple, but sometimes lengthy, two-step process:

1. If you're putting yourself down for having the fantasy, stop. If the fantasy is inspired by sexual abuse you suffered in the past, that's not your fault. If a disturbing fantasy comes from a secret desire, that's not your fault, either. Give yourself permission to let go of the guilt.

2. Modify the disturbing details of your fantasy in increments. If you fantasize that you're punching your partner, for example, try to fantasize slapping or spanking instead. Over time, make the slapping more and more gentle until it becomes a soft caress.

Controlling Fantasies When you are in control of your fantasies, they act as your own personal sex toys, stimulating the lust centers of your brain. However, when the fantasies take control of you, and the line between what is fantasy and what is real is blurred, they can destroy your relationship, get you fired, and even land you in jail. A fantasy is obsessive when it takes control of your thoughts—that is, when it plays over and over in your mind and you cannot stop it. A fantasy becomes compulsive when it controls behavior. For example, if a person has a fetish fantasy that they must act out whenever they have sex, or the person must watch porn video or chat on the Internet in order to get turned on, the fantasies are compulsive. The key word that makes this all problematic is *must.* (To the extent that you are operating on choice, it is not necessarily problematic.) Medication (such as SSRI antidepressants) is often quite helpful in controlling obsessive thoughts and compulsions. Sometimes it might take the right combination of medication and psychotherapy to do the job if an obsession or compulsion is severe.

To determine whether you have compulsive fantasies, ask yourself two questions: "Has my fantasy become essential for my arousal and orgasm?" and "Can I stop it?" If your fantasy is essential for your arousal and you cannot stop it on your own, you may want to seek professional help.

Internet Pros and Cons The Internet can be a wonderful place to explore sex, stimulate lust, and gather details for embellishing your own fantasies. It provides information on every aspect and manifestation of human sexuality from basic sex education to S&M. It features romantic stories, soft porn, hard porn, still images, videos, live chat, live shows, and much much more. Indirectly, the Internet makes people more comfortable about their own sexual desires and fantasies by helping people realize that they're not alone and that much of what they think and feel is perfectly normal.

A study by Al Cooper, psychologist and clinical director at the San Jose Marital & Sexuality Centre, and his colleagues in the *Journal of Sex and Marital Therapy* found that a vast majority of people do not consider their use of the Internet for sexual activity a problem. However almost 10 percent said they were addicted to the Internet. 8 percent of those men and women spend over 10 hours per week visiting Internet sex sites, some as many as 26 hours a week. The main reasons that people said they visited Internet sites were for distraction, education, coping with stress, exploring sexual fantasies, and socializing. Cooper points out that the Internet is a popular medium for those seeking sexual information and stimulation, because it is powered by what he refers to as the "Triple A engine of the Internet: access, affordability and anonymity." Cooper believes that the influence of the Internet could cause the next sexual revolution.

According to Jennifer Schneider, co-author of *Cybersex Exposed: Simple Fantasy or Obsession?*, "The Internet is the crack cocaine of sexual addiction." The Internet also makes it much easier to start an affair. In the real world, the challenge of approaching another person and determining whether the person wants to have an affair is often enough to thwart the thought. On the Internet, you can find a willing someone in any of numerous chat boards, plan the time and place, and even

GET PSYCHED

T. Egan found that 20 to 33 percent of Internet users engaged in some form of online sexual activity.

106

decide how far you're both willing to go. Of course, plenty of risks are still involved, so be mindful of what you are doing.

What You Can Do

Right now, here are some things you can do to fine-tune your fantasy life:

- ☐ Write one page of sizzling erotica, something that would arouse you greatly if you were to read it somewhere else. If you feel uneasy writing it down, keep it in your head.
- ☐ Use your fantasy breaks to embellish your page of erotica with additional stimulating details.
- ☐ Fantasize having a tryst with someone you pass during the day; this can be your partner, someone in line at the grocery store, someone you see driving next to you, an attractive co-worker, or even your favorite sexy celebrity.
- ☐ Record (in your mind, on paper, or on an audio recorder) a sexual experience you had that was truly spectacular. Work your current partner into a fantasy based on that experience. Embellish it with sensory details and additional action.
- ☐ Identify the primary sensual mode at work in one of your fantasies. Is it visual, olfactory, tactile, auditory, kinesthetic, or gustatory? Add sensory details; for example, if your scene is silent, make someone speak.
- ☐ Work one particularly arousing facet of one of your fantasies into your lovemaking this week. You need not even tell your partner about it.
- ☐ Most important, enjoy! Why else would you ever want to have a fantasy, anyway?

Ecstasy and Your Relationship

Passion alone can fuel a short-term relationship for quite a while, but a long-term relationship calls for something more reliable to keep it running. Most long-term relationships depend on a deep, interpersonal connection in which the partners accept one another, express mutual respect and admiration, display fondness, attend to one another's needs, and support each other in their struggles and pursuits. To the extent that a couple is able to establish a loving, caring relationship in which they both feel respected, appreciated, and secure, they have established a healthy environment that can foster the relationship connection that is such an important ingredient for sexual ecstasy.

In this chapter, we explore the factors that contribute to strengthening a long-term interpersonal relationship and explain why the non-sexy factors are so crucial to achieving sexual fulfillment, especially in a long-term relationship. This chapter also offers information and exercises that can help you and your partner become more knowledgeable of and more attentive to each other's physical and emotional needs. By the end of this chapter, you and your partner will have a clearer idea of what you can do to strengthen your relationship in order to experience sexual ecstasy together.

Connecting with Your Partner

In a long-term relationship, sexual ecstasy depends a great deal on the connectedness that partners feel toward one another. The strength and intensity of this connectedness is determined by several factors, including trust, love, intimacy, and physical attraction. Collectively, these factors form the two major *pillars* that characterize strong relationships: passion and comfort. The extent to which both passion and comfort are present in your relationship determines how solid your partnership is.

Early in a relationship, passion usually plays the greater role, since it is passion that usually gets you and your partner together in the first place. As a relationship evolves, comfort generally plays the greater role, as you work together to provide each other a safe, secure foundation on which to build your life together. Relationships can have passion without much comfort and vice versa, but most committed long-term relationships need a good amount of both to make the relationship work optimally for both partners.

> **GET PSYCHED**
>
> "It's not sex that gives you pleasure, but the lover."
> —*Marge Piercy*

Passion Passion is the emotional component of a relationship. Positive passion generally is what triggers that initial attraction that makes your partner so special to you at the early stages of your romance. It's experienced as love, sexual attraction, well-being, infatuation, desire, trust, and the joy you feel when you are around your partner or even thinking about him or her. Happiness, excitement, and sexual energy are all tied to *positive* passion. The *negative* side of passion, of course, consists of such things as anger, jealousy, fear, and longing.

A relationship based only on passion is usually marked by extreme highs and lows. Ultimately, it may be painfully stormy or short, or both. A relationship lacking passion altogether is typically something akin to a platonic friendship; the most you can probably hope for is to be good friends.

Passion is the spark that draws two people together and usually provides the ultimate motivation for keeping them together. However, passion does not provide the stability that a long-term relationship needs. For that, long-term couples depend on the other pillar, comfort.

Comfort Comfort—warm, easy, natural acceptance—is the day-to-day glue that allows a couple to have an enjoyable and peaceful coexistence. Couples who have stayed together for decades and who describe themselves as happy together, ultimately point to their comfort with one another as the ingredient that has sustained their relationship over time.

Comfort comes from knowing that it's okay to be yourself. More specifically, it is the extent to which you *can* be yourself, at ease, in a relationship without being obsessed with pleasing your partner or demanding that your partner constantly be attentive to your needs. Accepting your partner for the person he or she is, being able to deal with conflicts, and having enough in common (such as values and life goals) create the kind of psychological environment in which you can best nurture and sustain your relationship.

It is important to note that for comfort to be authentic in a relationship, it needs to be mutual. If only one partner has it, comfort is an illusion. When the element of comfort is mutual, it generally becomes the foundation on which you can build the strong framework to handle other issues and resolve most conflicts before they have a chance to damage your relationship. When both comfort and passion are sufficiently balanced in a relationship, that balance generally creates the foundation for sexual ecstasy.

111

you're not alone

Feeling turned on by your partner's nonsexual behavior is not only normal, but also very healthy. We asked several people what would turn them on, and found that for many of them, the answer pointed to an area that one might not think is related to sex:

"What would turn me on? And this might sound strange. But if I came home and she really appreciated me for what I do rather than giving me a list of things that need to be done around the house and with the kids. I know she works really hard during the day, but I do, too. Maybe giving me a little bit of a break would make me feel that she thinks that I'm more than a money machine." (Steve)

"It really helps to get me in the mood when he's romantic. It could be bringing home flowers or having a nice dinner together. We spend time talking to each other first and then somehow we wind up in the bedroom. It just feels like we've been connected and romantic for a while. It's so much more natural than when we've been apart all day and he expects sex when we meet in the bedroom at night. (Jennifer)

"What turns me on? Maybe this doesn't make sense, but I really find him most attractive when he's helping me take care of the baby. I love how he is with her and it just makes me feel that we're really a family and then I just get all warm." (Judy)

"I get turned on when he helps with the housework. I know many people wouldn't find that sexy, but it makes me feel that we're partners in this and also we wind up having more time together." (Karen)

Trust One important part of comfort is trust, the secure feeling you have when you believe that your partner is committed to you, is committed to the relationship, and will support you in your struggles and pursuits. Trust comes from knowing that your partner is there for you and will remain at your side, even if the going gets tough. Perhaps most importantly, trust is a prerequisite for intimacy. In a trusting relationship a couple is more open to revealing potentially vulnerable thoughts or emotions, because the partners are less concerned that there will be negative consequences for what they might reveal.

Intimacy Intimacy is the bond you have that enables you to share your innermost self with another person. Sometimes, but not always, this means opening that part of yourself to which no one else has access. No universal definition exists of what is the right amount of intimacy. All couples ultimately develop their own degree of intimacy.

According to Pat Love, author of *The Truth About Love,* "Passion implies intimacy—that there's an intimate connection between two people." She points out that one of the paradoxes of intimacy in a long-term relationship is that it is often more challenging to open up and become intimate with someone who knows you well. You might reveal a secret or vulnerability to a complete stranger, because the person doesn't know you and you are fairly certain you will never encounter the person again, thus no consequences. But when someone knows you intimately and you have more to lose if the intimate detail is not received well by that person, you might tend to hold back. Even though this reticence is understandable, Love points out that passion in a long-term relationship depends a great deal on a couple's intimate knowledge of one another (including what their real turn-ons are).

Of course, couples do sometimes need to be careful about becoming too open. Some couples actually split up because they have shared one or two things too many. (Often they've been able to predict the inevitable result.) We've heard others attribute their long-term success to understanding what is best left unshared. (In some cases, much is left unsaid.) Yet others claim that they are 100 percent open with each other. Rare indeed, but possible.

GET PSYCHED

Pat Love is an advocate of "vintage love." Vintage love, she says, is the sense that "We've been through some rough times. You really know me, warts and all. We've been through some struggles; we're not just living in the anxiety of infatuation. (That's a big part of infatuation, because part of your brain knows that this isn't going to last.) But this is a person who really knows me; he knows my fears, my vulnerabilities. And the courage to be vulnerable with someone who knows you is far greater than with strangers."

Q&A

What does intimacy have to do with sex?

In a long-term relationship, intimacy allows partners to openly communicate without fear of being judged or ridiculed in any way. It enables you to freely communicate your needs, fantasies, and desires to your partner, who is usually the only person that can attend to those needs, desires, and fantasies, within the boundaries of your monogamous relationship. When you can be intimate, you can let your partner know the real you. When sexually intimate, you can allow your partner to know what turns you on.

The degree to which you are able to establish this important bond of intimacy in your relationship can be measured by how much comfort you share as a couple. Indeed, many couples have told us in so many words that intimacy takes place not so much in the bedroom as in the living room. We suggest that you think of intimacy in the broadest way possible. Yes, intimacy means sharing many secrets—but it also means sharing many common, everyday, and humdrum matters of life. The ability to communicate about the widest range of subjects and concerns is what strengthens your bond of intimacy and enhances your growth as a couple.

Empathy Another part of comfort is empathy—the ability to understand each other's point of view, feelings, and motives. Of course, no one can *fully* understand the complex inner workings of someone else's mind, but to the extent to which you and your partner are able to see things from each other's perspective, you can minimize conflict and *mis*understandings while significantly increasing your understanding of one another.

Empathy also applies to romance and lovemaking in that it is important for partners not only to learn more about each other's needs and desires, but also to realize that their needs and desires can be quite different, and to acknowledge that having differences is okay. Most of all, empathy will help you to gain the understanding as well as the information about your partner to increase sexual pleasure for both of you in your relationship.

What Makes a Good Relationship?

When two people decide to stay together in a long-term relationship, what is it that *keeps* that partnership together? In general, the two important pillars we have already mentioned that support the relationship and make it more fulfilling for both partners over time: passion and comfort.

But in talking with many individuals and couples, we have discovered a number of more specific traits and attitudes that characterize the components of the best relationships. A checklist might look like this:

☐ They recognize that *an issue that affects one person will affect both as a couple.* These couples usually do not consider an issue resolved until they find a win-win solution that favors both.

☐ They value their relationship because it *fulfills the needs of each partner.*

☐ They think in terms of each other's *long-range* best interests and exhibit the ability to grow both separately and together.

☐ They *like, trust, and respect each other.* These feelings transcend any disagreements.

☐ They *mutually support each other's pursuit of what is important to him or her.* Each partner encourages the other to develop in his or her own unique way. When partners do things and make sacrifices for each other, they don't feel like martyrs. Instead, each is able to have genuine concern for the other partner.

☐ They share an acceptable number of *common interests.*

☐ *They share power.* Neither partner dominates the other. Instead, partners take turns being the balloon and being the string.

☐ *They do not rely on each other for all of their validation.* They are able to get many of their needs fulfilled outside of their relationship.

☐ Both partners have a degree of *self-reliance*. They are comfortable with and are able to accept themselves to the same degree they expect acceptance from their mates.

☐ They have *similar values* in most important areas and have worked out a way to handle disagreements in others.

☐ They are *sexually compatible* to a degree that satisfies each partner.

☐ They *enjoy playing together non-sexually*, as well.

☐ They are *interdependent*. They know they can rely on each other and believe that they are stronger acting together than separately.

☐ They give each other a sufficient amount of *attention and appreciation*.

☐ They *respect each other's privacy* and the need at times to "stand on one's own two feet."

☐ Partners together and separately take responsibility to *give their relationship the time and attention it needs and deserves*.

☐ Partners get at least *as much pleasure out of loving one another* as they do out of being loved by the other.

From: *The Art Of Staying Together*, By Michael S. Broder, Hyperion Books, 1993.

Always keep in mind that you and your partner are in a relationship that is about both of you. If the relationship is functioning well, you both benefit. If one of you is hurt, to some extent you both suffer. If one of you succeeds, you both share the rewards. So when you have a disagreement that's challenging any aspect of your relationship, work together to resolve it, to dismiss it as of little importance, or to set it aside as one of those issues that you will agree to disagree about. But most importantly, don't let it fester or build up anger and resentment.

GET PSYCHED

"Your needs to be loved are far greater than your needs to have sex."
–Stephen B. Levine, M.D.

The best couples can lovingly disagree about practically anything without letting their relationships suffer.

Setting Realistic Expectations

Long-term relationships call for realistic expectations. Few people expect to live together without having disagreements or sometimes needing to confront uncomfortable situations or issues, but often a person's expectations can rise to a level that exceeds what he or she can reasonably expect. What is important is that you form expectations that are reasonable.

Psychologist John Gottman, Ph.D., who has studied relationships for over 30 years, reveals the importance of establishing reasonable expectations: "In my research, I observed that only about one third of conflicts really ever get resolved in a relationship. People need to realize that this is the normal state of affairs in most relationships." Gottman goes on to say that fondness and admiration are two of the most important ingredients for a successful long-term relationship. He found that men who accept the influence of their wives are much more likely to be in healthy, thriving relationships, and he found that 94 percent of people (men and women) who have a positive spin on the beginning of their relationship still feel positively about their relationship. In his latest book, *The Seven Principles for Making Marriage Work*, Dr. Gottman makes the point that working briefly with your marriage every day will do more for your health and longevity than working out in a health club!

Working on your marriage everyday means spending couple time together. It can be playing together, talking, or doing a task that needs to get done. It means being together, hopefully enjoying each other. Even onerous tasks can become enjoyable or at least less burdensome when you do them together. What it doesn't mean is waiting for the

WEB TALK: For information and research about relationships and for quizzes and assessments of your relationship, visit:

www.gottman.com

weekend, until that big job is done, or until your children grow up to be with your partner.

Patience, flexibility, and forgiveness, or at least a sense of humor, are also important in sustaining a long-term relationship. These traits are often present early in an involvement, but over time, your partner's eccentricities, blind spots, hang-ups, and foibles, which you may not have noticed or might even have found attractive early in the relationship, can become less endearing, even to the point of becoming serious issues between the two of you. Sometimes, these issues can be addressed and resolved, but oftentimes, the answer is simply to work at assigning them a lesser degree of importance and overlook them.

Stephen B. Levine, M.D., offers two pieces of advice: "First, develop your patience—listen when your partner speaks. Second, give your partner the benefit of the doubt when you feel as though you've been mistreated." According to Levine, "Integrity, honesty, and respect breed love; love breeds good sex; and good sex breeds love. It's a beautiful and powerful vortex that can lift your relationship to new heights. Do not abandon your ideal of love just because your partner might not currently be meeting your standards of love or your exact requirements. Tell your partner how much you value your relationship and how much you value your sexual lovemaking."

> **GET PSYCHED**
>
> "Remember that when anyone gives love to another, happiness emerges from their mind, and they then are the biggest beneficiaries."
> —the *Dalai Lama, author of* The Art of Happiness

What Does This Have to Do with Sexual Ecstasy?

Sexual attraction is often sufficient for fueling a short-term, passionate relationship. Long-term relationships tend to depend much more on that pillar of comfort, which is highly connected to your ability to resolve conflict together. So when problems in a long-term relationship arise—whether they have to do with finances, child rearing, in-laws, or even household chores—those problems have the potential to diminish the degree of desire and pleasure you feel for each other in your sexual relationship. Conversely, successes you achieve resolving those conflicts can have a very positive effect on increasing the intensity of desire and pleasure you experience together. Sex can be a fairly reliable barometer in determining the current satisfaction level in a long-term relationship. Ilda Ficher, Ph.D., who specializes in treating couples, says from her clinical experience, "When the relationship is running smoothly, sex accounts for only about 20 percent of a couple's happiness in the relationship. When the relationship is experiencing rough times, due to unsatisfying sex, sex can be responsible for as much as 80 percent of their unhappiness!"

Dr. Barry McCarthy, co-author with his wife, Emily McCarthy, of *Getting It Right the First Time* and *Sexual Awareness For Couples*, says that in all his workshops, writings, and teachings, he has discovered "that the way to think about sexuality is that sex plays a 15-20 percent role in a marriage, and it's a positive integral role, but it's not that big a deal in the marriage. And that the role of healthy marital sexuality is a shared pleasure. It helps you deal with some of the stresses of sharing your lives and being married. So it really is meant to energize the bond, but that the much bigger issue is that the couple has to develop a respect-trust intimacy bond."

Q&A

My career and family life are so hectic that we never seem to get around to sex. How can we turn this around?

Making time for sex is more about attitude than about the number of hours in a day. You need to see your time to make love as a higher priority. Take a closer look at how you are spending your time. With rare exceptions, couples who are willing to cut down on TV, optional social functions, telephone chatter, and computer time are able to resolve this issue in favor of more sex. Also be flexible as to when you make love. If late nights don't work, early mornings or afternoon "naps" are possible options. Be creative together about this, and you will find the time for that which you value most.

According to Dr. David Schnarch, director of the Marriage and Family Health Center in Evergreen, Colorado, and author of *Passionate Marriage* and *Resurrecting Sex*, the personal maturity you develop in a long-term relationship is a critical component in helping to achieve sexual ecstasy: "The prime factor in having a long-term, satisfying sexual relationship is personal maturity. Given that emotionally committed relationships are people-growing machines, there is no better place to develop the personal maturity necessary for a profound and deep sexual relationship than in a long-term involvement."

Furthermore, it is important to realize that even though we can talk about interpersonal and sexual relationships as separate entities, they can have a very dynamic and synergistic effect on one other. Just as the enhancement of an aspect of your interpersonal relationship can improve the satisfaction you feel concerning sex, your sexual lovemaking can have a very positive influence on how you relate interpersonally. For most couples, sex serves not only to satisfy a biological need but also to attend to emotional needs. Dr. Stephen B. Levine makes this point quite clear: "As life gets complicated with children, work, fatigue, and so forth, sex becomes an important part of a couple's life, because it is a wordless reaffirmation that I love and I am loved, that I am part of a couple, that I am devoted to satisfying your needs, and I appreciate you, and I show my appreciation through our sexual behavior."

Strengthening Your Connection Through Romantic Love

One of the best ways to intensify the connectedness you and your partner feel with one another is to make a commitment together to rekindle the romantic feelings you may have had for each other early in your relationship. This calls for each of you to focus on your partner's desires. This means giving without being concerned about what you will get in return. When you rekindle romance your focus shifts to your partner. Or to paraphrase JFK, *think not what your partner can do for you, but what you can do for your partner.*

When you can *both* do that, you have discovered the ultimate aphrodisiac.

In his book *Five Love Languages*, Gary Chapman identifies and describes the five different ways that people express their love for one another: *words of affirmation, quality time, receiving gifts, acts of service,* and *physical touch.* The premise of the book is that people tend to give love in the way that they like to receive it, not necessarily in a way that the partner likes to receive it. For example, a husband might like to show love for his wife by painting the house (act of service), when the wife likes to receive love in the form of quality time. While the husband is painting away, thinking he's pleasing his wife, she's in the house stewing because he "never wants to spend time with me." So how can you get the result you want from this most noble of intentions? Most experts agree that the answer is for each of you to give love in ways that the other person appreciates receiving it. According to Michele Weiner-Davis, "Real giving is when you give to your spouse the things your spouse wants and needs whether you understand it or not, whether you like it or not, and whether you even agree with it or not. You do it because that's what real giving is all about."

Until you become aware of this simple truism, that different people like to give love and receive love (and whatever they consider loving gestures) in different ways, you may assume that while you're giving, your partner is simply unappreciative. But think about it; if a husband tells his wife how much he loves and appreciates her (words of affirmation) and gives her thoughtful gifts (thinking she likes receiving gifts), but what she most wants is for him to help around the house (act of service), his good intentions will most likely miss the mark.

Think back to a time when your partner delivered a loving gesture that you valued. What could he or she do now to bring that same loving feeling into your relationship? This might be a simple gesture, such as bringing you home a coffee from Starbucks when you didn't even ask or rubbing your back just before you fall asleep. Now create a wish list. Include in this list things you would want from your partner. When each of you has a completed list, make a date to meet for a half hour or so to exchange lists and discuss what you have learned about one another. Then, put them in action! You are well on your way!

you're not alone

Through a Partner's Eyes

"I was working with a couple who had been married for about 15 years. The husband was a real kind of soft-spoken guy and not one to complain about much. In fact, even when I would ask him a rather straightforward question about what he'd like to change he would talk around the issue. But finally, he cracked a joke and he said, 'I guess there really is only a two-hour window of opportunity on Friday nights from ten to twelve when she might be receptive to sex.' And he started to chuckle and with that she started to chuckle. And she said, 'Yes, that's about right, he's right about that.'

"I turned to him and said, 'Tell me, you've been married for 15 years, what's that like for you?' And after hemming and hawing a little bit he very slowly, but intently, told her, 'When I reach out for you and you're not there for me I feel incredibly rejected. I feel like you don't want me as a person and maybe that's not the way you mean it, but I feel unattractive, I feel as though you don't love me like you used to and I feel incredibly hurt. And then when you go to sleep and I'm staring up at the ceiling as I'm hearing you breathe, I can only tell you that I can't imagine any feeling of loneliness that's greater than the feeling of loneliness I feel lying next to you.'

"And, to this woman's credit she reached out and grabbed his hand, and her eyes filled with tears and she said to him, 'You know, for all these years that we've been together, when you touch me the only thing I ever do is check-in with myself. Am I in the mood? Am I not in the mood? I have never, not once, thought about what it's like to be in your shoes. And I am so, so sorry.'"
—*Michele Weiner-Davis, sex therapist, author of* The Sex-Starved Marriage

What You Can Do

The mere prospect of learning more about each other's needs and becoming able to lovingly give to your partner in a way that she or he appreciates can be so liberating and stimulating that many couples can't wait to make this a staple of their relationship. Here are a few things that you and your partner can do right now to begin weaving more romance into your lives:

- ☐ Plan one romantic surprise for your partner this week, and for the next four weeks. Pay special attention to what your partner might think is romantic, rather than what you yourself want. (Remember, what *you* want is your partner's responsibility.)

- ☐ Tell your partner something positive about him or her at least once daily. Tell your partner something you appreciate that he or she does for you.

- ☐ Plan one date a week to spend time alone together. If you have children, plan on getting away together for at least one overnight every other month, if possible. If not possible, try for at least an evening out together doing something you both find to be sexy and romantic.

- ☐ Think about a time when you and your partner first got together. What was it that first attracted you to your partner? How did it feel to be with him or her? How did you feel differently about your partner than about other people you may have dated around that time? Share your observations with each other.

- ☐ Think about a time in the recent past or even now when you felt particularly attracted to your partner. What is it that made this so special?

- ☐ At least once a week, ask your partner to do something special for you.

- ☐ If you're watching TV or listening to the radio, sit close together and hold hands or cuddle up to enhance your intimacy outside of the bedroom.

Communicating Your Ecstatic Desires

Few things are more exhilarating in a relationship than learning more about your partner, including what he or she truly enjoys, thinks, desires, feels, and dreams. If you completed some of the exercises in the previous chapter, you already have a taste of how rewarding it can be to know what your partner really wants and what makes your partner feel loved, appreciated, and connected to you.

This chapter encourages you to continue this process by taking a similar approach and openly communicating your sexual desires and needs. By practicing to become communicative about what turns you on and by explaining and showing each other what feels good to you sexually, you can begin to establish a climate that promotes uninhibited sexual expression, sharing, experimentation, playfulness, and that wonderfully delicious spice called novelty in just the right proportion for you.

Setting the Stage for Communication

True sexual intimacy calls for an openness that takes the guesswork out of pleasing each other. It empowers each of you by providing the knowledge that helps you do what your partner finds most pleasing or desirable. And it is this knowledge that is such an important ingredient in helping you achieve sexual ecstasy in your relationship. According to marital therapist

Michele Weiner-Davis, "You really have to have honest, open communication, to teach each other what works for you."

In communicating sexual desires or sexual concerns (whether about intercourse, birth control, masturbation, or anything else), it is best to start out by agreeing that you are on the same team, and that learning about what your partner wants will help you both to have a more satisfying sex life. Next, you must be clear with each other. Keep in mind that communicating about your desires can occur both inside and outside the bedroom, and can be carried out in two ways: by telling (talking) and showing (pointing out or demonstrating) to your partner what feels good. Telling promotes empathy, but showing leads to *visceral empathy*, a physical, instinctive empathy that is even more powerful for building the connection with your partner that helps bring sexual ecstasy to both of you.

Q&A

We've been married for 17 years. Shouldn't my wife know what I like by now?

Nobody can be expected to know a partner's sexual needs and desires unless communicated to them clearly. If you feel that what your wife is doing for you sexually is not satisfying you, don't blame her. She might not know how to please you, no matter how much she wants to. Teach her what you want, and then ask for it. And if you are uncomfortable asking her, ask yourself why that is. Then discuss your hesitation with your partner. Also, make an equally strong effort to learn what your wife truly wants as well. Do what you can to fulfill her needs and desires. In most solid relationships, when you see that your partner is making an effort to please you, your instinct will be to reciprocate or simply ask what you can do. This opens the doors of communication.

Breaking the "Conspiracy of Silence" Beverly Whipple— co-author of *Safe Encounters: How Women Can Say Yes To Pleasure and No To Unsafe Sex* and *The G-Spot and Other Discoveries about Human Sexuality*—believes that our culture has created a "conspiracy of silence" about sex: "Many women have grown up receiving very little information about sex and sexuality and have been taught that a woman shouldn't talk about it. Men are told they are sexually all-knowing and they're totally responsible. Now where are they supposed to get this information? And yet so many women don't tell their partners what they find pleasurable and so many men won't ask. Women won't tell their men because they don't want to damage that male ego and men can't ask because then they fear they would appear less masculine."

To ensure that your discussion will be as effective as possible in bringing you both a heightened sexual satisfaction, identify and resolve any of the issues that might be inhibiting your communication. Remove all of the obstacles that are standing between you (as a couple) and your sexual ecstasy.

you're not alone

Breaking the Ice

If you have any hesitancy about discussing sex with your partner, first understand that you're not alone. Most couples actually feel way less comfortable discussing sex than they are having it. So the challenge is to explore and address anything that might be holding you back:

- Do either of you feel embarrassed talking about sex? Why? Consider and talk about any beliefs or preconceived notions that might be causing these feelings.

- Do you feel guilty thinking that you should know what your partner needs or wants? Men especially believe that they should know what their partners want. And their women are often equally misinformed by assuming that men should know. Incidentally, both sexes can make either erroneous assumption. Ask.

- Are you being too vague? Many couples talk around the topic of sex. Try thinking in terms of what you want and what feels good. What makes you feel loved? What turns you on? If you fantasize or masturbate, what do you think about while you're doing it? Be specific. The key word is "do." The feedback you both give to and receive from your partner needs to contain things that are doable. For example, "Touch me here very lightly."

continues

continued

- Be optimistic that by discussing your desires, you will get what you want. That's the whole purpose—pleasure for both of you. Start, if necessary, by taking small steps. For example, tell each other three things you would like him or her to do or do more or less of. Choose one of them at a time to discuss or perhaps try.

- Communicate by showing, rather than telling. Your partner sometimes thinks he or she is doing something exactly as you want it. So the way to tweak this to perfection is to show your partner. Use your hand to guide your partner, or show your partner on him or her precisely how you like to be touched.

- Do you think that your partner will be angry that you didn't mention your desire earlier in the relationship? "We've been married for 15 years, and you're just telling me now?" Don't let fears like this spoil any potential opportunities for the next 15 years.

- Are you afraid that any solution is doomed to fail? "If this doesn't work, then what?" If you don't try, you are sure not to get it. Assume you will not get everything you want; however, if you and your partner have a good relationship, why wouldn't he or she want to please you?

- Are you afraid that your partner will be critical? Again, take responsibility; ask, don't demand; be up to hearing your partner's requests as well as open to his or her feelings about your request.

Learning to Ask for What You Want Nearly everybody has a notion of what he or she considers to be the ideal lover—usually somebody who knows exactly what to do and when to do it to turn him or her on and satisfy every sexual desire. By communicating clearly what you need and desire to feel more sexually fulfilled, you can begin to equip your willing mate with the knowledge that he or she needs to do at least a few things you might expect your ideal lover to do.

You are responsible for the pleasure you feel during love-making. That is, each of you has the ultimate responsibility for your own pleasure. That includes teaching your partner what pleases you—what you need and want physically, psychologically, emotionally, and spiritually—to feel loved, turned on, and sexually ecstatic.

If you are not asking or cannot ask for what you want, explore the issues that might be keeping you from communicating your sexual desires. Ask yourself the following questions:

- Am I assuming that my partner knows what to do for me, even though we haven't discussed it?
- Do I think my partner should know what I need without my having to ask for it?
- Am I afraid to ask for something that my partner already offered and I refused? It's okay to bring it up again; people's needs and desires can change over time.
- Do I feel selfish when asking for what I want? Remember that asking for what you want is truly a gift to your partner that helps take the guesswork out of sex and makes it easier for your partner to explore your needs!
- Is some other relationship issue at work undermining my desire to open up? If other issues are getting in the way of your sexual intimacy, identify them and talk them over or at least acknowledge them to yourself and allow yourself to let go of them for now; don't let them diminish your pleasure!

If you begin to feel like a martyr or think that the balance is tipping in favor of your partner, it's a good time to ask yourself, "Am I getting what I need?" Then talk about it with your partner. Remember, this needs to be a win-win-win situation; when you win, your partner wins, and your relationship wins.

Easing in to the Discussion You don't want something as potentially fun and pleasurable as your sex life to be a source of conflict, so keep it light. You don't need to start your dialogue about sexual pleasure by revealing your hottest fantasies, for instance. You might begin simply by talking about some of the great times you have had together in the past, or what you really like about the way you make love together.

you're not alone

B arry and Diane had been married for six years. Early in their relationship, Barry asked Diane if she would perform oral sex on him. He had never had it and thought it might feel pleasurable. Diane was reluctant to try it, and she expressed her reservations. Barry backed off from his request, honored her limits, and decided not to bring up the topic again.

Years later, during a therapy session, the issue came up again, because Barry was feeling that the relationship just wasn't sexually satisfying to him. The therapist asked Diane how she felt about giving oral sex. Her main concern was that she might choke or have to swallow the semen. Together, they discussed these concerns and explored ways that she could provide Barry with the heightened stimulation he wanted while at the same time avoiding what Diane thought might be unpleasant.

Barry agreed to shower beforehand, and Diane considered ways to perform oral sex without taking his entire penis in her mouth. She could manually stimulate him while licking the outside of the penis, for example, or take just the tip of the penis in her mouth. They experimented with several different ways, and Diane found it mildly pleasurable, while Barry's satisfaction increased significantly. They now regularly incorporate this in their lovemaking. In addition, this breakthrough led them to talk about and try many other kinds of sexual stimulation for both of them.

If you and your partner choose to make the discussion a little more direct, you can take a gradual approach with what you share. For example, if each of you lists your likes and dislikes, before you share them, rate them on a scale of 1 to 10, with 1 being the least risky (or risqué) and 10 being the most. Share your 1's first. If you don't have any problem sharing 1's, move on to 2's. Also, if you have a desire or fantasy that you think your partner might find a little disturbing, rephrase it; for example, if you fantasize about having a threesome with the neighbor, replace the neighbor with a celebrity or a complete stranger. After you have experienced success with relatively safe topics, then you can move on.

Another way to keep the discussion light is to set some rules in advance. For example:

- Agree in advance that if the discussion becomes uncomfortable for either one of you, you will end it, but then return to it later. This gives each of you an easy exit. In many cases, agreeing on a key word, gesture, or phrase for stopping an unpleasant discussion helps prevent any argument or other negative reaction. Keep reminding yourselves that the goal is pleasure, play, and ecstasy. Neither of you ever needs to feel *forced* outside of your comfort zone.

- Phrase anything you say as an "I" statement, which is merely a statement that starts with the word "I." An "I" statement softens what you say, because you take responsibility for saying it. "You" statements can cause your partner to become defensive, which usually results in inhibiting the conversation. Instead of saying something like "You embarrass me when you touch me in public," say something like, "I get really embarrassed when you show too much affection in public." At first, "I" statements might sound affected and insincere, but as you become more comfortable speaking in this gentler language, it will begin to feel more natural.

GET PSYCHED

In his research on couples, Dr. John Gottman found that conversations that start on a positive note, more often end that way. The same is true for starting in a negative or confrontational way.

- It goes without saying, but let's say it anyway: Anything either of you says remains between the two of you.

Always remember that the same rules apply to both of you. You cannot expect your partner to listen to your fantasies and desires without judging them if you yourself are unwilling to reciprocate. Most of all, be patient and remain committed. Your discussions will improve over time, and the pleasures resulting from them will begin to be motivation enough to keep the dialogue going. This can become one of the most exciting and erotic journeys of your life, so never allow this dialogue to shut down!

Talking Sex: Ideas for Getting Started

At this point, you and your partner are ready to carry on an open dialogue about your fantasies and your desires. You have an agreed-upon set of rules, you've left any baggage outside, and you're eager to become more intimately sexual with one another as a result of what you are sharing. So if you're ready to talk, go to it.

But if you need a little help in getting started, agree to set aside 15 to 30 minutes at least twice a week for one month to discuss how to better pleasure each other. Over the next month, do as many of them as the two of you agree are relevant to your unique situation. We have a couple of exercises that many couples have found helpful for generating a dialogue.

The first exercise calls for each of you to list 10 things you might like the next time you make love—10 things you would like to do during sex. Think in terms of specific behaviors and speech that are doable by each of you and that you would like or would like more of whenever you're making love, whether inside or outside the bedroom. For example, the woman might want to start out with a glass of wine, or hear "I love you," or have more attention lavished on certain parts of her body—buttocks, behind her ears, her breasts, or wherever it feels best. The man might want a massage, have his partner wear lingerie, stroke his genitals or someplace else where it feels pleasurable. Share your lists with each other. Talk about the doable desires first and see whether you can incorporate them the next time you are together. Share and explain to each other—if you'd like—why you want what you want. Also share any feelings you may have about your partner's requests.

Remember, you may not get everything you ask for. It's more important to enjoy what you do have to the fullest than to resent what you don't have or what may be missing. Also, if your partner wants something that turns you off, see whether you can come up with an alternative suggestion that you find mutually pleasing.

To help you generate ideas and begin talking to each other, try these exercises:

- Talk about the things you most admire about one another. (This is fairly safe for most couples.)
- Look at each other. Take turns making affirmative statements to one another using these models or something you come up with on your own:

  "I really feel close to you when ..."

  "What I like best about our relationship is ..."

  "The reason that I feel proud of you when I'm talking to others is ..."

  "We could be a lot closer if ..."

  "The things that we used to do that I miss the most are ..."

- Compose a statement that pertains more to your own sexual desires or pleasures, such as "The sexual fantasy of mine that I would really like to share with you is ...." Start with one that is fairly tame. As we suggested earlier, rate your fantasies on a scale of 1 to 10 with 1 being the most tame and 10 being the wildest, and then start with a 1 and work up as slowly or rapidly as you are comfortable with.
- As you become more comfortable, try a statement that provides more of a hint of what you desire, such as "Something that I've never done with you sexually that I would really like to do is ..." or "Something that I've always wanted you to do for me is ...."

Remember, you are sharing your thoughts and feelings and practicing openness and trust. When you're both ready, you can begin to negotiate what new things you will now try together. Most importantly, never get discouraged. The more you can communicate on this level, the closer you will be as a couple to sexual ecstasy.

Listening in on What Some Other People Want Realize that what turns you on sexually can range from the simplest romantic gesture (covered in Chapter 7) to fairly mild requests (such as a softer touch) to very direct requests for bold new sexual variations that may heretofore have only existed in your mind as fantasies that you would never even have dreamed of acting out. Here are some examples of sexual desires expressed by others:

> "I know my wife loves me and she seems to enjoy sex when we have it, but I really wish that she would be the one to initiate sex once in a while. It would really make me feel that she desired me and that I wasn't the only one in the relationship always pushing for sex." (Dave, age 37)

> "What I would really love my husband to do would be to go down on me. When I try to talk to him about it, I feel selfish and embarrassed, and I'm afraid he might think I was thinking about some old lover I was with before him. He's so jealous. I just think it would make me a little more, you know, juicy, and would make everything feel better." (Kathy, age 32)

> "I love when Sally dresses up for me in lingerie. I really feel she's super attractive and I know, and maybe this is silly, but it reminds me of looking at old *Playboy* magazines when I was a teenager. She's better than the models to me when she does it. And I also know that she's doing it to please me." (Jim, age 28)

> "I really love it when John and I are in bed talking and cuddling, when I feel really close and then I sometimes get extremely turned on. Sex is just great then!" (Anna, 42)

Sharing Your Fantasies When you and your partner feel as though you are becoming more comfortable talking about your sexual desires and turn-ons, you probably are ready to go to the next level, which is to explore one another's fantasies. But before you do, there are some things to consider. Wendy Maltz, M.S.W., and Suzie Boss, authors of *Private Thoughts*, points out that "when you share a fantasy, you run the risk of a partner becoming jealous or making false assumptions, such as that the fantasy is something you really want to occur in your real life. For example, if a woman fantasizes about large penises, her partner might think that she believes he's inadequately small or that she wants another man with a huge penis." Remember that in the fantasy world, the rules are different than in reality. In fantasy, anything goes, without consequences, and you and your partner are expressing pleasures that are often outside the realm of judgment—pleasure rules the fantasy world. But in reality, your choices—of which consequences do play a role—prevail.

If you find that you and your partner like to share fantasies and want to make more of your fantasy sharing, consider trying an exercise called a *fantasy rehearsal*. In this exercise, one of you begins to describe a fantasy, and then your partner joins in the conversation to collaborate on composing the fantasy, thus enhancing it. Through your words, you paint an imaginary picture of the scene—the time and place. You describe the roles you want to play, and what you see, taste, touch, smell, and hear. You describe what you're doing to your partner, and your partner describes what he or she is doing to you. There might even be other people involved, sex toys, or other accoutrements. The fantasy takes on a life of its own, often revealing to each fantasist involved things that the person wasn't aware he or she might like and what he or she might not have realized that the partner might like.

GET PSYCHED

Try fantasy rehearsals with your partner over the phone or on the Internet (in a private chat room or by using instant messaging software). This can become a profoundly erotic habit!

Q&A

How can I possibly not be jealous and angry when my wife tells me her fantasies about having sex with strangers?

First, in the privacy of your own mind, ask yourself whether you are *mentally* exclusive with your wife. If you fantasize about or ever find yourself attracted to other women, you are quite typical. Expecting her to be mentally exclusive with you is pretty unrealistic. Also, realize that when your wife shares her fantasies with you, she is offering them to you as a gift. These exist inside of her whether she shares them or not. By bringing you in, she is being quite intimate with you. Your wife is not trying to hurt your feelings or make you feel jealous, but merely to communicate in some way something that turns her on. So, if your wife shares a fantasy she has that disturbs you, try to let go of the jealousy and remember that this is merely a fantasy, that your wife is taking a risk in sharing it, and that chances are she is sharing it out of desire for you.

Negotiating Your Fantasies and Desires

As you take in all the details of each other's sexual fantasies and desires and learn each other's likes and dislikes, you will naturally want to put at least some of what you've learned into action. But just what do you choose to act out? That's completely up to you and your partner. The only limits are those that exist within and between the two of you.

Negotiating sexual fantasies and desires has no real downside. If you express a desire that your partner is unwilling or unable to go along with, you haven't lost a thing, but you've given yourself at least a chance of having it fulfilled. Also, when you have a list of 10 desires, you have a pretty good chance that your partner will agree to try at least one (and probably more) of them.

The only thing the two of you are negotiating at this point is what you might consider doing to please each other. You and your partner are merely exploring prospective opportunities to enhance your lovemaking together. You are only agreeing to what *might be* mutually pleasurable for both of you.

So here are some tips to make this pleasurable, fun, and erotic:

- Avoid thinking of a desire in terms of yes or no. Explore it in terms of how far you are each willing to go. For instance, you might not be willing to have sex in a public place, but you might be willing to have sex in a room with the curtains opened where you're fairly certain nobody can see in.

- Look at your desire or fantasy to see if it contains a negotiable component. Fantasies typically have several details that can inspire some creative thinking.

- Be open to trying something that doesn't, on the surface, highly appeal to you, if only to please your lover.

- If one of you has a strong desire to try something that the other simply cannot fathom doing, have a thorough discussion of it. Without making your partner feel wrong about it, address any and all fears, thoughts, and feelings concerning the desire or fantasy. If it is somewhat risky, discuss the risks or dangers, and discuss possible ways to reduce them or take the edge off. However, if at the end of the day, either of you says no, drop it. Chances are that there are many other avenues to explore.

Most important, understand, respect, and honor each other's boundaries. Don't turn your negotiation into intimidation or coercion. Keep it safe, be patient, and realize that your exploration of your sexuality together is a long-term and wondrous adventure.

Exploring Physical Communication

Up to this point, we have discussed the *telling* part of communicating with your partner about sexual fantasies and desires. There is also a *showing* part that takes place a little closer to the bedroom and, if you choose, during lovemaking. Just as you and your partner communicate what your minds consider sexually pleasurable and desirable, you can choose to *show* each other what your bodies feel to be most erotic.

Although you can do this during lovemaking, trying to provide instructions can also take you out of the moment and thus diminish the pleasure you feel. So, talk with each other beforehand and agree on what would be most helpful and when. If you both have the attitude that you're showing one another how to increase the pleasure for both of you, communicating during sex can significantly enhance your lovemaking and help it evolve.

Some people choose to remain silent and let the passion overtake them, others whisper affirmations, some moan, some scream, some talk dirty or raunchy, some instruct .... It's all up to you and your partner to do whatever is most pleasurable for each of you. For now, try communicating to see whether (and how much) talking and showing will enhance your love life and bring you closer to sexual ecstasy.

Practice making requests in a positive way. Instead of saying "That hurts, stop," which can interrupt the action for both of you, try making a gentle suggestion, such as "Press a little lighter" or "Move down a little, please." Or you might simply guide your partner's hand or finger to the place that feels best to you. Also, give positive feedback so your partner knows what you really like: "Don't stop." "Mmmmm, that feels great." "Just right." These are merely ways of sharing the experience more.

Putting It All Together

When you begin communicating and learning more about one another's needs and desires, you might find it useful to think in terms of the acronym TOUCH:

T Tenderness and talk. This can be verbal, physical, or emotional talk and gestures of tenderness. Talk about the things that are important to you and what you need to feel loved, appreciated, and desired.

O Openness. Few things are more erotic than knowing one another intimately. Open your heart and soul to your partner.

U Understanding. Build a sense of mutual empathy in which you begin to imagine how your partner might feel. Develop visceral empathy by teaching and learning from one another the types of touch that feel best.

C Chemistry. Acknowledge the chemistry that you had early in your relationship and realize that it still exists between you. Your only task here is to tap into it.

H Honesty. True intimacy requires honesty to build the trust that couples must feel in order to bare their vulnerable thoughts and feelings.

What You Can Do

Learning about your partner's sexual fantasies and desires can be so much fun that many people can't wait to get started! Here are a few things that you and your partner can do right now to begin enhancing your sexual intimacy:

☐ Give each other a sign of affection, such as a hug or a kiss at least three times a day. For example, acknowledge each other with affection, before leaving in the morning, on coming home at night, and before going to bed.

☐ Make a date with each other to make love, using some of the new ideas that you have learned by exploring them with each other. While instant transformation does happen sometimes, more commonly, progress tends to be gradual. Never lose the perspective that this is all for *your* pleasure.

☐ Take a bath or shower together and focus on *sensuality* rather than *sexuality*.

☐ Give each other body massages, or part of a body massage. Communicate to each other what parts of your body you prefer your partner to focus on.

☐ Prepare a list of things that would make you feel desirous of your partner, or a list that would make you feel more desirable to your partner. Share those lists.

☐ The next time you make love, ask your partner to do one special thing for you that he or she already identified as something he or she would be willing to do.

☐ Lying down fairly close facing one another, guide your partner's hands over your body to show your partner the parts that feel most sensitive and to apply just the right pressure. Then switch.

Part 2

Achieving Sexual Ecstasy

In a receptive, playful environment that's conducive to experiencing uninhibited sexual pleasure, you can begin to explore ways of embellishing your lovemaking with innovative sensory stimulations, erotic sexual activities, and variations that are limited only by your imagination. In this part, you learn how to add sizzle and spark by creating a special occasion each time you make love and by heating it up with seduction and flirtation, exploring the full potential of touch, and exploring ways to maximize your orgasms.

Sex Is Adult Play— A Primer

Children know instinctively how to play with their friends. They pick a game, gather anything they might need to play it, and then have fun without putting too much thought into it. If the game gets boring, they play something else. If they fight, they usually come to some agreement or let it drop, because that just cuts into their fun and playtime. Kids don't *try* to have fun. They just do! If only adults could follow this childlike philosophy of play, sexual ecstasy would be the natural result. The good news is that you can!

This chapter will help you rekindle your sense of play with your partner while introducing a variety of ways you can enhance your lovemaking, increase your desire, and electrify your passion and lovemaking. We present our ideas and suggestions simply as a menu of potential sexual delights. Order up whatever sounds appealing.

Understanding the Synergy of Sexual Play

When you and your partner go out to dinner at your favorite restaurant, the experience is much more delightful if you both have a good time. Your server is attentive without being intrusive, the ambiance is romantic, and you both find the cuisine delicious. You gaze into each other's eyes and see the joy and complete pleasure you both feel in the moment. And that shared joy makes the moment all the more enjoyable.

The same is true of sex. Sex is best when you both fully enjoy it, when each of you experiences that wonderful thing we call sexual ecstasy. And when this happens, the joy that each of you senses in your partner adds to that ecstasy, lifting your lovemaking to new heights. As you and your partner begin to play together, remember that what increases your pleasure increases your partner's pleasure, and your partner's sense of pleasure increases your own.

Q&A

Why can't we just focus on sex as a physical release and enjoy it for what it is?

The short answer is that you can! Sex is primarily a physical act, but it has other components that, if you choose to give them some attention, can help you enhance the ecstasy you experience. Dr. Don Moser, a past president of the Society for the Scientific Study of Sex, theorized that "people experience sexuality in three ways: through their bodies and the sensations they feel; through the connection with their partners; and through their sexual roles and fantasies—the sexual drama that plays in their minds. Most people lean toward one particular way of experiencing sex, but by expanding sexuality into other areas, people often discover that their ecstasy intensifies, as well."

Accenting Your Love Nest

Some innovative entrepreneurs have built businesses around providing couples with romantic getaway suites, complete with Jacuzzis, swimming pools, fluffy bathrobes, huge beds with silk sheets, and other romantic and sexually conducive amenities. They recognize the fact that a couple's surroundings can have a profound effect on their sexual mindset. If you have the money and can arrange a night or two at a romantic getaway suite, try it. They're wonderful.

Of course, you don't need to spend money to secure a favorable area for romance and lovemaking. Arrange an area in your house or apartment. You can enhance your current surroundings, and it might cost you little more than your time and effort. With the right attitude, you might just find the effort itself sexually arousing! Make it a joint project.

First, walk into your bedroom (or wherever you make love most often) and ask yourself, "Is this a room in which somebody would want to make love?" Answer honestly. Then, ask yourself, "How can I make this room a place where making love would be the first thing my partner and I would think of when entering it?" Your answers should provide you with plenty of ideas to get started. Here's a checklist that can help steer your attention to some important details:

> **GET PSYCHED**
>
> "Sex and laughter do go very well together, and I wondered—and still do—which is more important."
> –Hermione Gingold

- ☐ Room looks neat and tidy. Nothing strewn on the floor, no stacks of old magazines, no visible trash, dresser tops uncluttered and attractive.
- ☐ Bed looks its best—clean sheets and blankets.
- ☐ Windows and curtains are clean and in fairly good condition, no eyesores.
- ☐ Any photos or wall hangings are appealing or at least not distracting. No photos or pictures to take you out of the mood, such as a photo of your mother at the head of the bed or on the dresser.
- ☐ Distractions are minimal. TVs and computers can be distracting to some people but not to others. This is an option that you and your partner can discuss.
- ☐ Lighting is conducive. You need not rewire your room, but consider the lighting during lovemaking. If you typically have lights-off sex, consider turning them on, burning a candle, or adding an attractive lamp.
- ☐ Music or other audio is pleasant.
- ☐ Room smells good. No musty odors. Attend to any scents that you and your partner find pleasant.

For additional ideas, review your fantasies and your partner's fantasies. Do you find any colors particularly stimulating? Silk sheets? Rose petals strewn across the bed? Lace curtains? Colored light? Mirrors on the ceiling? Do you find any foods sensually stimulating, such as berries, cheeses, or chocolates? Sit down with your partner and make a list of things you would each like to add to your room to enhance the eroticism of the environment.

Nourishing Your Sexuality Over Time

Now, it's time to put that knowledge to use to form an aura of sensual sexuality around yourselves that will help guide you to the arena of sexual ecstasy. When attending to your own and your lover's needs and desires, keep in mind that they often change from day to day, hour to hour, minute to minute. Choosing to clean the house when your partner, at the moment, would really appreciate it more if you just sat down and listened for 15 minutes probably wouldn't be very effective. Remain vigilant to your own and your partner's ever-changing needs, and attend to them daily, not just when you want to have sex. Focusing on your own and your partner's desires over the long term will reap the rewards you are both seeking. Avoid forming those expectations that inevitably lead to disappointment.

GET PSYCHED

Continue to appreciate your partner daily for the rest of your lives. Love not expressed, is love not conveyed—the thought alone is not sufficient. —*Lonnie Barbach, Ph.D., psychologist, sex therapist, and author of* For Yourself: The Fulfillment of Female Sexuality *and* For Each Other: Sharing Sexual Intimacy, *among other books*

Attending to Yourself Pay some attention to your physical, sexual self. Do whatever you can do to feel more sexual. Think of yourself as a lover, your partner's lover. Take a shower remaining ever mindful that you are preparing yourself for your lover. Dry off slowly, paying attention to the feel of the towel against your skin. If your partner likes a certain perfume or cologne (or powder or lotion) that you don't mind wearing, put some on.

Dress in a way that makes you feel sexy or that you know your partner will think is appealing. You might purchase some naughty new underwear or clean and press your favorite outfit. Or, you might dress sexy underneath and wear a more understated outfit. It all depends on what you and your partner find alluring. Although all of these outer adornments might seem merely cosmetic, they can have a tremendous influence on how sensual you inwardly feel, and this sensuality usually finds a way to express itself outwardly. Many say it is even contagious!

Attending to Your Lover Once you know what your lover needs and wants, it's time to deliver. For example, if your partner feels a romantic connection when you help with the housework, grab a broom or dust cloth and start cleaning. If your partner just wants a few kind words of appreciation, start talking. If your partner wants a romantic dinner out, get on the phone and make reservations for dinner at his or her favorite restaurant. In the spirit of love, when you begin to realize that everything you do to attend to your lover's needs and desires heightens sexual ecstasy for both of you, the work and effort you put in magically morphs into playful recreation, which actually can function as a type of long-term foreplay.

Making Your Lovemaking a Special Occasion

When people are first dating or are having an affair, they often approach each encounter with a heightened sense of anticipation. Every date, every meeting takes on the importance of a special occasion, and the lovers often prepare meticulously for it well in advance. Before they make love, before they even reach the unofficial foreplay stage, they commonly engage in flirtatious banter, seductive touching, sensual kissing, and other highly erotic activity that brings their simmering sexuality to near boiling point before they reach the bed. Their entire encounter becomes an extended lovemaking session.

In long-term relationships, some couples treat sex as though it has an on/off switch. They ask each other if they want to "do it," and if they both agree, they do it. That's fine, if that's all they want, but sex can become much more satisfying if you and your partner become a little more attentive to one another throughout the day and let that intensity and anticipation simmer and build. You don't *have* to return to the days when you couldn't keep your hands off each other. (But on the other hand, if you can and want to, why not?) When spending time together, let go of any distractions that might have built up over the day and establish a more serene setting that's receptive to your thoughts about and feelings for one another.

Relax and restore your focus on each other. Make your relationship, romance, and sexual satisfaction priorities, even if you do it for only a couple of hours a week. Remember to date each other at least once a week, if possible. Leave your worries at home and most importantly, treat each other as if you're on a date.

> ## GET PSYCHED
>
> "Keep the erotic pot bubbling throughout the day. Little things mean a lot— little touches, little sayings …." –*Julian Slowinski, Psy.D., senior clinical psychologist, Pennsylvania Hospital, certified sex therapist and co-author of* The Sexual Male: Problems and Solutions

Heating It Up with Seduction and Flirtation

Seduction can generate intense sexual energy between you and your partner by pulling you together against some resistance that's pushing you apart. Early in a courtship, seduction plays an important role in helping the seducer overcome any barriers that stand between him or her and the object of desire. The seducer does a sort of mating ritual or dance to convince the person being seduced to engage in sex. In a long-term relationship, you and your partner no longer need to seduce one another; you have already agreed to be sexual together. But that doesn't mean you have to relinquish those delicious pleasures of seduction.

Lonnie Barbach, Ph.D., author of many books on both female sexuality and erotica, including *Seductions: Tales of Erotic Persuasion*, provides this vivid description of seduction: "When I think about the most erotic moments of a sexual experience, I am drawn to the delicious and unpredictable buildup, the dance of seduction. A sexual experience often lodges in memory most vividly because of the events that lead up to the actual physical lovemaking: the invitation to sensually provocative play, the anticipation of an experience charged with pleasure and delight. ... [Seduction] is a gateway to passion, enlivening a person's romantic interest and creativity, so it whets the appetite for lovemaking and increases the likelihood that sex will be exciting, fulfilling, and pleasurable."

Seduce each other. Start your morning with a soft, lingering kiss or a warm embrace before you go to work. Tell your partner how hot she looks in that outfit or how turned on you are by her scent. Walk up behind your partner when he's not expecting it and softly, teasingly press up against his body. Pat your partner's butt. Whisper sweetly into her ear how wonderful she felt last night. If you're away from your partner, phone in a few kind, affirmative words. Leave a love note where your partner is sure to find it. All of these little gestures of love and affirmation serve as subtle foreplay throughout the day and throughout your life together, increasing your level of sexual ecstasy.

When considering ways to seduce and flirt with your partner, don't limit yourself to physical options. If your partner likes to read, picking out just the right book for him or her can be a form of seduction. A rose left on the dashboard of the car can be a seductive gesture. A CD mix of your partner's favorite songs might be a turn-on. Even an intense intellectual discussion can act as a turn-on. Search yourself and your partner for the key to successful seduction. As Dr. Lonnie Barbach writes, "... our own personalities, our tastes, strengths, proclivities of every sort, put their unique imprimatur on how we seduce, or, for that matter, how we respond to a seduction."

Seduction is an art form—think creatively. Take a few minutes to sit down with your partner and each of you compose a list of five to ten ways you would love to be seduced. Exchange lists and discuss them, or, perhaps even better, choose not to discuss them and start *doing* them for each other right away.

Erotic Banter Sexual silence can be quite golden, but many people find sex talk very stimulating as well. In its broadest interpretation, sex talk is any audible utterance intended to sexually stimulate a person. It can be a form of foreplay or sex play. It can help reduce anxiety and bring you closer in the moment. Sex talk covers everything from innocent, romantic affirmations to squeals of joy to raunchy curse words. Even something as simple and reserved as whispering your lover's name near the height of orgasm can propel you and your lover to new heights of ecstasy.

The next time you and your partner have a discussion about sex, each of you might want to jot down, or simply recollect, what you like to hear during lovemaking. This can be music, romantic statements such as "I love you," your own name, soft or raunchy sexual language, moaning, screaming, silence, whatever. If you feel as though you're restraining yourself from uttering something during sex that you would really like to let out, describe that, too, and get your partner's feedback. Discuss your desires and options openly, so that you know you are on the path toward finding that optimal formula for maximum mutual fulfillment.

Teasing and Simmering In the movie *Vanilla Sky* the main character, David Aames (played by Tom Cruise), describes himself as a *pleasure delayer*, a person who delays pleasure in order to intensify his awareness and more fully appreciate the pleasure. The concept is not new. Many cultures and religions have it woven into their various customs and rituals. And there's a reason for that—a good number of people have found delayed gratification useful for intensifying the degree of a sensuous experience, one of the ingredients for sexual ecstasy. Just think of how much better your favorite foods taste when you've been without them for a week or a month.

Delaying pleasure in such dramatic ways is not for everyone, but a little delay to bring anticipation to a simmer can be quite appealing for many couples. The delay can even be more effective when accompanied by seductive sex talk and flirtation throughout the day. The simmering passions can draw you together as the commitment to delay can push you apart. The sexual energy that this often creates between partners can be quite astounding. The tough part is to be able to let the sexual energy build without forming expectations as to how the energy eventually will be released. If you focus on enjoying the energy itself, in the moment (another ingredient for sexual ecstasy), you really can't go wrong.

Spend some time with your partner discussing the possibility and potential benefits of delaying any sort of direct genital stimulation. Sex talk, touching, flirtation, and other forms of sexual activity that can help build anticipation and heighten your sexual charge are, of course, highly encouraged—many couples find them to be quite powerful preludes to great sex. Again, delaying pleasure doesn't appeal to everyone all of the time, but it's worth trying (or at least discussing).

Kissing Kissing can be one of the most intimate physical acts you share with your partner. In fact, an open-mouth kiss often is the first signal couples use to indicate that they find each other physically attractive and potentially sex partners. When this first open-mouth kiss occurs and is reciprocal, it commonly acts as an unspoken agreement that the couple is ready for a deeper, often more physical, connection. In a sexual relationship, kissing is commonly a signal marking the end of the teasing, flirtatious seduction and the beginning of more intense physical activity. Kissing is a nonverbal way of telling your partner that you want to connect with him or her, and it can still have tremendous power

WEB TALK: To take a kissing survey and read up on some interesting kissing tips, visit:

www.kissing.com

50 years or more into a relationship. Women especially find kissing to be a very stimulating physical turn-on.

Many therapists have observed that kissing and other forms of affection are sometimes (unfortunately) the first physical stimulants to leave a long-term relationship. Given that kissing is such a powerful, erotic way of showing love and affection, it's somewhat surprising that it gets phased out of so many relationships. Perhaps kissing is one of the pleasures that couples sacrifice when their lives become more hectic, or maybe couples think that any kissing that's more than a peck on the cheek *always* signals an agreement to have intercourse, and so they avoid it. Whatever the case, kissing is an activity that can heighten sexual ecstasy.

If kissing has been phased out in your relationship and you both feel that you might like to bring it back, you can start by agreeing that your kissing won't *necessarily* act as a cue for intercourse. Then, permit yourself to kiss the way you kissed early in your relationship—playfully. If necessary or desirable, prepare to kiss and be kissed by flossing, brushing, and using a mouthwash that you both like, to make the kiss taste as pleasant as it feels and to make yourself less self-conscious of how you might taste to your partner.

Discuss with one another how you like to be kissed and practice it together. In his book, *The Art of Kissing*, William Cane points out that there's much more to kissing than most people think, and more ways to kiss than many people have explored. Kissing doesn't have to be mouth to mouth. You can kiss any part of the body—the neck, behind the ears, the fingers, the thighs, the genital area. You can kiss with different amounts of pressure, open or closed mouth, using or not using your tongue. You can pucker your lips, lick, nibble, or suck. You can kiss with your eyes open or closed. You can kiss with a piece of ice in your mouth or a sip of champagne or a piece of chocolate, if you like.

Everybody has a kissing preference. Some people like French kissing and some don't. Some like only soft kisses, whereas others prefer a rougher style. It's up to you and your partner to explore and decide. You might start your exploration by each listing five parts of your body where you might like to be kissed or five ways you might like to be kissed. Or, in the nude, facing each other, show each other where it feels good to kiss and where it feels best to be kissed. Ask if your partner minds kissing a particular part of your body. If there's a part of your partner's body you would like to kiss, ask whether it's okay. Explore, experiment, and enjoy.

you're not alone

Ellen and Jan were in their late 30s. It was Ellen's first marriage; Jan had been married once before and has a 15-year-old daughter from that marriage. For the last 2 years of their 11-year marriage, they had not been having sex. They both reported that initially sex was extremely passionate and satisfying for both of them, but problems began when they tried to have a child and went through an unsuccessful infertility treatment. At one point they talked about adoption, but never pursued it. Ellen felt depressed and unsupported during this period.

They could not explain why they stopped being sexually active. The idea of needing to plan and talk about sexual activity and desire was difficult for both of them. When asked how they used to initiate lovemaking, they both looked puzzled, and then Ellen started to talk about how they would just start with these great kisses and great sex would come about from there. When asked why they stopped kissing, they couldn't remember. Their homeplay that week was to practice kissing. For them that was the breakthrough they needed. Both began to get turned on again just as before. And after several more weeks of learning to talk with each other about sex, their sex life was better than ever.

Connecting Through Eye Contact The eyes those silent tongues of love.—Antonio, in *Don Quixote*

Like your words and the sound of your voice, your eyes enable you to connect and make love without even touching. A loving look, a look of admiration and respect, or a leering look of lust can serve as a tremendous turn-on for many couples. Of course, some people become a little uncomfortable establishing eye contact and might even find it distracting during some stages of lovemaking, but if you and your partner think you might like it, establishing eye contact has the potential of adding to the intensity of your flirtations and your lovemaking.

By bedtime, neither of us feels very turned on. Is there anything we can do to liven things up?

When you're searching for answers, look outside the bedroom as well as inside, and don't be wedded to the idea of having to have sex before you go to sleep. If you're not turned on at night, early mornings, afternoons, or as a before-dinner appetizer are all possible options.

Anything you can do outside the bedroom during the day to build mutual affection, respect, camaraderie, cooperation, support, and a playful, romantic connection can help. Think of all of your daily niceties and flirtations as a form of outside-the-bedroom foreplay—things you do for one another that draw you away from the phone, the TV, and the computer and toward the bedroom. Do whatever it takes to make you feel more connected. Each of you write down five to ten suggestions for completing the phrase, *I feel like making love to you when ...* , and then share your responses. What makes you want to put down this book, hang up the phone, turn off the TV, and go have sex? When you or your partner can answer that and effectively communicate it to one another, you are definitely heading in the direction of ecstatic sex.

Discuss it with your partner, and if you decide you might like to try having a little more eye contact, work it into your relationship. You can try it at dinner by sitting across from one another instead of next to each other, or try to sneak a glance during your next kiss. Eye contact during foreplay or intercourse also can add a great deal to the feelings of connectedness and the mutual appreciation of your sexual experience together.

Foreplay—Inside the Bedroom Let's go inside the bedroom. Without changing anything about the way you actually make love, you and your partner will likely experience more intense and satisfying sex due to any added attention you have given to foreplay outside the bedroom. With the right prelude, sex exactly the same way you have done it for years will probably feel better and more fulfilling for both of you. So, you don't need to focus on changing anything. *More important, never stop doing anything that's working for you now, that you both enjoy.*

We do have some ideas that you and your partner might want to consider that can add to or enhance your foreplay inside the bedroom, but we caution couples to avoid thinking of these ideas as techniques or tools to help you reach any ultimate goals such as that of ecstatic sex. Approach these ideas with an attitude of playful exploration and experimentation *free of expectation.* Consider them merely as potential ways to expand your sexual play.

As you and your partner have already begun to learn new ways to explore, touch, and communicate your desires, this time we're going to suggest you become more focused in order to take it a little further. The following is a list of questions that you and your partner can answer separately or together to learn what might appeal to you both. If you do these already, play together to find more ways to make them even sexier. If not, simply add them to your smorgasbord:

> **GET PSYCHED**
>
> "Extended foreplay is to marriage what taste is to a good meal; a small amount may augment a full-course meal, while a large amount alone may suffice in itself. Prolonged lovemaking can enhance a relationship sensually and emotionally." –Ilda Fisher, Ph.D., Emeritus Professor, Institute for Graduate Clinical Psychology, Widener University, founder of one of the first sex therapy centers in Philadelphia, PA

- Would you like to undress your partner? Would you like your partner to undress you? Would you like to undress for your partner in a provocative way?
- Would you like to kiss in the nude?
- Would you like to give or receive a massage? Do you like to caress, fondle, and make out before sex?
- Where on your body do you most like to be touched? Mention as many spots as you can think of. How do you like to be touched? Squeezing, rubbing, pinching, patting, spanking?
- Which parts of your partner's body do you like to touch that are consistent with the places your partner likes to have touched?

GET PSYCHED

"Skin is our chief extragenital sex organ, underrated by men, better understood by women."
–*Alex Comfort from* The Joy of Sex

- Would you like to have oral sex performed on you? Would you like to perform oral sex on your partner? If so, how?

- What do you not like doing or having done to you?

It's important as well as fun to fine-tune your foreplay by providing feedback, but provide feedback in a positive way that's less likely to make either you or your partner self-conscious. When receiving feedback, think of foreplay as a menu of options from which to choose; chances are, not every option is going to appeal to you, and everyone has a preference for how a particular item on the menu is seasoned and served. These are simply preferences, just as some people prefer their food with a little more spice or a little less.

While exploring what feels good to each of you, and even during sex itself, it's often helpful to have an agreed-upon nonverbal signal to stop something and talk about it later. Or, instead of telling your partner you don't like something or to stop doing something, ask to have it done differently or request another alternative. For example, if your lover is licking your neck and you find it unpleasant, ask your partner to lick a different area or kiss your neck, instead. Afterwards, and in a light, playful, and helpful way, discuss what felt good and what didn't. Be sure to explain why, if you so choose, but positively. In some cases, something might usually feel good but does not on a particular day. You might not want your partner to completely stop doing it, so explain that it just didn't feel good right then (but please try it again next time).

Incidentally, just as in the case with deep kissing, foreplay doesn't necessarily have to lead to intercourse; it can act as an activity sufficiently pleasurable in and of itself. Use foreplay not only to increase desire on the way to intercourse but as a method of connecting to your partner and expressing your love through sensual touch. Your exploration doesn't even have to be a turn-on, although it usually is.

In our practice, we use a six-step protocol that has helped provide many couples with a more structured approach to their mutual exploration of one another's bodies:

1. Explore without talking. Examine each other's bodies and touch each other without saying a word. Focus on your partner's body other than breasts and genitals.

2. Explore with giving feedback. While touching each other, provide feedback on which parts of your partner's body are most sensitive and how you like to be touched. Again, the focus is on your partner's body other than breasts and genitals.

3. Explore by showing with feedback. Show your partner where you like to be touched and how. This can include guiding your partner's hands. Remain focused on body parts other than the breasts and genitals.

4. Explore this time including genitals and breasts and explain or demonstrate types of touch that feel pleasurable. If you use oils or lotions, be sure to use only water-soluble lubricants, such as K-Y Jelly or Astroglide, around and inside the vagina. (Oil-based lubricants and lotions can cause irritation.)

5. Have your partner explore your genitals (and breasts, for the woman) while providing feedback on the types of touch that feel pleasurable.

6. Explore with penetration to become more aware of the subtle sensation of the penis inside the vagina. An exercise called the silent vagina is often helpful—you practice penetration or partial penetration (usually with a partially erect penis), and stay inside without moving. Try it with eyes open or eyes closed.

Enhancing Play with Sex Toys Although human touch is incredibly sensuous, the skin can experience many other pleasurable sensations through the sense of touch. Warm oils and lotions can often feel soothing. Ice or other cold objects on certain parts of the body, such as the nipples, can be quite erotic. Silky fabrics or feathers (or a clean feather duster), rubber or leather, lace or fur can all stimulate the highly sensitive skin. Some people like to have their skin rubbed down with oil or lotion or be caressed through a slippery layer of soap in a shower or bath. Others like to be stimulated with a vibrator or other sex toy. If you and your partner think that some additional accoutrements might be interesting, think creatively of what you might already have available in your house or apartment, go shopping together at a nearby erotic novelty store (if one is available), or peruse the offerings of adult novelty shops on the Internet.

WEB TALK: The Internet has several tasteful online stores where you can shop for sex toys:

www.howtohavegoodsex.com
www.goodvibes.com
www.evesgarden.com

Playing Out Your Fantasies We explored fantasies in Chapter 6 and revisited the topic in Chapter 8 to see how fantasies could be rehearsed and examined to discover more about what you and your partner might find arousing. Perhaps in one of your discussions you have already talked about the possibility of playing out one or more of your fantasies. Fantasies can be very useful, erotic, and a lot of fun, even if you choose not to make them any more than just fantasies. You and your partner are free to choose whether to keep them private, share them, rehearse them, masturbate to them, play them in your mind during intercourse, or even fully play them out in some way.

If you and your partner are open to the idea of actually playing out your fantasies, discuss any limits beforehand, especially if the fantasy includes elements of being tied up, being controlled, or spanking. The basic agreement that's important to have is to stop when either of you gives the signal to stop, no questions asked and no judgments passed. (Come up with a signal or a codeword or even some gibberish that signals the end of a certain activity.) Remember this: If one person keeps going when the other wants to stop, the one who wanted to stop is likely to be much more reluctant to play next time.

Once you come to that agreement, pick one or more fantasies you might want to try and then decide on the one that you both find most appealing. The fantasy can be about anything you think might feel good. What do you want to play out with your partner? This might be a striptease, whipped cream with or without oral sex, watching your partner masturbate, receiving a long massage that's not over till you say stop, wearing leather lingerie or chains, being tied up or blindfolded, being tickled, pretending you're different people, pretending one of you is a virgin, pretending or actually having a *ménage à trois,* picking each other up at a bar or restaurant .... Whatever sounds like it might feel good and is agreeable to both of you is fair game.

The Segue into Intercourse

One thing that sexologists are discovering today is that the model for how we once viewed the sexual response cycle—a step-by-step linear progression from desire to arousal to orgasm to resolution doesn't hold up for what many women and men experience. The goal-directed model is like climbing stairs. First you touch, then kiss, and then ... until you reach orgasm.

Beverly Whipple, Ph.D., director of the International Society for the Study of Women's Sexual Health and co-author of *The G-Spot and Other Discoveries about Human Sexuality,* suggests that the sexual response cycle can follow a circular pattern in which the focus is pleasure, not orgasm (see the following figure). Dr. Whipple says, "We know that women are circular, that we don't have to have desire before arousal, and so on. But it seems that both men and women really don't like to be put into a linear pattern. And many of them do not respond in a linear path. We're now developing tools to evaluate the importance of pleasure and satisfaction to individuals and to couples rather than just focusing on orgasm. Although much of my research has been on women's experience of orgasms, the goal of my research has been to validate the experiences of women who enjoy pleasurable things that didn't fit into the normative pattern of sexual response as defined by Masters and Johnson." In this model the focus is on pleasure, and each experience is satisfying and an end in itself. The diagram that follows shows some different types of sexual response cycles. The "?"s in the circular model are there for you to complete with any additional experiences that bring you sexual pleasure. Think now about what kinds of stimulation you would include in your own personal response cycle. You may want to share this information with your partner.

SEXUAL EXPERIENCES

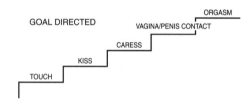

The goal-directed model of the sexual response cycle.

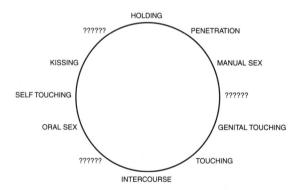

Whipple's Sexual Response Illustration: Printed with permission of Beverly Whipple, Ph.D., adapted from Timmers, et. al. 1976, "Treating Goal-Directed Intimacy," Social Work, 401-402.

Rosemary Basson, M.D., M.R.C.P., also describes a circular model of sexual response where some women need more emotional intimacy or physical stimulation to initiate desire and arousal and that the increase in desire and arousal breeds more emotional and physical satisfaction, as well as intimacy. Some women become more aroused after orgasm. By following this model, couples can become more relaxed in their lovemaking, realizing that they don't need to take a step-by-step, goal-oriented, linear approach that leads from desire to orgasm and resolution. In other words, they can try "jumping in" at different points in the response cycle to determine what they both like.

All the romantic and sexual activity you do leading up to intercourse serves to make each of you more aroused, full of desire, and ready for it. As the transition to intercourse nears, sometimes it's helpful to slow down and provide additional stimulation if one or both of you is not quite ready—extended foreplay, caressing and kissing, a change in positions (as discussed in the next chapter), or manual or oral stimulation of the genitals. Some women prefer to have orgasm before intercourse; others prefer to spend more time having intercourse. The key is to clarify your preferences with your partner in order to become more in tune to each other's readiness and preferences.

In relationships where the man is usually ready for intercourse before the woman, many couples find it helpful to agree that the woman will initiate intercourse when she is ready. Often it is helpful for her to guide her partner's penis inside her. Also, intercourse does not have to be continual thrusting to orgasm; you might try stopping, just feeling the sensation of being enveloped and enveloping, and then starting again. You can also try different speeds and ways of thrusting, changing positions, or simply positioning your legs differently. If one of you typically does most of the thrusting, you might change roles or experiment with both of you moving together. Talk and experiment with new ways to experience intercourse. Allow yourselves to discover new ways of enjoying this glorious form of adult play.

Ecstatic Afterplay

Orgasm does not have to signal the end of sex. Your entire love-making session, which, perhaps, was an experience of sexual ecstasy, calls for celebration and appreciation of what you just had together. This is a time when you can deepen your bond, a time when men typically feel more open and emotional and couples feel more intimate. Although the energy that surrounds you after sex differs from the energy you feel before or during sex, it can lead to a different experience of sexual ecstasy just the same.

Instead of falling asleep right away, consider holding one another close or continue touching and caressing one another. Some couples like to take a shower together afterwards or get up and cook breakfast or have a snack. Others like to talk about what they just experienced or laugh if their lovemaking had been particularly playful. Some couples like to reminisce about old times or simply savor other aspects of their relationship. Use this time as another opportunity to peacefully connect. And yes, still others like to be silent or go back into their own space.

After a particularly ecstatic experience, don't necessarily be in a hurry to let it go. Write a note about it or call and remind your partner how good it was. Don't expect or demand an exact repeat performance, but use the great experience you just had to build on and enhance the overall sexuality in your relationship.

GET PSYCHED

"There is no better way to end a sexual experience than to prolong the intimate feelings. Think of ways you can extend those loving moments.

Give or receive a light back-scratch or gentle massage.

Cuddle in spoon position.

Have a verbal instant replay of how great the sex was.

Talk about how much you love each other.

"As love deepens, afterplay becomes foreplay for the next sexual experience." *–Lonnie Barbach, sex therapist,* 50 Ways to Please Your Lover

What You Can Do

As you were reading through this chapter, you probably came up with many ideas for taking a more playful approach to your lovemaking. Here are a few more specific things you can try:

☐ Decorate your bedroom, or wherever it is you most frequently make love, to make it more conducive to sexual lovemaking.

☐ Each of you list five to ten new things you would like to try the next time you make love, based on what you've learned in this chapter and your discussions.

☐ Discuss ways to play out one of your fantasies. Modify the fantasy, if needed, so it fits within the limitations of each of you.

☐ Based on what you learned in this chapter, introduce one sexual surprise this week into your lovemaking. It's best to try something your partner has not articulated but you picked up from what your partner told you.

☐ Write a letter or poem or note or card telling your partner what you found most enjoyable the last time you made love.

☐ Make a date to have a bout of lovemaking when you have time to do it in a relaxed way. Plan your encounter one or two days ahead of time in order to increase the anticipation.

Ecstasy and Your Bodies

Simply by freeing the mind to be more receptive to everything the body takes in, you and your partner can achieve a heightened level of ecstasy. But giving some additional attention to parts of your bodies that are particularly sensuous and receptive to pleasure can enhance your sexual ecstasy even more.

This chapter teaches you and your partner various ways of sharpening your senses, locating each other's erotic hot spots, and experimenting with different positions and techniques that can help you experience new sensations or experience the old sensations more fully. This is not a how-to manual packed with diagrams, photos, and tricks of the trade. Plenty of books and other resources on the market serve those needs. Our mission here is to maximize pleasurable sensory stimulation and make your mind more fully aware of everything that turns you on and heats you up!

Heightening Your Senses

Any sensation can turn a person on or off—whether you see it, hear it, smell it, taste it, or touch it. One way to heighten sexual ecstasy is to become more attuned to each sense in turn and to let each communicate its preferences and turn-ons to you. Here, we lead you through a sensual tour of your five senses—touch, taste, smell, hearing, and sight—and explore various ways to titillate each of them.

The Potential of Touch Sex, especially during foreplay and intercourse, involves a great deal of touching, so we begin our tour of the senses with a sensual massage or *sensate focus* massage, originally developed by Masters and Johnson. The sensate focus massage consists of taking turns giving each other sensual experiences that focus on all areas of the body except the genital areas and the breasts.

As preparation for your massage, you might identify for your partner the places on your body where you feel the most pleasure and provide specific guidance as to how you like to be touched in those places—stroking, patting, kissing, licking, squeezing, and so on. Beverly Whipple and Gina Ogden, co-authors of *Safe Encounters: How Women Can Say Yes to Pleasure and No To Unsafe Sex*, recommend that each partner fill out an extragenital matrix,

like the simplified matrix shown in the following table. Alone or together, you and your partner can fill out the chart using numbers from one to ten to create a map that shows just where and how you each prefer to be touched. You can do this before you begin or use this as a guide during the massage.

The extragenital matrix suggests many possibilities, but you don't have to try them all, and you might even think of more. That's why we included the "other" column. Your bodies are unique; your responses to touch are also unique and quite changeable. What felt good last time might not feel so good this time, so allow yourselves to remain open and flexible.

In the following table, rate from 1 to 10 (1 not at all, 10 ecstatic) how much you enjoy various kinds of touch on different parts of your body.

GET PSYCHED

"In terms of sexual ecstasy, you can have an ecstatic experience by looking at your partner, being someplace together, listening to music, seeing a sunset, or hearing the ocean. All of our senses are involved; and we can have pleasurable and satisfying sexual and sensual ecstasy though experiences that don't even involve the genitals. Whatever it is that brings this sensual and sexual pleasure about individually or as a couple is ecstasy."
—*Beverly Whipple, Ph.D., sex researcher, vice-president, World Association for Sexology Director, International Society for the Study of Women's Sexual Health*

Marty (age 33) and Gwen (age 31) are a professional couple. After the birth of their twins 14 months ago, they have rarely had sex (four times in the last year). Gwen now stays at home raising their children, and Marty has a demanding job as a lawyer. Initially they had sex almost every day, sometimes more, but for Gwen, it was over more quickly than she had wanted. She had had previous lovers who were both more passionate and sexually intimate than Marty. She never said anything about it, because she didn't want to hurt his feelings and everything else was so good. But now when Marty touched her, she would withdraw much of the time.

Through sensate focus, they began to reconnect, and they started going out on dates together one night a week. They also went to bed at night spooning in the nude (his penis touching her), an idea that Lonnie Barbach, Ph.D., recommends. Through sensate focus, they each learned what the other wanted more of and were able to better provide it for one another. In fact, they discovered when they talked that both wanted things to go a little more slowly, but they had been assuming that the other one was wanting to move faster.

They started talking during sexual encounters, which felt more intimate to both Marty and Gwen, and they finally began to feel that when they had sex they were making love. The quantity never returned to what it was early in their relationship, but they were quite satisfied with having sex about once a week, with additional affection and sensual contact on other nights. They both agreed that the quality of the sex they were now having together was more than they had known was possible for them.

Before you start, make a pact with your partner that the massage will be completely focused on sensual pleasure and any possible discomfort will be avoided or immediately addressed. Discuss in advance any potential areas of discomfort, including parts of the body to avoid, pressure that might feel uncomfortable, and scents, sounds, or sights that you might find distracting. Also agree to provide only positive instructions and directions and agree not to take offense at any suggestions your partner might offer. Make this as positive, enjoyable, and sensitive a learning experience as possible. You can do the massage with just your bare hands or with the addition of oils, lotions, or powders. Let the receiver make the call as to what he or she prefers.

GET PSYCHED

One way to enjoy touching each other is to take a bath or shower together and just let yourselves enjoy the sensations of soaping each other's bodies.

Extragenital Matrix*

Where on My Body	Touching by Hand				Touching by Mouth					
	Soft Stroking	Deep Stroking	Rubbing	Other	Patting	Kissing	Licking	Sucking	Nipping	Other
Head and Face										
Hair/Scalp										
Cheeks										
Lips										
Ears										
Neck and Torso										
Neck										
Shoulders										
Stomach										
Back										
Buttocks										
Arms and Hands										
Arms										
Elbows										
Wrists										
Palms										
Fingers										
Legs and Feet										
Legs										
Ankles										
Feet										
Toes										
Full Body										
Other										

*Modified from "Your Personal Extragenital Matrix," printed with permission of Beverly Whipple and Gina Ogden, Safe Encounters: How Women Can Say Yes to Pleasure and No To Unsafe Sex (New York: Pocket Books, 1990).

We suggest you set aside at least one hour for your sensate focus massage, so you won't be rushed. During this time, you and your partner will take turns acting as the *giver* of the massage and the receiver. The giver provides the receiver a variety of experiences of touch. The receiver's responsibility is to focus on the sensations that he or she feels during the massage—this is why it's called *sensate focus*. The only other responsibility of the receiver is to not judge or direct the giver. This frees the giver to explore many possible ways of touching his or her partner without the fear of being judged or the demand to "get it right." However, if something feels uncomfortable, the receiver should certainly let the giver know in a gentle and instructive (as opposed to judgmental or critical) way.

As the giver, you are encouraged to experience the sensation of touching your partner as well. Focus on how you feel being the giver and exploring each part of your partner's body as if you had never touched it before. What are the different textures, temperatures, and scents of your partner's body? Learn them and, most importantly, find new ways to enjoy them. For this massage, avoid the genital area and the breasts, because this massage is intended to focus on sensuality, *not* sexuality. The essence of this sensate focus is for each of you to explore your preferences and desires when giving and receiving. There is no right or wrong way to do this; you are learning what pleases you both. Once one partner has received the sensate focus massage, it is the other partner's turn, so reverse roles. As a bonus, you might want to end the massage by hugging and holding each other in order for you to savor the pleasure.

> **GET PSYCHED**
>
> "Man consists of two parts, his mind and his body, only the body has more fun."
> —*Woody Allen*

After completing the massage, take some time to share how the experience felt to each of you, and be sure to emphasize the positive aspects of what you shared together. Describe what you liked and, even more importantly, what you would like more of. Set aside another time to do this again. This time talk beforehand in order to let each other know what you want.

Tasty Turn-ons For many people, specific flavors can have a strong effect on the way they experience sex. A kiss after eating a chocolate, for instance, can be delightfully erotic. You might find a type of mouthwash or lotion that your partner uses to be more or less pleasing than another. It's important for you to know which flavors turn you on and which ones turn you off and to discuss your preferences with your partner.

You and your partner might consider incorporating certain flavors more directly into your lovemaking, especially if either of you tends to connect sexual pleasure with certain flavors, such as chocolate or wine, for example. Something as simple as setting a plate of berries or cheese nearby and nibbling on the treats while you play together is one option. You might dip a finger in chocolate syrup and lick it off as a tease or let your partner suck it off. You might share a kiss after a sip of champagne or flavor your foreplay with whip cream. If you prefer to keep food and sex separate, you might find other options appealing, such as edible flavored oils or gels. You can even incorporate flavors into your sensual massage.

Erotic Aromas Scientists have known for some time that many creatures including humans emit chemicals, called *pheromones*, which can sometimes help attract members of the opposite sex. In fact, many perfume and cologne companies use research on pheromones to design products intended to mimic the effects of pheromones. Frequently, however, a scent that appeals to the wearer does not appeal to his or her partner, so it's important to become aware of the scents that you and your partner find pleasant and unpleasant and agree to share your preferences, so you can be sure that at the very least you are not working against your goal of maximizing these potential pleasure enhancers.

Norma McCoy and her colleagues at San Francisco State University found that women wearing perfume laced with synthetic pheromones saw an overall increase in the frequency of kissing, heavy petting, affection, and sexual intercourse. Of the

36 women tested, 74 percent of those who wore their perfume spiked with the pheromone experienced a significant increase in sexual activity. Only 23 percent of those wearing their perfume laced with a placebo reported any increase.

So if a particular perfume or cologne your partner wears doesn't appeal to you, gently communicate that. Another selection might appeal to both of you. Ask your partner whether there's a perfume, shampoo, deodorant, or cologne that he or she would like you to try. Or better yet, go out and buy one for your partner that pleases you. And remember, for many couples, the best turn-ons of all are the natural scents radiated from each other's bodies.

Also, focus on scents around the house, especially in the bathroom and bedroom. Modern society is well equipped to eliminate odors and freshen the scent of almost every aspect of your life with air fresheners, scen-ted candles, bath soaps, carpet fresheners, incense, and an assortment of other great-smelling stuff. And if those options don't appeal to you, sometimes opening a window or adding a bouquet of fresh-cut flowers is just the thing to set the right climate.

Stimulating Sounds Many species of animals, including humans, use sound in their courtship rituals. Male frogs and toads croak, humpback whales sing, bull elephants blare a trumpetlike call, and birds call seductively to one another. Poets and troubadours have used the rhythms of language and song to woo prospective mates as well. Even the sound of a partner's voice can sometimes act as an *aphrodisiac*.

Some people find music erotic and can feel the music in their bodies as an enhancer to whatever erotic feelings they are experiencing.

PsychSpeak

A **pheromone** is a chemical that a creature can emit to influence the behavior or development of others of the same species. Pheromones often serve to attract members of the opposite sex.
An **aphrodisiac** is a substance that increases or excites sexual desire. The word comes from the Greek *aphrodisiakos*, which means sexual pleasure. Aphrodite was the goddess of love and beauty from Greek mythology whose allure was irresistible to gods and men alike.

Music can be a way of setting a romantic mood. Some couples have their favorite song, which can trigger feelings of love and connection. Still others find music a way to relax and let go of the day. Then once they're relaxed, they can begin to feel desire building. Consider experimenting with different kinds of music or sounds. Do you like nature sounds—the ocean, for example? Or do you prefer quiet? Do you like to listen to your partner's breathing? Moaning? Romantic whispers? Sex talk? Consider listing or discussing some types of sounds and think about incorporating one or two into your lovemaking next time.

Sensual Sights For many people, especially men, the sense of sight has a commanding sexual presence. The contours of the human body, certain colors and textures, and specific styles of fashion can significantly stimulate desire in both men and women. Many couples focus on their own appearance and choose to accent their bodies in various ways to feel sexier about themselves and feel more appealing to their partners, but background sights can also help establish a visually enticing setting. Different types and colors of light, candlelight, and the appearance of the room in which you make love can all enhance the pleasure you experience. Erotic photos and videos, or video clips of you and your partner making love, can be another enticing choice for some couples.

Of course, you always have the option of blocking out visual stimulation altogether to increase the mystery or to make yourself and your partner more aware of other sensory stimulation. Sometimes closing your eyes or wearing a blindfold while your lover massages your body or treats you to other pleasant sensations can be highly erotic. Simply turning out the lights if you typically make love with the lights on can even serve as a novel variation.

GET PSYCHED

"In long-term relationships it's important for people not to get into a rut. Acknowledge that there are multiple ways that people can have sensual and sexual pleasure and then experiment with what you find pleasurable. Take the time to find what's pleasurable, what brings you ecstasy with your body and with your mind." –Beverly Whipple, Ph.D.

Mutual Erotic Touching

Up to this point, we have intentionally shifted focus from breast and genital sensation to increase awareness of other sensations that often go unnoticed in moments of passionate lovemaking. As foreplay progresses, however, breast and genital sensation often intensify and become the key sensations that can trigger orgasm. Exploring the types of direct genital and breast stimulation that you and your partner prefer can intensify pleasure and perhaps increase the frequency and intensity of orgasm. One of the most effective ways to explore and teach one another the types of stimulation you find most titillating is through mutual erotic touching. In that regard, here is something you and your partner can do together: Try doing the sensate focus massage again. Only this time, include the breast and genital areas. Again, the focus is on pleasure, not performance or reaching orgasm; although, if orgasm happens, enjoy!

Locating Your Body's Hot Spots Some people know where they like to be touched and which areas of their bodies act as pleasure buttons, but many people have not yet explored all of their potential hot spots or passed that information along to their partners. Give your body a sensual physical exam to find out what feels good and where it feels good, and then communicate the information you discover to your partner. To help, we've created a Female Genital Matrix and Male Genital Matrix (see the following table) that you and your partner can complete to identify your chest/breast and genital hot spots and become more aware of how you like to be touched in those places. As you read through this section and the next, you might want to complete the chart that pertains to you, and use it for future discussions.

In the following tables, rate from 1 to 10 (1 not at all, 10 ecstatic) how much you enjoy various kinds of touch on different parts of your body.

Female Genital Matrix*

Kinds of Touch

Where on My Body	Touching by Hand						Touching by Mouth					Other	
	Light Touching	Firmer Pressure	Circles	Slow Stroking	Fast Stroking	Other	Kissing	Licking	Sucking	Nipping	Other	Toy	Vibration
Genitals													
Mons pubis													
Labia													
Clitoral hood													
Clitoral shaft													
Clitoral glans													
G spot													
Vagina													
Torso/Belly													
Breasts													
Nipples													
Buttocks													
Buttocks													
Anus													
Other													

*Modified from "Your Personal Extragenital Matrix," printed with permission of Beverly Whipple and Gina Ogden, Safe Encounters: How Women Can Say Yes to Pleasure and No To Unsafe Sex (New York: Pocket Books, 1990).

Male Genital Matrix*

Kinds of Touch

Where on My Body	Touching by Hand					Touching by Mouth					Other	
	Light Touching	Firmer Pressure	Slow Stroking	Fast Stroking	Other	Kissing	Licking	Sucking	Nipping	Other	Toy	Vibration
Genitals												
Penis tip												
Penis shaft												
Testes												
Perineum												
Prostate												
Torso/Belly												
Chest												
Nipples												
Buttocks												
Buttocks												
Anus												
Other												

*Modified from "Your Personal Extragenital Matrix," printed with permission of Beverly Whipple and Gina Ogden, Safe Encounters: How Women Can Say Yes to Pleasure and No To Unsafe Sex (New York: Pocket Books, 1990).

Externally, the male genitalia has three main hot spots: the penis, the scrotum (which includes the testes), and the perineum (the area between the genitals and the anus). Many men find the tip of the penis especially sensitive. Internally, the prostate gland, sometimes referred to as the *male G spot*, can deliver intense pleasure if stimulated externally by pressure to the perineum or internally through the anus; some men find this pleasurable, whereas others do not. Some men also find the nipples and buttocks to be quite sexually sensitive.

If you and your partner are comfortable with masturbation and are willing to masturbate in the presence of each other, masturbation can be one way to teach each other what feels good to you. In addition, for many, this can be a very erotic turn-on in and of itself! Show your partner the areas of your genitals that you like to touch and have touched. Demonstrate how you like to be touched. You might even guide your partner's hands and fingers to the right spots and provide feedback to help fine-tune the pressure and motion of the touch. If possible, explain when you like to be touched in specific areas. For example, women often find clitoral stimulation most pleasant after they are already aroused by intense foreplay or stimulation of the labia. And many women enjoy touching in all areas of the genitals, including the labia and vagina. Any details you can pass along to your partner will help. As always, make the exercise a pleasurable learning experience. And most importantly, avoid any feedback that might sound to your partner like a putdown for not already knowing what you like.

For men, your partner can add variations by touching, kissing, or licking the penis in areas previously unexplored, such as the crown of the penis or around the testicles. Your partner can also help stimulate other areas, including the perineum and the prostate gland, the nipples, and other erotic areas in ways that feel quite different than your own touch during masturbation.

For women, the breasts and the areas around the breasts can be quite sensitive to touch, although sensitivity varies a great deal.

Some women can reach orgasm with the proper stimulation of their breasts, whereas others do not enjoy it at all. Others find it pleasurable only at certain times during their menstrual cycle. Sensitivity frequently changes when a woman is pregnant or breastfeeding and as the woman passes through different phases of menopause. (Postmenopausal women may experience a change in sensation in their breasts and their genitals.)

PsychSpeak

The **mons pubis** is the fatty mound of flesh over the pubic bone in women which is normally covered by pubic hair. It is a highly sensitive area and can transmit sensation throughout the genital area when touched or moved.

The most sexually sensitive area of a woman's body is the clitoris, the portion of the female genitalia that has the most nerve endings. Clitoral stimulation, for many women, is the key to sexual arousal and can be an important component in achieving orgasm. Although the external part of the clitoris is the most sensitive and accessible, it also has a sensitive shaft that runs from the gland to the vaginal opening. Stimulating the clitoris too early in a lovemaking session can be uncomfortable for some women. Stroking or licking the labia or other areas around the clitoris first, until it becomes excited and aroused, is often helpful before touching the clitoris itself. As the clitoris becomes more sensitive, any direct pressure can actually hurt, so communicating at various stages how it feels is very important. If the clitoris is dry, use an appropriate lubricant, such as saliva, K-Y Jelly, or Astroglide.

The vagina, especially the two inches nearest its surface, is another quite sensitive area. Although the majority of women require clitoral stimulation to achieve orgasm, some women can achieve orgasm through vaginal stimulation alone or accompanied by additional sensory stimulation and erotic thoughts. You can explore the vagina by inserting your finger and moving it around in different ways. The silent vagina exercise, discussed in Chapter 9, is also useful. Women usually need some degree of overall sexual arousal before they experience genital arousal or before genital stimulation is even felt as pleasurable. Again, this is an individual matter.

Once you know your hot spots, consider how you prefer having them touched; and perhaps try different options and techniques alone or with your partner. Some women, for example, prefer having the clitoris stimulated in an up-and-down or back-and-forth motion, some prefer small circles, and others like the touch varied. Try a lighter touch early with more pressure as the clitoris becomes enlarged. Women often like to have all the areas of their genitals stroked, and also their thighs and breasts. If you like, try a sex toy or vibrator for additional stimulation. If your partner is exploring different ways to stimulate you, provide feedback in the form of verbal instructions, moaning, or body movement, or show your partner how you like to be touched.

Mutual erotic touching can be performed with variations such as in a bath or a shower, with appropriate lubricants or powders, or even completely or partially clothed. If you feel comfortable touching one another in public, you can sneak in an erotic touch on a plane or in your car, or at a restaurant or movie. Mutual erotic touching can be part of a tease or seduction, or as a form of lovemaking in and of itself. Some people can bring themselves to full orgasm with their clothes on. Of course, as with everything, whether you choose to perform mutual erotic touching and how and where you choose to do it is completely up to whatever you and your partner feel is comfortable.

Who discovered the G spot and what led to the discovery?

In 1981 after listening to women's histories describing what was pleasurable to them, Dr. John Perry and Beverly Whipple realized that the Master's and Johnson monolithic model of clitoral stimulation did not apply to all women. Reports from these women included descriptions of intense pleasurable sensations from vaginal stimulation and in some cases expulsion of fluid. Perry and Whipple rediscovered what they named the Grafenberg Spot (or G spot) after Ernest Grafenberg who initially described this sensitive area in 1950.

The G Spot—His and Hers The *Graffenberg spot*, commonly referred to as the *G spot*, is a physiological structure in most (if not all) women that is believed to be analogous to the male prostate and that has the reputation of being able to induce deeply pleasurable sensations. It is a small area inside the vagina on the front wall about 2 inches from the entrance. For a woman, locating her own G spot can be difficult, because she might not be able to reach her fingers deeply enough into her vagina, but a partner can often help by inserting two fingers or a sex toy and moving it up two or three inches along the top surface of the vaginal wall. The G spot frequently becomes larger when stimulated. A deep stroking motion is usually most pleasurable. The orgasm that some women experience from G spot stimulation can sometimes cause the woman to ejaculate a prosthetic fluid (not urine) from the urethra. Many women find this pleasurable, and many do not.

Hitting the G spot and triggering female ejaculation are goal-oriented approaches (and we do not generally recommend goal oriented approaches), but it can be fun and rewarding to explore G spot stimulation as yet another way to intensify pleasure. Sometimes, a particular position during intercourse can make it easier to reach the G spot. For example, the rear entry position—the woman on all fours and the man entering the vagina from behind—is sometimes helpful in stimulating the G spot, and some women find that the missionary style (partners facing each other), with the woman on top works well, or the missionary position with the woman on bottom drawing her legs up slightly toward her shoulders and tilting her pelvis back to bring the G spot more in line with the tip of the penis. You might want to try some different positions in order to see whether it enhances your pleasure. Remember, not all women find G spot stimulation to be pleasurable. So if this doesn't work for you, not to worry. There are many other ways to experience pleasure!

Although the G spot refers specifically to female anatomy, the male anatomy has its own "joy button"—the prostate gland. The prostate gland surrounds the urethra at the base of the bladder, controls the release of urine, and secretes a fluid, which is a major constituent of semen. Many men find stimulation of the prostate to be very sexually arousing, but others might find it uncomfortable or even painful. The prostate can be stimulated either by applying pressure to the perineum or by inserting a finger or other suitable object carefully into the anus with the aid of a water-soluble lubricant.

Superb Oral Sex

Depending on whom you ask, *oral sex* can be a complete turn-off, a scintillating main act, an invigorating warm-up, or a pleasant departure from the routine. Some people would rather perform oral sex than receive it. Others prefer receiving over giving. Some enjoy giving and receiving at the same time. And others have an ever-changing preference.

PsychSpeak

Oral sex consists of using one or more parts of the mouth to stimulate the partner's genitals. When a woman performs oral sex on a man, it is referred to as *fellatio.* When a man performs oral sex on a woman, it is called *cunnilingus.* When the man and woman perform oral sex on one another simultaneously, they do it in a position commonly referred to as the **sixty-nine (69) position.**

Oral sex can serve as a part of foreplay or it can lead to orgasm without intercourse. It also can serve as an excellent replacement when you and your partner cannot have intercourse or when one partner desires sexual release more than the other. Many couples prefer oral sex over manual stimulation because the lips and tongue provide their own lubrication and apply a softer, gentler touch.

If you're new to oral sex, if it is something that at least one of you desires, and if you're both willing to discuss it, know that there are ways you can ease into it and make it more appealing to try for the two of you. Discuss with your partner any reservations either of you might have. In some cases, an obsolete belief or a notion from the past might be generating some discomfort. Or, you could be afraid that you might not do it properly or in a way that your partner will find pleasurable.

If the idea of bringing your mouth in contact with your partner's genitals is inhibiting, a gradual approach might help you become less sensitive over time. You can choose to kiss or lick around the genitals and gradually move to the penis or vagina. If hygiene is an issue, request that your partner shower or bathe beforehand or apply an edible, flavored gel or liquid (only water-soluble for women). If you're a woman who dislikes the idea of having semen in your mouth, lick from the base of the shaft upward to avoid the tip, or ask your partner to wear a condom or signal when he's about to ejaculate. You might choose to agree to use oral sex only as foreplay and bring your partner to orgasm manually or during intercourse. Some women are just comfortable knowing that as long as the partner has no sexually transmitted disease, the semen is perfectly harmless. It contains protein and can even be considered healthy according to Gordon Gallup of NY State University.

Oral Pleasure for Her Because the clitoris can be the most erotic of hot spots for women, men usually need to pay more attention to it during oral sex, but it's not necessarily the first area to visit. Most women need to be sexually aroused in other ways before the clitoris is ready. Remember all of a woman's body can be an erogenous zone. So you might want to start on top (kissing) and slowly make your way down. Once you're at the genital area, begin stimulating the vaginal lips. Going from the vaginal to the clitoral area and back is often helpful, with the receiver providing feedback concerning the types of stimulation that feel

GET PSYCHED

The National Health and Social Life Survey, studying the sexual practices and beliefs of Americans, found that almost three quarters of those studied had tried oral sex at some point and at least twenty percent engaged in it during their last sexual experience. It was slightly more common among men, the young, and the more educated in the population.

GET PSYCHED

Dr. Ava Cadell, sex educator and author of *The Pocket Idiot's Guide to Oral Sex* (Alpha Books), gives some additional pointers:

- Make oral sex a ritual, bathing each other before oral sex.

- Women generally like less pressure than men on their genitals.

- The cleanest orifice in the body is the vagina. Make sure anything you put into it, including fingers and sex toys, is clean. Anything containing oils or sugars is bad for it, so if in doubt, leave it out.

- When giving a man oral sex, the penis and testicles deserve equal attention.

- When giving a woman oral sex, don't go south too fast, and never chew on her clitoris.

- Ask your partner how he or she wants to be pleased; be comfortable taking directions.

good—kissing, licking, sucking, soft or firm pressure, up and down or circles, fingers involved or not involved, and so on. Once vaginal stimulation arouses the clitoris, it is more ready to feel the pleasures of oral sex. For many women, direct stimulation of the clitoral head is too intense. So if this is the case, play around it, and ask for and give feedback.

To ensure that oral sex remains as comfortable and safe as possible for the woman, the man might consider shaving (if he has any stubble) before performing oral sex, and both partners should find comfortable positions (or agree to change positions if one or the other indicates that preference). A woman can often increase the pleasure by moving or shifting positions while her partner is performing oral sex. In addition, men should know not to intentionally blow air directly into the vagina, which could possibly (although this is rare) cause an air embolism. This doesn't mean you need to hold your breath, but just remember to avoid blowing directly into the vagina.

Oral Pleasure for Him There are many ways to pleasure a man through oral sex, and most men find all of them erotic to some degree. So the first thing women should know is that however you perform oral sex and whatever level you take it to, your partner will probably appreciate it—assuming, of course, that he enjoys receiving oral sex. And you can certainly discover many wonderful ways to do it as you learn more about what your partner enjoys. But first, it's a good idea to discuss whether you will bring your partner to orgasm with the oral sex or whether you're doing it as a part of foreplay.

You can begin by caressing your partner's body with your hands and then moving to the genitals—the penis and the testes. Lick the shaft from the base of the penis up to the tip, or lick the testes. You need not take the entire penis into your mouth, although some women like to. The *coronal ridge* (around the head of the penis) is a highly sensitive area. In *The Sensuous Woman*, the author, "J," writes about drawing a butterfly design around the ridge of the penis, to envision an area of very exquisite sensation. Lick around the ridge or suck the head of the penis into your mouth and use your lips to massage the ridge. Any additional stimulation, including sucking and caressing the penis with your tongue, can increase the pleasure. Using your hand to stroke the testes (no hard squeezing unless he specifically asks for that), rub or squeeze the buttocks, touch or pinch the nipples, or even provide anal stimulation (explored later in this chapter) can add greatly to the intensity of his pleasure. Licking or sucking the testes or perineum is extremely pleasurable for some men.

Some women enjoy taking the whole penis into their mouth. If you want to try this, concentrate on your breathing to avoid the gag reflex, and use your hands as well as your mouth. But no matter how you do it, remember to share positive, constructive feedback. By doing that, things can only get better and better!

Oral Pleasure Together Giving oral pleasure to each other simultaneously can often lift some couples to new heights of sexual ecstasy. In the *69 position,* partners position themselves so that their faces are aligned with each other's genital area. They can be lying down or one partner can be atop the other, straddling his

WEB TALK: To read more about Dr. Ava Cadell's specific suggestions, check out her website at:

www.sexpert.com

or her face. The 69 position can be quite pleasurable in that the focus on your partner can often make you more receptive to other sensations you're experiencing. This position also can free your hands and place them in easy reach of other highly erotic areas of your partner's anatomy; you can manually stimulate your partner, insert a finger or vibrator into the woman's vagina, or add anal stimulation, if your partner finds it pleasurable. Again, the 69 position is not for everyone, but if you both like to give and receive oral pleasure and you haven't done it before, it is definitely worth a try.

Anal Stimulation

The anal area has a concentration of nerve endings that make it a potential pleasure zone. Many couples enjoy some type of anal touching to some degree during intercourse, oral sex, or even foreplay. The area around the anus is very sensitive, as well, so some couples prefer stimulating just around the ring of the anal area, rather than trying any form of penetration. Many couples also choose not to include it as part of their lovemaking.

If you do decide to incorporate some form of anal stimulation into your love-making, follow a few precautions: Keep anything that touches the anal area, including your fingers, away from the vagina; wash your hands and any objects you use before touching them to or inserting them in the anus; do not insert any sharp objects, including fingers with long fingernails, into the anus; and lubricate the anal area before inserting anything into it.

GET PSYCHED

The National Health and Social Life Survey found that about 25 percent of American men and women have tried anal sex at some point in their lives, ten percent within the last year, and only two percent during their last sexual experience.

Other forms of anal stimulation include analingus (licking the anus) and anal intercourse, in which the penis is inserted into the anus. If you and your partner would like to try analingus, it's best to do after showering. Some women find that using the tongue on the clitoris, and one finger on the vagina and another finger in the anus or around the anus provides intense erotic stimulation. If you choose to perform anal intercourse, always wear a condom, make sure the anus is well lubricated with a water-soluble lubricant, and, most important, wash off before entering the vagina.

My boyfriend likes to touch my anal area during sexual play. I feel aroused by it, but I also am not comfortable with it. It gives me some pleasure but is he doing something perverted?

There are numerous nerve endings in the anal area, and many people find this kind of anal play to be stimulating during sexual activity. If it is something you both find pleasurable, there is no difficulty; just be sure that, if he stimulates you in the anal area with his finger or penis, he does not insert that into the vaginal area before washing because it can transmit bacteria. As long as you mutually consent, follow healthy hygiene, and perform it safely, anal stimulation can be quite pleasurable and is certainly not perverted!

Intercourse—The Grande Finale?

To some, intercourse equals sex. But as we now know, this is only one of many sexual activities available to you. Someone once referred to sex as a deck of cards with 52 varieties. All pleasurable sexual activity, romantic components, and interpersonal bonding contribute to sexual ecstasy. When you and your partner are ready to initiate intercourse, there's not much more to tell you than what you already know: In the bedroom, keep doing what works for you and consider anything extra or different that might make it even more enjoyable. Intercourse can be the ultimate culmination of a long, titillating seduction; a playful recreational activity; a stress reliever; a way to show your love; or anything else that you and your partner decide to make it.

Experimenting with Positions Although the standard missionary position (man and woman face-to-face) might seem uninspired to the more "savvy" lover, with the right mindset, this position is quite suitable for experiencing all degrees of sexual ecstasy. You might choose to add some variations to the position by taking turns on top, holding your legs a little differently, thrusting at different speeds (or taking turns thrusting), partially penetrating (sometimes with the woman holding her legs in the air), or thrusting at different angles. In the missionary position, you can rub your torsos together, use your free hands to stimulate other erotic zones, kiss, connect through eye contact or keep them closed, whisper in your lover's ear, or even reach behind to provide anal stimulation. It's a position that accommodates a great deal of variation.

My husband would like to experiment more with positions and with doing different kinds of things. The problem is that when we have tried in the past to change positions, I have stopped being aroused. I don't want to do anything wrong. Can you help me with this?

Your reticence might be the result of an assumption about how sex is supposed to be. Most people believe that once you begin to be sexually involved, you need to get more and more aroused until you have an orgasm. The reality is that human bodies often don't work that way, particularly if you want to be adventuresome and experience different kinds of sexual activity. If there's a transition between one position or one activity and another it's quite normal to lose arousal. Problems often arise when you begin to worry about that. Look at this as a time of teasing when your arousal can go up and down indefinitely. It's perfectly normal that switching positions at times will decrease arousal. This does not indicate that you should stop. However, if intercourse becomes painful, stop the activity and engage in holding or touching. That may mark the end of your lovemaking session, or if you begin to engage in more touching or kissing, you might find yourself aroused again. Don't worry about it and certainly don't force it.

However, it can be fun to try different positions, and experimenting often leads to innovation, so feel free to research and try something different. You can find a plethora of books and articles that describe the more intriguing positions in great detail and contain plenty of illustrations or photos to show you just what to do and how to do it. Videos are also readily available. If your partner is open to trying different positions, you might find it fun to purchase a book of positions and flag the ones that each of you finds appealing. Together, you can rule out any that look uncomfortable to either of you and then take turns trying the rest. Try a new position more than once before you give up on it—some positions take a little practice and finesse. If something's not working, switch positions, switch back to manual or oral stimulation, or just play around and enjoy the moment. Remember, your only real mission here is the pleasure that's there for both of you!

Kegels—The Art of Muscle Control To help treat urinary incontinence problems in women, Dr. Arnold Kegel developed some exercises (*Kegel exercises*) to help women strengthen the muscle responsible for cutting off the flow of urine. Surprisingly, some of the women who performed the Kegel exercises began reporting increases in sexual responsiveness and sensation. The increase was traced to their *pubococcygeal* (P.C.) muscle, the muscle that surrounds the vaginal opening—the main muscle that contracts during orgasm. Men also have this P.C. muscle, and learning to relax and control it can help them as well. To feel this muscle, try to stop the stream of urine when you are urinating. Your stomach and buttocks muscles should feel relaxed, but the pelvic muscles should tighten.

To strengthen the P.C. muscle, first contract and then release the muscle ten times, three times a day, until it starts feeling easy for you. Next, contract or squeeze the muscle for a count of three, and do ten repetitions three times a day. When that begins to seem easy, try another exercise called the "flutter": squeeze and release rapidly; do ten repetitions three times a day. You can try to work up to 20 repetitions, 5 times a day or more. This can be done almost anywhere: while standing in line, stopped at a red light, or sitting in a meeting. For women, if you are comfortable with masturbation, you can try a variation of the Kegel exercise by inserting a fairly firm (not hard) dildo or even your finger into your vagina and tightening and relaxing your P.C. muscle around it, or do it with your partner's erect penis.

For both sexes, doing the Kegel exercises can increase your own awareness of your sexual response as well as increase orgasmic control and intensity. What's more, doing the Kegel exercises during intercourse can increase pleasure for *both* you and your partner.

What You Can Do

This chapter is dedicated to helping you become more aware of what your body and your partner's body enjoy and find sexually stimulating. You probably have learned a great deal already about your body's likes and dislikes, but here are some additional ideas for helping you learn more:

- ☐ This week, introduce two new sensory stimulants (one for each of you). Repeat this for four weeks until you've treated each of your five senses.

- ☐ Take turns performing sensual massages, but this time have the recipient close his or her eyes (or use a blindfold), and introduce stimulation other than physical touch—scents, sounds, or flavors.

- ☐ If you both enjoy oral sex (or are at least open to it), discuss ways in which you would like or might like to have oral sex; see if you can try something new and different that you haven't done in the past.

- ☐ Discuss anal stimulation to determine whether you or your partner might find it appealing. If you do, make a commitment to explore your options and explain to one another how you might like to approach it.

- ☐ The next time you make love, turn on the lights or burn a candle and keep eye contact during your lovemaking. If this is how you usually do it, try the opposite.

Maximizing Your Orgasm

Ironically, the best way to maximize orgasm is to minimize the importance of achieving it! In other words, to the extent that you can shed any goals you might have with respect to reaching orgasm or making your orgasm more intense, you have taken the biggest step possible toward maximizing it. In addition, the degree to which you and your partner are able to incorporate the five ingredients of sexual ecstasy into your lovemaking fosters an environment that is not only more conducive to orgasm but certainly more favorable for experiencing all aspects of sexual ecstasy. So once the ingredients are in place, if you can relax playfully with one another and enjoy your lovemaking in whatever form it takes, you have set the stage for great orgasms to happen.

Orgasm is a sensation that many people describe as intensely physical and even deeply spiritual. They can be profoundly strong, mildly pleasurable, or anywhere in between. Your experience of orgasm may differ each time as a result of physical factors, including fatigue, the amount of time that has passed since your last orgasm, or any medication you may have taken. It is also affected by your mood, feelings about your partner, and, of course, your expectations. Scientists have even discovered that measuring the intensity of muscle contractions does not necessarily correspond with how satisfying the orgasm felt. Orgasm is not essential for experiencing sexual ecstasy, but anything you can do to intensify it or make it last longer with your partner can certainly heighten your feelings of pleasure.

In this chapter, you will see how to enhance your orgasms without making them a critical ingredient of ecstasy (since all forms of pleasurable sexual activity can be really fulfilling in and of themselves). We provide the latest information to dispel the myths surrounding orgasm. We also describe several methods and different approaches that can help prolong and intensify your orgasm.

Facts and Myths About Orgasm

Orgasm is a reflex, an unintentional contraction of the genital muscles that involves the discharge of accumulated sexual tension. It is physiologically analogous to a sneeze or a hiccup. The whole body is involved, and the orgasm is marked by fast and heavy breathing, a racing pulse, and contractions of the pelvic muscles, as well as muscles elsewhere in the body (at .8-second intervals). The contractions help expel the blood that was trapped in the genital area, which causes the pleasurable sensations, followed by an enjoyable release of muscle tension throughout the body. In men, orgasm is almost always accompanied by ejaculation—the forceful ejection of semen, usually experienced at the peak of sexual excitement. Often orgasm is experienced as sexual ecstasy.

PsychSpeak

Orgasm is also commonly referred to as *climax*.

Although some people can be brought to experience orgasm through only one type of stimulation (physical stimulation or intense fantasy, for instance), it can follow as a result of any and all forms of stimulation that positively affect you sexually—including physical, emotional, psychological, intellectual, and spiritual stimulation. When it all comes together in a feeling of bliss, orgasm is often the result.

Unless guilt or pain are in some way triggered, most people who have experienced orgasm have found it to be anywhere from mildly pleasurable to one of the most intensely ecstatic feelings they've ever had:

"Incredibly pleasurable convulsions taking over my entire body."

"It feels like waves of electricity passing through my brain!"

"Delicious sensations wash over me—sometimes my whole body, sometimes just my genitals—and then a sense of pure bliss and satisfaction and feelings of closeness towards my partner."

"A real and pure feeling of well being."

"It's like arousal, tension, desperation for release, an altered state, sometimes a fantasy is playing in my head and sometimes not. I have a release and then am in a great mood for the next day or two."

"I am fully and deeply in my body, feeling the sensation of my body touching his and his, mine. He is deeply inside of me and our bodies are synchronized in motion. I can hear his excitement, his breathing, and then I hear my sounds and can hardly believe that these sounds are coming from my body. I am building up to my climax. I can feel my clitoris and vagina swelling and pulsating. It is as if I have become my genitals."

"My orgasm happens gradually and then seems to explode all of a sudden. My body contracts as if my head and feet want to meet. Sometimes I feel like I lose consciousness for a few seconds. I am totally connected to his body; there is no separation. I continue to feel the pulsing for many minutes and often cannot speak. I am just sound and sensation."

The ability to experience and enhance orgasm depends so much on the attitude you have about it, that an important first step toward maximizing orgasm is to dispel any myths surrounding it. Here are the straight facts about orgasm and how it relates to your sexual experience:

- *You can have good or even great sex and achieve ecstasy without orgasm.*

- *You and your partner can have a pleasurable sexual experience even if only one of you reaches orgasm.* Simultaneous orgasms can be magnificent, but in reality, they're fairly uncommon. Through open communication, you might increase your chances of experiencing orgasms simultaneously, but never rate your lovemaking—no matter how subtly—based on this; in fact, not having simultaneous orgasms allows you to experience two orgasms, to fully enjoy yours and to vicariously share in your partner's. If you're having orgasms at the same time, you might miss your partner's completely.

- *You can be a good lover even if you don't experience great orgasms, multiple orgasms, or any orgasm at all.* Being a good lover is about much more than being sexually wired for orgasm. Identify something in your lovemaking you enjoy, ask your partner for it, and then give yourself permission to fully experience it. And remember to validate your own sexual desires, whatever they might be. If you can experience some form of sexual pleasure, you communicate your needs and desires to your partner, and you are attentive to your partner's needs and desires, consider yourself a good lover!

- *You can experience orgasm even when your partner doesn't do exactly what you want at a given moment.* Barring any complications, your capacity to orgasm is within you, irrespective of your partner.

- *Sexual ecstasy can include orgasm, but orgasm is not a necessary component of sexual ecstasy.* Orgasm can enhance your ecstasy and play a very important part in it, but it's not an essential ingredient.

- *And remember, you don't give your partner orgasms.* Each person is responsible for reaching his or her own orgasms.

Orgasms are very powerful, pleasurable experiences, and they are certainly something to desire; however, no one knows the exact formula for achieving the perfect orgasm every time. We just know that it's important to be open to pleasure and connected to your partner in the present moment during lovemaking. And then, if orgasm happens, great!

His and Her Orgasms—Understanding Each

It's no surprise that orgasm produces some different sensations in men and women, but the differences go far beyond the physical sensations. By learning and developing a deeper understanding of how the opposite sex experiences orgasm, and by communicating your unique experiences to one another, you and your partner can become more attuned to what brings each of you closer to the orgasm you desire. And once you know, you can begin to approach your lovemaking in a way that can maximize orgasm for each of you.

Male Orgasms Men's sexual response generally starts with desire, leading to increasing arousal, rising through intercourse to the plateau phase, and culminating in orgasm and ejaculation. Many men commonly become more or less aroused throughout the period of lovemaking, but they usually experience orgasm every time they have sex. Afterward, men undergo a refractory period in which they cannot have another erection or ejaculation for several minutes or even several hours. This period gradually gets longer as men age, and can even last several days.

For a man, maximizing orgasm usually calls for delaying it to experience more pleasure before orgasm, to make intercourse more satisfying for his partner, and to intensify the orgasmic release during climax. However, conscious attempts to delay orgasm and any expectation for experiencing more or better orgasms can sometimes lead to the opposite effect, so it's important not to focus too much on trying to hold back.

Prolonging pleasure before orgasm usually calls for focusing more on pleasure and less on the orgasm itself. Sometimes men try to slow down orgasms by distracting themselves during sex. Sometimes this works, but this can actually lead to a speeding-up of orgasm. To slow down orgasm, concentrate on the sensation and think of it as just another pleasurable feeling rather than as a sensation that will ultimately result in an orgasm. Sometimes, if you and your partner can stop moving and allow yourself to feel comfortable inside for a moment (as with the silent vagina exercise), you can relax enough to resume another round of pleasurable lovemaking before you ejaculate.

Sex feels great to me, but I don't come through intercourse, and my husband feels disappointed. I try to explain that he really does feel good inside me, but he wants me to have an orgasm. What can we do?

It's natural for you not to reach orgasm through intercourse alone, and it's understandable that your husband feels disappointed. But he needs to understand that this may be an unrealistic expectation. He obviously wants you to feel as good as he does. There are some things you can try. Extending foreplay can help. Keep in mind that many women prefer to have orgasm before intercourse; if your husband is open to it, he might find it very erotic to manually or orally stimulate you or even use a vibrator or other sex toy to intensify the stimulation before intercourse. The most important thing, however, is to continue your dialog with your husband and keep trying new things in a playful way without goals, expectations, or disappointment.

Female Orgasms The female orgasm differs from the male orgasm in two important ways: the physiological experience itself and the sexual response cycle leading up to orgasm. Unlike men, who typically experience orgasm as genital muscle contraction followed by ejaculation, women can experience various types of orgasm: clitoral, vaginal, pelvic floor (which includes the G spot), and a blended orgasm (a combination of these three), depending on the kind of stimulation she receives. However, the resulting contractions and other body responses are the same and are experienced the same way in the brain. Preferences vary depending on the woman and on how she feels at a particular time. During orgasm, the vagina actually changes shape; the vagina, uterus, and rectum might experience pleasurable contractions; and there is typically a reaction in the breasts. The entire physical experience of orgasm is quite different for women.

The latest research and findings concerning female orgasm have been significant in validating the way many women actually experience their own sexuality. Recent studies have dispelled many myths and given women more accurate information to help them better understand their experience:

- *Having intercourse without experiencing orgasm is natural and very common for women.*
- *Seven to ten percent of women* never *reach orgasm.* Moreover, only about one third of women can have orgasms with intercourse alone.
- *Women commonly require more time and stimulation than men to become aroused and to have orgasms.*
- *As a woman ages, it is perfectly natural for her to need more stimulation to reach orgasm.*
- *Women do not have the refractory period between orgasms, making it more possible for them to experience multiple orgasms.* Women do have what is called a *resolution phase* after sexual activity ceases, in which the body returns to a relaxed state.
- *Women reach their sexual peak later in life than men.* Women tend to reach their sexual peak in their 30s, whereas men tend to reach their sexual peak in their late teens. In long-term relationships, the woman's ability to reach orgasm might be on the rise while the man's is on the decline.
- *In a long-term relationship, women generally are less driven to be sexual and less driven by the need to have orgasm.* Rather, their satisfaction is more about intimacy—the connection with her partner and other aspects of her relationship.
- *The intensity of a woman's orgasms may vary depending on the amount and quality of time spent during foreplay.* Intensity may also vary depending on where she is in her menstrual cycle.

Extending and Increasing the Frequency of Orgasm

Examining the differences between male and female sexual response cycles and the way men and women experience orgasm leads to an interesting conclusion: Extending foreplay and intercourse is generally what will maximize the pleasure of orgasm for *both* you and your partner. For the man, prolonged lovemaking provides more pleasure and arousal before orgasm and can intensify his orgasm. For the woman, extended foreplay, additional stimulation, and prolonged intercourse increases arousal. So, simply by taking your time to enjoy everything you do leading up to potential orgasm, you will naturally increase not only the likelihood of orgasm, but also the intensity of it. Here are some more specific techniques that you both can try to incorporate these realities into your lovemaking:

- Kiss one another in various ways and on various places. Many couples like to French kiss during intercourse. You can kiss all around your partner's face and neck and ears. Perhaps lick or suck your partner's nipples, but don't stop there. Remember, the rest of the body can be quite erotic, too!

- Use your pubococcygeal (P.C.) muscle to heighten pleasure and to make you more aware of sensation in the genital area. Kegels can help firm up this important muscle, as well as greatly increase your partner's pleasure.

you're not alone

Joan and Scott, a couple in their 30s who had been living together for two years, were struggling to decide whether to get married. They got along well and had good sex, but Scott was upset that Joan could have orgasms only with oral sex. Scott couldn't help wondering that maybe he was an inadequate lover and that Joan might leave him for someone who could satisfy her more. At other times, he would wonder if there was something wrong with Joan. Joan used to really seem to enjoy making love to Scott, but recently it seemed as though she had lost some desire. According to Joan, while sex was still good and Scott is the best at oral sex, she's uncomfortable that Scott always has to talk about what could

- Focus on pleasure. Communicate to each other what feels good to each of you. This will almost always increase the intensity of orgasm. Particularly for women, as they usually benefit from extended periods of play.

- Tease yourself and your partner and let your preorgasmic lovemaking simmer. Get aroused and then relax and back off to make it last. If the man loses his erection during sex play, don't be concerned about that. Continue pleasuring each other, and most often the erection will return.

- Stimulate other parts of your own body. Tense up the whole body, and then release and relax it. Point your feet down away from your body or up toward your head, and then relax them. Go with the flow of your body.

- Make noise. Immerse your whole body in the moment and vocalize that. Let your voice and body be in harmony.

- Try sex toys to intensify stimulation during foreplay and enhance orgasm. Vibrators have been used to help women who have had difficulty reaching orgasm. Men also can use vibrators to give a different type of sensation. Start slowly and gently, then work up as it feels naturally pleasurable.

Once both of you have reached orgasm, it doesn't mean that sex is over. After intercourse, there could be more orgasms with manual or oral stimulation. And remember, of course, the reverse also might work—experiencing orgasm manually or orally and

have made it better for her.

Joan and Scott needed to be educated about the various response patterns that women experience; since Joan was easily orgasmic with oral sex, and she did not experience it as a problem, it wasn't a problem. Scott was also able to share for the first time with Joan his feeling insecure because she seemed to have had more sexual experiences than he had before they met. He was sure that she had orgasms with her other lovers and was not telling him, just to be kind. Once they knew more about how they each felt and understood differences in sexual response patterns, they could put some of that behind them and begin to enjoy their sexual activities again. This kind of information can be quite powerful!

then through intercourse. In either case, allow yourselves the time to savor the sensations and build on them once orgasm occurs!

What a Woman Can Do for a Man A few methods are available specifically for women to help their men extend and intensify their orgasms. If the man typically sets the rhythm and progression of foreplay, switching roles to give the woman more control can often slow down the pace. Discuss this with your partner to see if it is an option. Here are a few specific techniques for intensifying the man's orgasm and possibly extending it:

- Increase stimulation of the penis by doing Kegels during intercourse and by fondling or massaging the base of the penis with your hand.
- Apply mild pressure to the prostate gland either by stroking the perineum or through anal stimulation.
- Massage or pinch your partner's nipples, or kiss, touch or massage other areas of his body during intercourse in ways he feels are pleasurable.
- To extend lovemaking before ejaculation, stroke his testicles and pull down on them gently. The testicles must be retracted during ejaculation—pulling down on them gently decreases the ejaculatory inevitability.

What a Man Can Do for a Woman Several techniques can help men, specifically, to help their partners maximize orgasm. Simply allowing your partner to have more control over the pace of lovemaking and agreeing to let her initiate intercourse when she is ready can be very effective. You can also try a few additional techniques:

- Provide more genital stimulation for your partner during foreplay, or bring your partner to orgasm first.
- Increase stimulation of the clitoris during intercourse. You can do this with your finger, have your partner

massage her clitoris with her own finger, or use a vibrator or other sex toy.

- Massage, caress, or lick your partner's breasts and stimulate her nipples, if she likes, or stimulate other parts of her body in ways she has communicated she prefers.

- Change positions. Take turns on top. Many women find that clitoral and G spot stimulation is much more intense when they're on top, and many men find that they have more control over ejaculation by being on the bottom.

- If possible and desirable, add some form of anal stimulation, either using your finger or a suitable object. If you choose to do this, it is important to remember not to touch the vagina with the finger or object you use before washing it.

> **GET PSYCHED**
>
> "There are two words I would tell a young man who's just starting out being sexual, 'slow down.'"
> —*Wendy Maltz, L.C.S.W.,* author of Private Thoughts

Ecstasy and Spirituality

Orgasm can transcend the physical experience and deliver a sense of spiritual ecstasy—an awakening of one's soul, a feeling of connectedness to all things, a merging of one's self with another being—your partner—in a mystical dance of love. In the throes of orgasm, you can completely lose any sense of self and attain the peaceful awareness that Eastern mystics might characterize as nirvana. Some people feel as though they black out for an instant or become weightless. Others might see intense colors or feel an inexplicable flow of energy taking over their entire being. The feeling can be so sublime that many people throughout history have sought to experience this state of spiritual bliss sexually. And many have certainly succeeded.

The approach to sexual ecstasy that we recommend throughout this book can bring you closer to experiencing your lovemaking as sacred and spiritual. By relaxing and becoming more aware of all sensual stimulation in the very moment that you and your partner are making love, you are opening the channel to the experience of spiritual ecstasy, as well. There is a definite element of *spirituality* that connects to sexuality. Some people find their definition of a higher power, life force, or religion when making love to someone they truly love. We all have our own paths for getting to that sacred place. Sex is but one of those paths.

Gina Ogden, Ph.D., sex researcher and author of *Women Who Love Sex*, studied almost 4,000 people, asking them to respond to questions about sex and spirituality. Ogden found that in people age 50 and over (both men and women), more than half had at least one spiritual experience related to their sexuality. Even in her population of 30 and younger, some had had this experience. Some of what people described included the experience of time stopping; seeing colors; and experiencing a higher power through their senses, their body, mind, heart, and soul. Sometimes both partners experienced the same phenomena at the same time.

An essential ingredient of spiritual sex, according to her study, was the feeling or sharing of love. Sexuality was a way of truly knowing oneself and one's partner. Her study suggests the evolving nature of sex through the couple's lifespan. As couples grew older, they reported feeling much more accepting and appreciative of and connected to their sexual encounters as well as to their partners and themselves.

Another way Ogden demonstrates the similarities between sexuality and spirituality is to point out that both sexuality and spirituality share many of the same symbols and

WEB TALK: To learn more about Dr. Gina Ogden and her work, visit:
 www.womanspirit.net

GET PSYCHED

Spirituality is the *internal* connection you have with your sense of purpose, a higher power, and all things larger than yourself and what you can explain as a part of the material world. At its best, it is usually experienced as a blissful and peaceful vision of your world and beyond. While each person's actual experience of spirituality is unique, the one similarity that most people report is that connection in the present moment to a higher self or wonderful life force that encourages oneness and unity with the universe and everything and everybody around us.

rituals, such as candles, incense, special foods, flowers, the laying on of hands, music, and dancing, to name a few.

There is no exact recipe for experiencing sex more spiritually. Not unlike orgasm and sexual ecstasy itself, you and your partner just need to be open to the possibilities, and let it happen.

Tantric Sex Techniques For couples who would like to explore additional ways of experiencing sex more spiritually, other approaches, such as Tantric exercises, can help. Tantra is a mystical approach to understanding and experiencing the universe through meditation. It is an approach that has been developed and practiced for thousands of years to make followers more aware of themselves as manifestations and extensions of universal energy and matter. In Tantric thought, all matter and energy are one. Meditation dissolves the sense of separateness and enables you to experience your connectedness to all being, in the moment. This awareness delivers a sense of peaceful, all-encompassing, spiritual bliss.

It can also significantly enhance the connection you feel to your partner. Tantric teacher Andrew Milberg explains that the primary principle of Tantric sex is that the "human body in its physical form represents divinity. Tantric sex calls for you to experience yourself and your partner as physical manifestations of the divine. You look at each other as a god or goddess and approach your lovemaking with great reverence, appreciating and honoring your lover as a divine being, and serving this divine being in love."

In addition to approaching one another with great reverence, Tantric sex calls for enhanced eye contact and breathing. You can practice Tantric techniques as part of

GET PSYCHED

"What Tantric breathing can bring up is the willingness to be vulnerable with your partner. To just sit with your partner and look into his or her eyes and breathe together can for some bring up very vulnerable feelings. For a couple that is willing to expand their experience of intimacy with each other, this exercise can be very powerful. It can also trigger fears as well. But if you can move through them, your reward may be a feeling of connection that's really incredible and very timeless." –Andrew Milberg, Tantric instructor your foreplay or during intercourse. Try these exercises. First, sit facing one another and focus on your breathing. There are actually different ways you can breathe together—one in which you both inhale and exhale at the same time, and the other in which you alternate. If you're just sitting with each other, you can experiment with the different energies that are created by each method. Try both and be aware of how you feel with each. Then try it while making love.

WEB TALK: To continue your exploration of Tantra and Tantric sexual techniques visit:

www.Tantra.com

Tantric breathing can help you and your partner connect and bring you both closer to and more aware of everything you are experiencing together in the moment. Through practicing these techniques, you can enter a state that is more receptive to the experience of both sexual and spiritual ecstasy. With that fully present mindset, anything you experience can enhance and transcend your physical sensations and give you and your partner a unique and very intense sexual experience that may also be quite spiritual.

The deep breathing that Tantra promotes can be enhanced through various Yoga disciplines, especially Kundalini Yoga. Any good Yoga class can help improve awareness and thus increase your experience of sexual ecstasy by teaching your body to become more relaxed, and by developing muscles in ways that are generally more natural than those developed through common exercise regimens that strengthen muscles. You might even want to consider taking a Yoga class together!

The Kama Sutra The Kama Sutra offers another approach to sex that is rooted in a spiritual tradition. This ancient text of sexual lovemaking acts as a how-to manual, but it presents sex as a journey rather than a destination. Like Tantra, the Kama Sutra recommends a more reverent approach to sex that focuses on your partner's pleasure as well as your own. It presents various kissing techniques, positions, tips for how to treat one's marriage partner and concubines, recipes for aphrodisiacs, and much more.

The Kama Sutra recognizes the advantages of building passion over time. When couples first wed, for example, the Kama Sutra recommends that the marriage not be consummated for ten days after the wedding. Couples are advised to spend the first ten days gradually getting to know each other—talking, gentle kissing, and then a little bit more each night until the tenth night, when consummation is allowed. This is something you might even want to try sometime for ten nights—engaging in progressively more erotic activity starting with conversation and kissing, gradually escalating to caresses and embraces, and finally consummating in intercourse.

WEB TALK: To view information and illustrations from the Kama Sutra, visit:

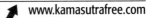 www.kamasutrafree.com

The Kama Sutra is much more than a formula for lovemaking. It helps couples combine all five senses with the intellect and the spirit, consciously and intentionally exploring the full and complete pleasure of bodily contact.

Western religious traditions (Jewish, Christian, and Transcendentalism) have their own unique ways of incorporating human sexuality into their spiritual framework, many of which are probably influenced by ancient Eastern tradition. Most practices center on slow, mindful, reverent sexual union that—at its best—leads to sexual ecstasy.

All these approaches recommend a slower, more mindful approach to lovemaking that increases intensity over time and enhances your awareness of all of the wonders of the universe, including the divine spirit that manifests itself in each of us.

What You Can Do

At this point, you don't *need* to do anything more than accept your conscious mind for what it is and let it go. Then, let your body take over. To add to your ecstasy and perhaps even maximize your orgasms, here are some things you can do right now:

☐ Momentarily let go of your desire for pleasure and put your focus on your partner. Breathe in unity—the deeper the better—make eye contact, and accept with gratitude whatever comes back to you as a pleasant playful surprise.

☐ You and your partner list ten things you enjoy about sex other than orgasm. Discuss the items on your lists, keeping in mind that sex can be great even without orgasm.

☐ If you have experienced orgasm, use a metaphor to describe one or more of the orgasms you have had. If you're doing this with your partner, share your descriptions.

☐ You and your partner write down anything you have done to yourself or have had done to you that you feel has enhanced an orgasm. Use the information to begin teaching each other how you best experience orgasm.

☐ The next time you make love, agree to try one of the techniques described in this chapter for maximizing orgasm. For example, you might agree to try more kissing, breathing, or eye contact and anything else the two of you can come up with that will give you that slower and more mindful connection.

☐ If you have the time, money, and inclination, sign up for a Tantric sex workshop or getaway with your partner. Or enroll in a Yoga class together (or even alone).

Part 3

Overcoming Your Barriers to Sexual Ecstasy

Is sexual ecstasy still eluding you? Then perhaps some unidentified barrier is standing in the way. In this part, we help you systematically remove your barriers to sexual ecstasy—sexual dysfunctions, relationship issues, and any health- or age-related conditions that might be slowing your progress or dampening ecstatic sensation. By the end of this part, you and your partner should have a clear path for your journey toward sexual ecstasy!

If Sexual Ecstasy Is Still Eluding You

I f sexual ecstasy is still eluding you, it's time to do some detective work to identify the obstacles standing in its way and then do whatever is necessary to remove them. In this chapter, we explore the physical, emotional, and cognitive obstacles that prevent you and your partner from experiencing sexual ecstasy. These can be anything from medication you might be taking to anxiety and depression to sexual dysfunctions, or any combination of these factors. We explore and explain the most prevalent sexual dysfunctions in order to help you identify any that might be acting as obstacles. And we provide information, resources, and advice that can help you and your partner improve your situation on your own or with the help of a qualified professional.

Nearly every potential obstacle to sexual ecstasy can be identified, addressed, and overcome. Whether your problem is physical, psychological, or emotional, it is usually more common than you might think, and more treatable than you might imagine. By teaming up with your partner and approaching whatever issues may exist with openness, optimism, and resolve, your chances are excellent for getting back onto the path of sexual ecstasy.

I love my husband very much and I think he's a good lover and all, but in the last couple years, I just don't get aroused like I used to. Sometimes intercourse is uncomfortable and even painful. My married friends all seem to like sex, at least the way they talk about it. Am I abnormal?

The fact that you don't become as aroused and lubricated as you used to may be the cause of your discomfort, and you may be experiencing a sexual dysfunction. Recent research indicates that sexual dysfunctions are very common in both sexes. One study published in *JAMA* (*The Journal of the American Medical Association*, 1999; Laumann, Paik, and Rosen) estimates that 43 percent of American women and 31 percent of American men have experienced some kind of sexual dysfunction. The study also indicates that slightly less than one third of women do not regularly experience orgasm during sexual activity and almost a quarter reported that at some point, sex was not pleasurable. About a third of the men in the study reported having persistent problems with climaxing too early.

Both you and your husband need to realize that you're not alone, and that whatever is causing you to feel less aroused can usually be identified and resolved, either by working on it together or with the help of a medical or mental health professional trained in the treatment of sexual dysfunctions.

Sexual Dysfunctions: What They Are and What Can Be Done About Them

A sexual dysfunction is an inability (as opposed to an unwillingness) to respond sexually in a way that you expect to (or want to). Most people, at some time in their lives, experience an inability to become aroused or a lapse in their sexual response. This could be due to physical exhaustion, taking a medication that negatively affects sexual desire or arousal, or feeling too much anger at your partner to become turned-on. These are all examples of things that can trigger sexual difficulties, but they rarely require treatment unless they become persistent and begin to interfere with your sexual satisfaction for an extended period of time. Part of the definition of every sexual dysfunction is also that it must cause distress to you or trigger some degree of difficulty in your relationship.

It's important to realize that a sexual dysfunction is something a person has, as opposed to something a person is. It does no good to blame yourself or your partner. In fact, worry, blame, guilt, and other negative emotions about a sexual problem can worsen the situation and perhaps even contribute to turning a temporary inability to respond sexually into a chronic dysfunction! So it's important to try a more positive approach:

1. Acknowledge that something is not right.
2. Blamelessly identify the symptoms or what you think may be amiss for you sexually as an individual or couple.
3. Learn about the possible causes or reasons behind the problem.
4. Learn effective ways to eliminate or address the symptoms and causes of, or reasons for, the problem.
5. Work with your partner as a team to take action. (And be aware that sometimes learning and understanding the nature of the problem can be all that's needed to resolve it.)

The principal approach to sexual dysfunctions we use in this book is commonly referred to as *bibliotherapy,* which is simply a way of learning about the nature of an issue and strategies to resolve it by reading specific materials that clearly show you how. Bibliotherapy is effective in several ways— it helps you identify an issue, understand that other people have similar experiences, recognize possible causes, and then learn how to solve the problem or (at the very least) how to accept those circumstances that you might not be able to change. This chapter (this entire book, in fact) can be thought of as a form of bibliotherapy.

If you cannot find a satisfactory resolution for a sexual dysfunction by using your

> **GET PSYCHED**
>
> **Bibliotherapy** is a form of self-help and a supplement to psychotherapy in which carefully selected reading materials are used therapeutically to assist a client in learning about or resolving an issue. **Audiotherapy** refers to exactly the same approach, except that audiotapes or disks are used instead of information in print format.

own resources or the guidance we offer in this book, we encourage you to seek help from a qualified professional. With proper therapy or medical intervention, most couples are able to overcome sexual dysfunctions in a very short period of time. The success rate for the treatment of sexual dysfunctions is very high!

Why Sexual Dysfunctions Occur

A sexual dysfunction can occur for any number of reasons. In some cases, a single incident can trigger it—possibly a painful sexual encounter, a physical injury that makes sex uncomfortable, or a suspicion that one's partner has lost interest. A medication (prescription or over-the-counter) might trigger a dysfunction. Financial concerns, anxiety over a career change, or a relationship issue (as you'll see in the following chapter) can also be the culprit. More often than not, it is a combination of physical and psychological factors that work together to give rise to the dysfunction. Here is a sampling just to give you an idea of how varied the causes can be:

- Anger at your partner
- Depression
- Sexual boredom or lack of novelty
- Attitudes about sex or sexual performance that conflict with one's sexual pleasure
- Poor self-image
- Negative thoughts about your partner (such as feeling that your partner is unattractive due to hygiene, aging, or weight gain)
- Inadequate physical stimulation
- Partner having sexual problem or dysfunction

GET PSYCHED

If you or your partner is experiencing a sexual dysfunction, get help now. Sexual dysfunctions can negatively affect a person's quality of life. The *JAMA* article on "Sexual Dysfunction in the United States" (1999; Laumann, Paik, and Rosen) reports that for women, all sexual dysfunctions had strong positive associations with low feelings of physical and emotional satisfaction and low feelings of happiness. Men with erectile dysfunction and low sexual desire experience diminished quality of life, but those with premature ejaculation are not affected.

- Fatigue or stress
- Attraction to someone outside the relationship
- Thinking of your partner more as a best friend or roommate rather than as a lover

So, as you can see, any number of things can trigger a dysfunction, and all sexual dysfunctions have one thing in common: To the degree that they are present, they certainly inhibit sexual satisfaction and therefore sexual ecstasy! So, it is certainly important that you and your partner team up to identify and address any situation as soon as you become aware that a problem exists.

Performance Anxiety Performance anxiety is any excessive concern that you might not be able to perform sexually at all or at the level that meets your or your partner's expectations. People who suffer from it commonly unintentionally turn themselves off by experiencing anxiety either during sexual activity or just before sex is about to begin. It can prevent a man from obtaining or maintaining an erection. And it can negatively affect lubrication and inhibit orgasm in a woman. Any of the causes mentioned earlier can trigger it and should be considered. Performance anxiety often intensifies over time—anxiety hinders performance, which generates more anxiety, which further impedes performance, thus leading to even more anxiety. In other words, it is a vicious circle that will spiral more and more out of control until you can identify it, address it, and break the cycle.

The most time-tested procedure for overcoming other types of performance anxiety, such as the anxiety related to public speaking or a job interview, is generally to ignore the anxiety and push yourself to do whatever it is you're anxious about doing. Over time, people generally become less nervous. They either experience some success doing the "dreaded act" or they learn that even if they do meet with failure, it will not be nearly as awful as they thought it would be. However, this approach doesn't usually work for sex, especially with men, because the anxiety itself can make it impossible to get or maintain the erection needed to perform sexual intercourse with any degree of success. However, many couples have found some approaches to be very effective.

you're not alone

Defeating Sexual Dysfunction

Leslie and Kurt, a couple in their mid 50s, were no longer having intercourse. Kurt had lost interest in sex years ago when he stopped having erections. Leslie was feeling as though Kurt no longer loved her. He stopped showing her any physical affection, and when she tried to be affectionate to him, he would pull away.

The couple decided to think back and consider anything else that might have been going on at the time when they stopped having intercourse. Kurt brought up that he had been diagnosed as having high blood pressure and started taking a medication the doctor had prescribed. Neither of them had previously considered that a medication could affect their sex life, but when they began to recollect the progression of events, it was clear that the medication was probably the cause of Kurt's loss of interest.

Kurt remembered how he felt at the time. He and Leslie would start making love, and he would become only partially erect—enough to penetrate but not like it used to feel. He was embarrassed and concerned that any attempt at sexual intercourse would lead to failure, so he began to avoid intercourse and any physical affection that he thought Leslie might interpret as an invitation to have sex. At the same time, Leslie was trying all sorts of enticements to seduce him—lingerie, being more attentive, acting more sexually aggressive, but Kurt ignored her or pulled away. She suspected that Kurt had fallen out of love with her or was having an affair.

Through their discussions, Kurt and Leslie learned that all the assumptions they were making about each other and their relationship were unfounded and that the medication Kurt was taking was probably the root cause. Kurt agreed to visit his doctor for a physical exam and evaluation. The medication was changed and the couple began to become more physically affectionate again.

Through their research and reading, the couple learned that given Kurt's age, his erections probably would not be as spontaneous as they once were. Together, they learned to approach sex differently—first by being physically affectionate, then by pleasuring each other sexually without intercourse, and then by returning to sexual activity with intercourse. Recovering their lost sex life took time and effort, but with the right information and their commitment to work together, it was well worth it.

One way to lessen performance anxiety is to set realistic expectations. Keep in mind that in long-term sexual relationships not every lovemaking session reaches the level of sexual ecstasy. Many times your sexual experience will just be good or good enough and you can even assume some to be just so-so or disappointing for one partner or the other. Approach your sexual encounters with eager anticipation that's free from expectation, and your anxiety level will usually decline. In other words, if you can free yourself of the expectation and demand that any given lovemaking session has to be ecstatic, great, or even good, you will have very little to be anxious about.

Another approach that many couples find useful is to *take away the need to perform altogether.* You and your partner can do many things together sexually that do not require an erection or natural lubrication. Often, taking away the need for erection or lubrication paradoxically makes it come back. As a couple, you can engage in a wide variety of very pleasurable sexual activities without penetration, no matter how anxious either of you might be. Try having sex in ways other than intercourse, until you feel more comfortable together. Give each other a sensual massage, have oral sex, or engage in erotic touching. Do virtually anything except attempting intercourse. And try not to set any target dates for when you think you might feel ready to try—simply concentrate on enjoying the pleasure of whatever sexual activity you choose to engage in. Not only will this reduce the anxiety associated with performance, but it can generate increased sexual energy, as well. At some point you will probably become more turned on than anxious, and as long as you don't go back to setting performance goals, your performance anxiety will dissipate.

Pleasure Anxiety Pleasure anxiety is any self-conscious thought about feeling sexual pleasure that prevents you from fully experiencing pleasurable sensations. You might experience pleasure anxiety if you believe that you are not entitled or worthy enough to feel pleasure. You might even worry about what you might do or become if you were to allow yourself to let go; for example, a woman might think that if she likes sex too much, it means she's immoral or loose. A man who has sexual fantasies might consider himself sinful or perverted. Pleasure anxiety often arises from religious beliefs acquired in childhood or—especially for a woman—a belief that it takes more time for her to feel pleasure than she is entitled to. She might then worry that her partner will become tired or lose patience.

The main cure for pleasure anxiety is actually one of our ingredients for sexual ecstasy: *Give yourself permission to feel pleasure.* To the extent that you can give yourself permission, you will overcome pleasure anxiety. Adore sex, fantasize about it, look forward to it, and create new fantasies with your partner. When you have sexual thoughts during the day, be attentive to them and treat those thoughts as gifts. Then give yourself permission to play them out in your mind and, later, in your bedroom.

Lack of Accurate Information   Many sexual dysfunctions arise from naiveté, the lack of accurate information, or the presence of misinformation (including false assumptions). Fortunately, once you know that the problem is, in fact, a result of insufficient information, obtaining the right information is often all you need to do. Knowing, for instance, how common it really is to experience performance anxiety can often serve to lessen the anxiety itself.

Helpful information can come from a variety of sources: biblio- or audiotherapy (books, articles, tapes, videos, and so on), websites, physicians, therapists and other experts, and friends, to name a few. And never overlook the two wealthiest sources of information regarding your unique sexual preferences—*you and your partner.* An open and ongoing dialogue about your sexuality (your turn-ons, what feels good versus not-so-good, what you would like to try, and so on) can be way more valuable than practically any other resource. But many times, no matter how smart a person is and how intimate the couple, the answer can only be found by exploring other resources, including those in this book and the resources listed in Appendixes B and C. Any time a situation has you baffled, start asking questions and looking for answers. And if you and your partner still do not experience sexual satisfaction, seek help from a professional; a qualified therapist can often point you in the right direction.

Medical and Chemical Issues Whenever you experience a significant and lingering decline in sexual desire or arousal that cannot be traced to an obvious cause, consider any changes to your health or medicines you might be taking, and consult with your physician or a therapist who has expertise in sexual dysfunctions. It's best to rule out possible health or medical conditions first, because they might be triggering secondary causes, such as psychological or emotional issues. Health and medical issues cover a wide variety of possible causes:

- You might have a cold and be afraid of passing it to your partner.
- Arthritic pain or a backache can make sex uncomfortable.
- Heavy drinking might prevent a man from obtaining or maintaining an erection or a woman from experiencing sensation or orgasm.
- A particular medication or combination of them can lessen desire and arousal. Even an over-the-counter antihistamine can trigger dysfunction.
- Depression or anxiety might be at work. Or, the medicines to treat depression or anxiety could be dampening sensation.
- A woman's hormonal makeup might have changed due to her menstruation cycle, a pregnancy, breast-feeding, menopause, or some other factor.
- Diabetes, thyroid conditions, and any illnesses involving the neurological or vascular systems can trigger problems.
- Even healthy exercise, such as extensive bike riding with the wrong type of bicycle seat, can sometimes affect a man's ability to maintain an erection.

My wife and I are college grads and have been having sex for 10 years. How is it possible that there's something we don't know about sex?

If you and your wife are satisfied with your sex life, the knowledge you have is sufficient for your needs. But in a long-term relationship, changes often occur over time that call for additional information or a new way of doing things. You might know little or nothing about a given area simply because you never really *needed* to know about it.

A surgeon once came in for therapy because he couldn't believe he had lost his ability to have erections and couldn't identify the cause. His formal training had nothing to do with sexual matters and since he had never experienced an inability to obtain an erection, he never needed to be informed about the topic. So, when it happened to him, even though he was very intelligent, he was ill-informed about erectile dysfunction. And because he thought that, as a physician, he *should* know, he was reluctant to ask for help. But once he did, the problem was quickly resolved.

If you notice a sudden change in your sexual behavior or ability to have satisfying sex and it corresponds with any change in your health condition or the medicines you take, it's quite possible that you've uncovered the cause; consult with your physician to determine available options.

If you observe no clear connection but the problem persists, ask your physician to perform a physical examination and evaluate any medications you might be taking. Even if you don't suspect that the problem is related to health issues or medicine, a physical evaluation can help you rule out those possible causes, so you can look elsewhere for the answers.

Male and Female Sexual Dysfunctions

Some dysfunctions, such as Inhibited Sexual Desire (ISD), affect both men and women. Some, such as erectile dysfunction, are obviously specific to men; whereas others, including sexual arousal disorder, affect women. First, we will look at the sexual dysfunctions that apply to both sexes, and then we will explore those that are specific to men and to women.

Inhibited Sexual Desire Inhibited Sexual Desire (ISD), sometimes known as Hypoactive Sexual Desire Disorder (HSDD), is the suppression of normal desire in an intimate relationship. ISD can be categorized as *global* (not desiring sex in any form with anyone or even by yourself) or *situational* (not desiring sex in any form with your partner). People who have ISD commonly report feeling that they love their partners and like being affectionate, but if they were never to have sex again with that person, it wouldn't matter to them; they might say that they "feel dead, sexually," or they might start to question whether or not they've fallen out of love with their partners. It's not that the person isn't in the mood occasionally or that he or she desires sex less than the partner, but that the person's desire level now compared to what it was before is significantly lower. Also, people with ISD—if they have sexual relations with their partners—can function and become aroused and even enjoy their sexual encounters once it gets underway. This odyssey can make the problem even more confusing to both partners.

ISD is one of the most frequent sexual problems that couples experience and is about twice as prevalent in women as in men. Laumann and others estimated that 22 percent of women and 5 percent of men have experienced ISD at some point within the last year. What's more, people of any age can experience ISD, even those in their 20s or 30s who have been together only a few years. Many of the causes mentioned earlier in this chapter can trigger or worsen ISD.

If you are experiencing ISD, first determine whether your ISD problem is global or situational. If it's global (no desire for sex in any form), a medical evaluation is necessary to help determine if the problem is related to health or medicine. You may also want to be evaluated for depression, since loss of libido is a common symptom of depression.

If it's situational (lack of sexual desire only toward one's partner), an approach that focuses on the relationship, both interpersonal and sexual, can be very effective:

- Identify and resolve any relationship issues that might be getting in the way, especially anger and control issues, as explained in the next chapter.

- Agree to hold off on having sex for a period of time, but retain and increase physical affection to allow the desire to build. Be especially attentive and affectionate to your partner throughout the day.

- Focus on pleasurable activities together, other than sex.

- The person with low sexual desire is advised to be more attentive to any sexual feelings that occur during the day.

- Set aside a few minutes a day to indulge in sexual fantasy that can allow you to re-experience your own sexual potential.

- Stress and the pressures of time commitments can drain away the relaxation that enhances the growth of sensuality. Quiet time and focus on the body provided by activities such as exercise, yoga, and receiving massage can help you refocus and reconnect without the stresses and strains of the "daily business of life."

- Read up on how to reignite desire in your relationship. Some excellent books on the subject are *For Each Other*, by Lonnie Barbach; *Rekindling Desire*, by Barry and Emily McCarthy; *The Sex-Starved Marriage*, by Michele Weiner-Davis; *Hot Monogamy*, by Pat Love; and *Resurrecting Sex*, by David Schnarch. (See Appendix C for more resources.)

Sexual Aversion Unlike ISD, which is a disinterest in sex, sexual aversion is a strong dislike, an anxiety, or fear of sex. A person suffering from sexual aversion might find the idea of having sex repulsive or frightening and thus consciously avoid it, or even experience panic attacks with relation to sex for no clearly identifiable reason. There can be an aversion to one specific aspect of sexual experience, such as intercourse, or an aversion that is generalized to any form of sexual contact. The aversion can crop up any time in a relationship, even after a person has been sexually active and satisfied for many years. It might arise from a physically painful sexual encounter such as a rape (recent or past), a traumatic experience, a vision from the past, or unresolved feelings related to sexual abuse.

If you feel an aversion to sex, focus first on resolving what you believe to be the cause—perhaps a recent painful experience or a problem in the relationship—and then gently resume sensual and sexual activity other than intercourse. Make sure you wait until you feel comfortable and ready before resuming intercourse. Should this be something that you or your partner recognize is, in fact, connected to past trauma or abuse, it is best to seek professional help as soon as possible. This is not something to be resolved by self-help alone.

GET PSYCHED

"People who have experienced sexual abuse need to heal from the past first. Then, they need to deal with the present-day realities of how they approach sex. Their challenge is to see sex as something positive once again (or perhaps even for the first time). Healing from the sexual issues caused by abuse is possible–it involves changing attitudes and behaviors and learning new skills. Resources do exist to help you do this, as well as hearing about people who have been successful in overcoming sexual trauma. If you and your partner work on the issues together, you will increase your intimacy, and it will greatly benefit your sex life and your emotional life together."–*Wendy Maltz, M.S.W., sex therapist and author of* Sexual Healing Journey

Male Sexual Dysfunctions

Three sexual dysfunctions are exclusive to men—premature ejaculation, erectile dysfunction, and retarded ejaculation. Further compounding the problems inherent in these dysfunctions are the resulting psychological and emotional issues that commonly accompany a man's inability to perform in a way that's satisfying to himself or his partner. A man cannot usually "fake" response, and if his ego is tightly wrapped around sexual performance, any lapse in it that he experiences can lead to self-blame, anxiety, and even negative feelings that can result in him putting himself down regarding this as well as other areas of his life. Obviously, these factors can further aggravate the problem.

To effectively deal with a dysfunction, first understand that it's a condition that can be addressed, not a personal failure! With persistence, the dysfunction can be eliminated.

Premature Ejaculation The most common of male sexual dysfunctions is premature ejaculation (sometimes called rapid ejaculation). It occurs when a man cannot exercise what is to him or his partner an acceptable amount of control over ejaculation. It needs to be addressed if it becomes problematic for one or both partners. Studies estimate that 29 percent of men at some point experience premature ejaculation, making it even more common than erectile dysfunction. The problem can become worse if a man *tries* to control the ejaculation by consciously distracting himself from feeling genital stimulation or by simply being afraid of ejaculating too soon.

According to Michael Metz, Ph.D., co-author (with Barry McCarthy, Ph.D.) of *Coping with Premature Ejaculation: How to Overcome PE, Please Your Partner & Have Great Sex*, premature ejaculation can be triggered by one or more physiological and psychological factors. Physiological factors include being biologically hardwired to ejaculate quickly, taking medicines that can cause it, suffering trauma to the pelvic area, or experiencing age-related issues. Other factors include conditions such as bipolar or obsessive-compulsive disorder, relationship issues, or other forms of psychological distress.

In their book, Metz and McCarthy caution couples not to seek quick fixes, such as using a condom or a special lotion to deaden sensation in the penis. Instead, they encourage couples to develop a custom approach that addresses the cause or causes that apply to their unique situation. Their recommendations support many of the same ingredients to sexual ecstasy described in this book. They recommend that couples first attend to any health or medical issues, address any psychological or relationship problems, and then focus less on performance and more on enhancing pleasure and intimacy.

If premature ejaculation is diminishing sexual pleasure for you or your partner, Kegel exercises can help you develop the pelvic and sphincter muscles that control ejaculation, but you should combine toning exercises with exercises that teach you how to relax those muscles and train yourself to enjoy a slower rhythm:

1. You can practice a simple start-and-stop technique by yourself, by masturbating up to the point just before you feel that ejaculation is inevitable, and then letting the sensation go down. Focus on the pleasure you feel and learn to relax the pelvic muscles. Increase sensation again, and then stop. Do this four times, and then let yourself ejaculate.

2. Repeat Step 1 using a lubricant to simulate the sensation you might feel with vaginal stimulation. This process can take several weeks. Sometimes men "teach" themselves to orgasm quickly during masturbation, and they need to retrain themselves to establish a slower pace. Retraining takes time.

3. Repeat steps 1 and 2, but this time have your partner masturbate you. Communicate to your partner when to start and when to stop. Again, don't focus on control, but focus on the sensation itself and on relaxing your pelvic muscles.

4. Finally, practice the start-and-stop technique inside your partner. Remember, if a lubricant is required, make sure it is water-soluble. After penetration, allow the penis to become acclimated to the vagina and allow yourself to feel the sensation of being inside your partner. Start, stop, and change the rhythm, focusing on the sensation.

Continue to practice this both alone and together. And be aware that it can take some time to unlearn a rhythm that you and your partner have established over a long period of time. Approach this with patience.

Erectile Dysfunction *Erectile dysfunction* (ED), often referred to as *impotence*, is a man's inability to obtain or maintain an erection sufficient for intercourse. *Global ED* is characterized by an inability to have an erection under any circumstances—no morning erection and no erection with any form of sexual activity, including self-pleasuring. Global ED is often a sign of an underlying physical cause. *Situational ED* is an inability to become erect during sexual activity with one's partner. A man experiencing situational ED might wake up with a morning erection or have no trouble obtaining an erection through masturbation. Most, if not all, men have experienced an inability to obtain or maintain an erection at some time. He might have been too tired or inebriated; he might have been angry with his partner or nervous about something; he might have taken a cold pill that had a negative effect; or perhaps he experienced something else (the possibilities are numerous) that decreased his arousal.

If you experience ED, first determine whether you get early morning erections or can obtain erections with any other stimulation, such as masturbation. If you do not, your first step should be to consult a physician (preferably a urologist) to see whether it requires medical intervention. If you can obtain erections, the chances that your ED is a result of medical factors are slim. However, don't rule out health or physical issues entirely. Sometimes alcohol, cigarettes, certain medicines, and even bike riding can reduce the sensitivity of the penis and decrease blood flow to it. Conversely, proper nutrition and moderate exercise often can help. Consult a professional if any question remains.

In addition, try taking a slower approach toward sexual activity that centers more on pleasure. Agree with your partner not to engage in intercourse for a while. During this time, connect with one another through other activities, including erotic touching, romantic interludes, or even outings that you both find to be fun and stimulating. If you do achieve an erection, don't be in a hurry to have intercourse. Let things simmer a while.

In fact, here is a strategy that might even sound paradoxical, but it's highly effective: Let your erection subside, even if you have to do something to make it go away. Try this for a little while. Chances are if you focus on the pleasure rather than performance, your erection will return on its own, and be even stronger. (Even if it doesn't come back right away, the pleasure will be gratifying if you haven't gotten hung up on being or not being able to perform.) Let the excitement sizzle for some time. A man can do things to arouse and pleasure his partner and perhaps even bring her to orgasm, further increasing his desire, but no intercourse or masturbating himself to orgasm until the agreed-upon time.

Another technique to try after this is penetration with a *flaccid* penis. With your partner on top, just lie together and experience the feeling. Either of you can move around to heighten the pleasure. Again, do this with no expectations.

If you are still experiencing problems with ED, several drugs specifically designed for treating ED have proven to be very effective. PDE-5 inhibitors, the first and most famous of which is Viagra, have been a godsend for many men, even men who are quite elderly. Julian Slowinski, Psy.D., and co-author of *The Sexual Male: Problems and Solutions*, explains how PDE-5 inhibitors work: "Any form of sexual stimulation triggers a release of a number of chemicals in the man's body that affect the blood vessels in the penis. One of the chemicals (or transmitters) enables the blood vessels to expand to pump more blood in the penis and cause an erection. The body also releases another chemical, called a PDE-5, which contracts the blood vessels and relaxes the penis. PDE-5 inhibitors hinder the release of the second chemical, so as long as the stimulation occurs, the erection is maintained. A PDE-5 inhibitor *does not cause the erection; it allows the erection to be maintained*. If a man takes the pill and is not sexually stimulated in some way, nothing is going to happen." *PDE-5 inhibitors do not act as aphrodisiacs to stimulate desire.* They merely allow the penis to respond more spontaneously to whatever sexual stimulation is present.

Stanley Althof, Ph.D., sex researcher, and professor of psychology in the Department of Urology at Case Western Reserve University, says: "One positive side effect of PDE-5 drugs is they help men to get their confidence back." But he adds, "Having erections alone may not be enough if the couple has not had sex in 3 or 4 years, since there are barriers that are built up which may not be easily reversed." Althof and his colleagues are presently doing research on men who stop using these drugs. They believe that medical treatment alone may not be enough; the couple needs to incorporate the drug into their sex life in a way so that both can achieve sexual satisfaction.

Before trying a PDE-5 inhibitor, discuss it thoroughly with your partner. Over a period of time, your relationship may actually have adjusted to accommodate some degree of erectile dysfunction. If you begin taking a PDE-5 inhibitor and immediately begin having erections like you had 5, 10, 15, or even 20 years ago or more, that can have dramatic ripple effects on your relationship that you might not be ready to handle. So thoroughly learn about and anticipate any possible side effects—physical, psychological, and emotional—of the drug you are considering.

WEB TALK: For more information about new drugs that can help you with ED, visit: hisandherhealth.com

Retarded Ejaculation Retarded ejaculation is an inability to ejaculate for an inordinate amount of time once obtaining an erection, or not being able to ejaculate at all. If a man can ejaculate normally during masturbation, the problem usually is not medical in nature, and of course, if it isn't perceived as a problem by either partner, it's generally not anything that must be addressed.

Sometimes retarded ejaculation is caused by the fear of getting your partner pregnant, the fear of "letting go," control issues, or even the experience of a fetish or sexual fantasy the man finds unacceptable. Bernard Apfelbaun, Ph.D., sex therapist, suggests that men who experience retarded ejaculation are "sexual workhorses, who have difficulty focusing on their own pleasure."

I'm a man in my 40s. I love my wife very much and find her quite attractive, but I don't seem to respond sexually to her the way I used to. She suspects that I'm no longer attracted to her. What should I do?

For a man, it's perfectly normal to slow down sexually in your 30s and 40s—you might not be able to run as quickly or bicycle as long either. It often takes longer to become physically aroused, and even when you feel sexually aroused, the erection might not be as spontaneous as it once was. In other words, you might be turned on before your penis shows any signs that you are aroused. You might need more stimulation—physical and emotional—to get as turned-on as you need to be in order to have intercourse. This is not a reflection on you or your wife, and it's not a problem unless either one of you perceives it to be. Many women welcome the need to take additional time to build up to intercourse, and it can actually enhance the experience for both of you.

Since your wife is feeling as though you desire her less, address her needs, as well. You can communicate the way you feel and reassure her with additional attentiveness and affection that doesn't necessarily have to lead to sex. This is how you can work together to bring sexual ecstasy back into your relationship!

If retarded ejaculation does cause concern, and you are able to ejaculate during masturbation, the problem might be that you have trained yourself over a long period of time to experience sexual pleasure in a certain way that is different from the way you experience sex during intercourse. The steps provided earlier in this chapter for dealing with premature ejaculation can often help you learn to masturbate in different ways that are more in line with the way you experience intercourse. This can help you focus more on what gives your body pleasure and arousal. Then you can teach your partner how to bring you to orgasm—first through touching, and then by incorporating those elements into intercourse.

Painful Intercourse Painful intercourse is much more prevalent in women, but it does call for some mention here, because it might be a sign of infection or other medical problem that can affect both you and your partner. If you feel any soreness after intercourse, it's likely that your partner might experience some soreness as well if adequate lubrication wasn't present. Later in this chapter, we discuss possible ways to increase lubrication or use a substitute, water-soluble lubricant. If you have any sores on your penis, have them checked out by your family physician—they can be a sign of an STD (sexually transmitted disease) or an allergic reaction to a soap, lubricants, or some other substance or material that comes in contact with your penis.

You should also be conscious of any painful discharge when you ejaculate. Pain or burning sensations in the urethra might be signs of an STD or of prostate or bladder problems that should be checked out by a physician. Testicular pain can also be a sign of infection or another medical problem. Some infections can be passed on to your partner, so if you have any of these symptoms and choose to have sex before you see the doctor, be sure to use a condom.

Finally, if you are experiencing difficulties ejaculating, or differences in sensation when ejaculating including a change in the volume and force, you may have a type of lower urinary tract dysfunction. If this is the case, consult a urologist as soon as possible.

Female Sexual Dysfunctions

Women might not have as much pressure to perform as men do, but many women experience sexual dysfunctions that inhibit their ability to fully or even partially experience pleasure. An inability to lubricate can make sex painful, as well as trigger anxiety in a woman. An inability to achieve orgasm might trigger feelings of inadequacy or give her the feeling that she's missing out on something she really wants to experience. However, women typically are less prone than men to place emphasis on performance. For most women, a solid, romantic relationship with an adequate amount of fulfilling sex is satisfying. Some women can be satisfied sexually even when they do not experience an orgasm. However, only you can define what you find to be fulfilling.

If a sexual dysfunction is getting in the way or you think it may be, it's important to recognize it and take action to get beyond it.

Sexual Arousal Disorder *Sexual arousal disorder* is a persistent or recurring inability to obtain adequate lubrication or to experience physiological changes associated with arousal, including swelling of the genital tissues, increased clitoral or labia sensation, or increased nipple sensitivity. A medical condition or medications including some birth control pills and antihistamines, hormonal changes, or any number of physical, psychological, or emotional issues can cause sexual arousal disorder in women. If you suspect that you are experiencing sexual arousal disorder, it's important to have a medical evaluation first and then address any psychological or emotional issues that might be causing you to feel less aroused.

Sexual arousal disorder frequently responds well to the ingredients of sexual ecstasy we have described throughout this book. Sometimes, a partner's increased attentiveness and affection can enhance desire. You can also try some of these additional strategies and techniques:

- Look at what you have found to be arousing in the past and clearly communicate that to your partner.

- Add novelty to your lovemaking.

- Set aside a longer period of time for making love. You might just need more time and additional stimulation to become optimally aroused. Most women tend to need more tactile stimulation. Remember, you owe it to yourself to explore all of the possible roads to the ecstatic sex you are seeking.

PsychSpeak

Sexual arousal disorder, as described by Jennifer Berman, M.D., urologist, and Laura Berman, Ph.D., sex educator and therapist, in their book *For Women Only,* is the "inability to attain or maintain adequate genital lubrication, swelling, or other somatic responses, such as nipple sensitivity. The main symptoms of arousal disorder include a lack of vaginal lubrication, decrease clitoral or labia sensation, decreased clitoral or labia engorgement, or lack of vaginal lengthening, dilation, and arousal."

- Continue to engage in pleasurable sexual activity free of intercourse for a period of time, to see whether your desire will build to the point at which arousal naturally follows.

- Use a water-soluble lubricant to engage in intercourse if you do not maintain adequate self-lubrication.

- Introduce a vibrator or sex toy into your lovemaking.

- Remember that more time and focus on clitoral stimulation can induce and enhance the responsiveness of your vagina.

Orgasmic Disorders An orgasmic disorder is an inability to climax. Women can experience it as a *preorgasmic* or *anorgasmic* disorder. Preorgasmic implies that the woman has never had an orgasm or is unaware of having orgasm; she has yet to experience orgasm through intercourse, masturbation, or any other sexual activity. Anorgasmic means that the woman has had an orgasm and might be able to achieve orgasm through masturbation, but that she is unable to be orgasmic with her partner. Either form of orgasmic disorder can be caused by health issues, certain medicines, sexual inhibition, lack of knowledge, feelings of guilt or anxiety, inadequate stimulation, or any combination of these. Most women are capable of experiencing orgasms with some form of stimulation.

If you are preorgasmic, you can often become orgasmic by learning more about your body and what turns you on. The exercises in Chapter 5 can help you acquire knowledge about your sexual self that can help you bring yourself to orgasm and then teach your partner how best to pleasure you. Explore your own body and give yourself adequate time; a thorough, relaxed

GET PSYCHED

Lonnie Barbach, Ph.D., author of *For Yourself: The Fulfillment of Female Sexuality* and *For Each Other*, suggests that you ask yourself, "What makes sex good for me?" According to Barbach, the answer to that question and the responsibility for carrying it out lies within each woman: "Look to yourself to discover what's right for you and to build on what works. If you don't know, try lots of different things. Disregard anything that is not arousing and maximize those that are. Don't try to fit in to someone else's model, form your own unique vision."

examination of your whole body including your genitals involves setting aside at least an hour each time you do it over the course of several weeks in order to get comfortable with your body and fine-tune exactly what turns you on. Experiment with touch, erotica, fantasy, clitoral, and vagina stimulation. Try a toy or a vibrator to add extra spice.

Once you have been able to have an orgasm by yourself, you are ready to share with your partner all the unique ingredients necessary to turn you on.

Anorgasmia commonly results from not giving yourself permission to feel pleasure or not communicating what feels pleasurable. In other words, you might know what turns you on, but you may feel unable or unwilling to show your partner what you want, or perhaps you think he should already know without you telling him. Perhaps you want the sexual activity to proceed at a slower pace, but you're afraid that it will then take too long and that your partner might become uncomfortable or impatient. Anorgasmia can often be overcome by giving yourself permission to feel pleasure, asking or showing your partner what you want, extending foreplay, and adding stimulation both before and during intercourse, perhaps with manual stimulation of the clitoris or by using a vibrator. Different positions can also help vary the types and intensity of stimulation.

If you are able to have an orgasm with your partner, but not through intercourse, it is not necessarily a problem. However, if you would like to try to have orgasms during intercourse (and can have orgasms with your partner in other ways), you might try any of the following:

- Try positions in which either you or your partner can stimulate your clitoral area during intercourse manually or with a vibrator.
- Try positions that will stimulate your G spot, such as the rear entry position or with you on top.
- Ask your partner to include anal stimulation during intercourse.

Painful Intercourse Although intercourse can be painful for both men and women, painful intercourse is *far* more prevalent in women. Painful intercourse is often a symptom of a lack of lubrication or an involuntary contraction of the vaginal muscles that makes penetration painful or impossible (the latter is known as *vaginismus*). It can be caused by a host of health and medical conditions, including infections, diseases, inflammation, irregular tissue formations, or ovarian cysts; so, if intercourse is painful for you, first get a physical evaluation by a qualified gynecologist who specializes in pelvic pain. Sex is not supposed to be painful, so don't try to tough it out. If you try to live with the pain, your mind might even begin to associate sex with pain, which could lead to anxiety and some degree of sexual aversion or inhibited sexual desire.

If the physical evaluation shows that everything is normal, you do have some options for reducing or eliminating the pain. Oral stimulation before intercourse can help, as can extended foreplay. If you remain dry, water-soluble lubricants, such as K-Y Jelly or Astroglide, are very safe and effective substitutes and can often be applied in stimulating ways as a part of foreplay.

You might also experience painful intercourse if you haven't had intercourse for some time. Penetrating more slowly and gradually can often help. If your vaginal muscles are contracting involuntarily, perhaps inserting a finger or having your partner insert a finger to stimulate the vagina and help it dilate before penetration can reduce the pain. Sometimes, backing away from intercourse and engaging in additional foreplay can help the vaginal muscles relax and give the vagina additional time to respond. Practicing Kegel exercises, tightening and relaxing the pelvic muscles, can also help you develop muscle control over time.

WEB TALK: For more information about what to do if sex becomes painful or you have other female sexual dysfunctions, visit:

www.newshe.com

If sex remains painful, continue researching other possible causes. *For Women Only: A Revolutionary Guide to Overcoming Sexual*

Dysfunction and Reclaiming Your Sex Life, by Drs. Jennifer and Laura Berman, is one possible resource.

What You Can Do

Some form of sexual dysfunction affects almost every couple to some degree sometime during their relationship. So, having the dysfunction itself is not nearly as significant as how you choose to approach it. If you suspect that you or your partner is suffering from a sexual dysfunction, here are some positive steps you can take right now:

☐ Discuss your concerns with your partner, so he or she can be both an emotional and physical source of support for you, by using many of the strategies we offer in this book. Remember, a sexual problem that either of you experiences affects both of you, so team up to resolve it.

☐ If you have any doubts about a medication you're taking or you suspect a medical reason, get a physical evaluation, preferably by a gynecologist or urologist who specializes in sexual dysfunction, or go to a sexual dysfunction center or clinic. Most teaching hospitals can be relied on as excellent resources.

☐ Do additional research on the Internet or at the library to learn more about a specific dysfunction. (Be skeptical of any products that are touted as miracle cures or quick fixes; some might even make the problem worse.)

☐ Consult Appendixes B and C for additional sources of bibliotherapy and audiotherapy that have to do with various types of disorders that you or your partner might be experiencing.

☐ If intercourse is uncomfortable for any reason, but you still find pleasure in other forms of sexual activity, take a brief hiatus from intercourse. Sometimes, the problem will resolve itself once the pressure to perform is removed.

☐ Do not hesitate to seek out a mental health professional who has particular expertise in human sexuality. They are trained to help you assess what is needed to resolve your particular questions or problems. Sex therapy is a focused, short-term, results-oriented therapy with a demonstrated rate of success. Your concerns may be solved in only a few sessions.

Overcoming Relationship Barriers to Ecstasy

When enough passion is there, even a couple in a troubled relationship might be able to have great sex sometimes, but the undercurrents of unresolved issues or the ongoing effects of anger and other barriers will eventually begin to present unexpected challenges to the sexual side of their relationship.

If you and your partner believe your relationship is working as well as you want it to, feel free to skip this chapter for now, but remember to come back to it any time you need to. The advice and guidance we provide here can help you and your partner identify and remove obstacles whenever they might occur in order to make your journey toward sexual ecstasy that much better.

Feelings About Your Partner That Can Hinder Sexual Ecstasy

How you feel *about* your partner strongly influences how you feel *with* your partner. Obviously, if you and your partner respect, appreciate, and adore one another, your lovemaking will likely be way more enjoyable than if one or both of you harbor resentment, jealousy, or other forms of negativity toward the other. With enough attraction and passion, practically any couple can sometimes sidestep negative emotions long enough to enjoy a round of great sex, but in the long run, those negative emotions usually serve to undermine sexual pleasure.

In the sections that follow, we address the negative emotions that can act as barriers to sexual ecstasy in practically any relationship. Keep in mind that negative feelings can arise from two sources: feelings about your partner generated by unresolved issues between you, or any unrealistic expectations regarding your partner, your relationship, or relationships in general that may have formed long before you even met.

Anger—The World's Leading Anti-Aphrodisiac Few emotions can interfere with good sex more than anger. But you don't have to let anger get in your way. A very effective, though temporary, fix is to make a conscious decision—a pact with your partner—to *leave anger out of the bedroom.* Do this right now, even before you begin working on any long-term solutions. If something is bothering you so much that it's getting in the way of your sex life, it is crucial to *resolve the issue* or *let go of it!*

If you choose to let go of an issue, let it go forever. John Gottman, Ph.D., co-author of *The Seven Principles for Making Marriage Work,* estimates that over two thirds of conflicts never get resolved in most relationships, and that's perfectly normal. You need to accept that you will always have some differences. Then focus on working out the issues that can be resolved and on the strengths in your relationship instead of the weaknesses.

> ## GET PSYCHED
>
> "I think that many couples are so angry and alienated that they say they are not going to become sexual again until they resolve their issues. I think that's the wrong strategy. You need to deal with those differences and keep the touching and sexuality alive." *—Barry McCarthy, Ph.D., marital and sex therapist co-author of* Getting It Right the First Time *and* Rekindling Desire

Q&A

I like to party on Friday nights, and my husband just wants to stay home and read. What can I do to make him want to go out and have fun with me?

With some effective negotiation, you might be able to make this a win-win situation for both of you. First, think about why your husband might be reluctant to go out. Did you party on Friday nights earlier in your relationship? If so, what's different now? Did you spend time together when partying or did you leave him alone? Maybe he felt ignored. Did you generally like to stay longer than he did? If your situation changed, when did it change? If he's open to discussing this, you might be able to figure out, between the two of you, why your husband is reluctant and address that issue. Talk with him and work out a compromise together that gives each of you something you want. Perhaps going out to a bar at happy hour and then going out to dinner or a movie or back home would work. Or maybe take turns; do what he wants one Friday and what you want the next. Or plan an evening that mixes in a little of what each of you finds enjoyable. The key here is to choose to do things together that you both enjoy. Sometimes this requires compromise, and sometimes one of you will enjoy an activity more than the other. But when you can each get some of what you want, you will be much more likely to yield to your partner on the other things.

If you cannot completely let go of an issue, however, don't let it fester; revisit it later when you and your partner can take a calmer, more rational approach. Unresolved and often unrelated issues that continue to gnaw at either one or both of you can poison virtually any aspect of your relationship, especially your sex life.

Anger toward your partner may be a result of unmet expectations, so whenever you're feeling angry with him or her, first take a look at the expectations and demands you're placing on your partner and on the relationship in general. For example, if you're telling yourself, "My relationship must give me all of the fulfillment and desire that I want and must never fall short," that belief, in and of itself, is the factor within you that's probably igniting your anger, perhaps on a constant basis. Ask yourself in a

GET PSYCHED

Long-term relationships call for a short-term memory.
—Mari, married 35 years

private, non-angry moment whether the expectation you have is in fact reasonable. (For example, suppose your partner expected that same thing of you?) If the answer is "No," then it is important to lower your expectation(s). And the sooner, the better! This can be a major step toward resolving your anger and feeling better about your partner and your relationship. If you believe that your expectations are reasonable, however, explore whether it's possible to get what you are looking for from your partner.

you're not alone

Cindy (age 31) and Matt (age 34) were married for 8 years and experienced chronic money problems. Cindy thought Matt didn't make enough money or work hard enough. He thought that she spent too much money. They went back and forth about money issues, constantly jabbing at each other for several years. Occasionally they would get into incredible arguments, name-calling and blaming one another for their bleak financial situation, but never resolving it. At the end of an argument, or after a certain amount of time had passed, one of them would say, "I'm sorry I said what I said." And then the other would say something like, "I'm really sorry, too." And they would hug and embrace, and 5 minutes later, they would be up in the bedroom having usually quite passionate sex.

As you can see, they unwittingly used arguments as "foreplay"–their negative passions of anger would ignite positive passions of lust. They would get angry, make up, feel close to one another, and have good sex, but never really resolve the issue. In reality, sex reinforced their anger!

Cindy and Matt did eventually seek help, and in therapy had quite an awakening when they realized that they were using sex as a payoff for fighting. They both learned to deal with their anxieties about money and developed the ability to problem-solve together. This included setting aside time for "business meetings" each week with each other to calmly discuss issues. Once they were able to do this, they no longer needed to fight, and their sex life got much better, as the anger was no longer necessary.

When unresolved issues are causing your anger, agree to work quickly with your partner to address them. Remember that a problem that affects one of you affects the relationship and thus both of you. First agree that you're on the same team and that you are going to look for a solution that works for both of you, a win-win situation. To make this process happen, *remember to work on your issues at a time when neither of you is angry*. Rarely, if ever, does anything get resolved in the heat of battle. Issues get resolved when you're calm and you can talk things through—when you can make concessions and are more open to seeing your partner's point of view as well as your own.

Much of what couples usually fight about has no right or wrong but is a matter of preference, style, or taste. Whether it's about how to spend money, how often to visit the in-laws, or how to raise the children, rarely is "being right" worth the havoc that the battle can wreak on your relationship in the long term. When you're feeling angry, usually all you want to do is defend yourself, convince your partner that you're right, attack, or retreat. And that obviously doesn't lend itself to good sex, intimacy, closeness, or trust. In fact, vicious statements made during arguments can sometimes destroy trust and intimacy and often generate guilt as well. Even if heartfelt apologies follow later, the negative effects of hurtful words can linger.

Anger can also be used intentionally to avoid sex. It's common for some couples to pick a fight about something that they know they will disagree about before going to bed. If this sounds familiar and is done intentionally to avoid sex, you need to explore the reasons why one or both of you might want to do this; perhaps sex is not fulfilling for one or both of you, or there is a sexual dysfunction you are trying to avoid. Sometimes, picking fights before bed is unintentional—a pattern that you have developed over time—in which case,

PsychSpeak

A **marital business meeting** consists of sitting down together as a couple and addressing any areas of your life that might need some attention. You can use the time to schedule the week's activities or talk about finances, vacations, and other "business" issues. You can make an agenda or just show up. Many couples find this to be an extremely helpful and timesaving way to deal with ongoing issues, family matters, or simply things in their relationship that may be otherwise neglected until they reach that "fever pitch."

you can choose to break the pattern. One suggestion is to agree not to address difficult issues or conflicts after a certain time in the evening, say 8 or 9 P.M. Usually, if you stay up until 10 or 11 P.M. arguing, you're both tired, vulnerable, and less willing to make concessions or engage in any type of rational problem solving. Consider scheduling a *marital business meeting* once a week, perhaps sometime during the weekend, to manage the "business" of maintaining your relationship.

If you do feel anger encroaching on your thoughts at bedtime, practice a technique called *thought-stopping*. When any negative thought pops into your head, resolve to stop it (if you really want to stop it) because otherwise it will obviously interfere with your sexual pleasure as well as your partner's and certainly with your overall sense of peace. Tell yourself "stop!" and then substitute a positive image right on the spot—maybe a vision of a time when the two of you really connected. Some people find it very helpful to wear a rubber band around their wrist and to snap the rubber band, giving them a slight amount of harmless pain when they begin to have an unwanted thought. This is an easy way of deconditioning thoughts before they have a chance to linger too long and become obsessions.

PsychSpeak

Thought-stopping is a technique in which you choose to end a negative or disturbing thought or replace it with a positive, pleasurable one. Thought-stopping is effective for blocking out thoughts and feelings that produce such things as anger, guilt, jealousy, anxiety, and spectatoring.

Then, make a commitment that before you get into bed together again, you will figure out how you're going to deal with the issue, or make a commitment to let go of it. Consider adopting the 72-hour rule: If something is not dealt with (or at least scheduled to be dealt with at a time when you can address it rationally) within 72 hours, you will let it go *forever!*

If you do notice that a disagreement is heating up, try to defuse the situation as quickly as possible. Rarely do both partners feel the same intensity of anger immediately or at the same exact time. Typically, one partner gets angry, the other partner reacts, and it escalates. Make a pledge to each other that the one who is least angry will defuse the situation. Agree and make a commitment that both of you will back off whenever either of you gives the de-escalation signal. The calmer one of you might say, "Let's take a timeout." Or maybe you can work out a code word or signal to indicate when one of you realizes that the discussion is going nowhere, such as "peace" or "sushi." Set a procedure that you can both agree to follow, at a time when you are in a peaceful or solution-oriented mode.

> ### GET PSYCHED
>
> "If your heart rate exceeds 100 beats per minute you won't be able to hear what your spouse is trying to tell you no matter how hard you try. Take a twenty-minute break before continuing."
> —John Gottman, Ph.D., marital researcher and co-author of *The Seven Principles for Making Marriage Work*

Many people think that letting off a little steam is natural and even healthy, but usually, letting off steam only gets people angrier. If unleashing your anger were a healthy approach to resolving conflict, therapists the world over would be teaching people how to yell more loudly at each other. Usually, when someone starts yelling, they become more convinced that they're right, and it can feel so good to be right and to yell, that the next time they get into an uncomfortable discussion, they're likely to follow the same unworkable strategy. And the puzzling thing about this is that people who follow this pattern usually never realize that although it might help them to feel better at the moment, it's not bringing them any closer to getting what they really want—peace and fulfillment with their partner.

> **WEB TALK:** To learn more about John Gottman's research with couples and for more of his advice go to:
> www.gottman.com

My wife and I have some pretty heated discussions that usually spin out of control and leave us both a little resentful. Do you have any suggestions on how to temper our discussions?

One of the keys to having a productive discussion about an issue that ends with a sense of closure is to know how to enter into a discussion and how to exit it.

John Gottman, a clinical psychologist who has done extensive research on couples interactions, suggests some effective ways for doing this. His first recommendation is to "soften your startup." Arguments first start up because a spouse sometimes escalates the conflict from the get-go by making a critical or contemptuous remark in a confrontational tone. You can soften the startup to a discussion by thinking about and editing what you're about to say before you say it. His second suggestion is that you "learn to make repair attempts." Happy couples know how to repair the situation before an argument gets completely out of control. Successful repair attempts call for de-escalating the tension, either by requesting a time-out or being conciliatory in some way. Stroke your partner with a caring remark, "I understand that this is hard for you," making it clear that you are on common ground and backing down. In a good relationship you may have to yield so you can both win. Gottman suggests that at the end of an argument you "soothe yourself and each other," including physically calming down, and "be tolerant of each other's faults." Offering signs of appreciation for your partner and his or her feelings can go a long way. You may also want to read *The Art of Staying Together*, by Michael S. Broder, for more effective ways of dealing with conflict.

To the extent that you can learn how to put these issues away, by resolving them or letting go of them, you are going to prosper sexually, as well as in every other area of your relationship!

Anxieties and Fears About Your Partner Sexual intimacy, the ability to reveal your most private sexual desires to your partner, is a key ingredient to ecstasy. Without it, you cannot adequately communicate what turns you on, show or tell your partner what feels good to you, share your fantasies, or try new things. So, if you find yourself withholding your sexual desires and wants from your partner, you are, in effect, erecting barriers to sexual ecstasy for both of you. If you cannot be intimate about sexual matters with your partner, your sexual relationship will almost certainly be stifled to some extent, and that's not going to bring you to the level of ecstasy that you are seeking.

We urge anyone who feels unable to be sexually intimate with his or her partner to adopt an attitude that is more open. An attitude that can quickly turn this around allows you to tell yourself, "I've chosen my partner, we're intimate in many other ways, and in my relationship it is important for me to risk being more open." Taking risks is an important part of being in a relationship; it helps you both develop as individuals and as a couple. If you find that you can't risk openness with your partner, honestly explore the possible reasons why. In many cases, a couple is not sexually intimate because one or both partners are afraid that if they openly express a particular desire, some kind of rejection will follow.

Realize that by taking the initiative to be intimate, you really can't lose. If you find that your partner is accepting and genuinely interested in teaming up with you to help fulfill your desires, great—your relationship and sex life together is probably about to get a whole lot better! But if your openness reveals the results you most feared—that your partner rejects you or turns you down—then you've learned a great deal about your partner, your relationship, and where it stands. You learn what needs immediate attention. It might be something you can work on together, something you can choose to change this moment to turn your relationship around, or not; but at least you know something more about the direction you need to take in this important area of your life.

GET PSYCHED

I believe that the most important component of emotional intimacy is feeling loved and respected for all of who you are, including your weaknesses and vulnerabilities whether they are intellectual, career-wise or emotional. I think you really do feel much more loved and accepted when your spouse knows all about you, including your weaknesses, and still loves and respects you. *–Barry McCarthy, Ph.D. marital and sex therapist co-author of* Getting It Right The First Time *and* Rekindling Desire

Another approach that can help you feel more comfortable expressing an unfulfilled desire is to ask yourself where your fear of expressing your desire is coming from. Sometimes, thinking that your partner won't be receptive can be a sign that you're not very receptive to that desire yourself. Be as accepting of the desire yourself as you would like your partner to be. Switch roles: If your partner told you what you are afraid of telling your partner, how would you react? Would you be okay with it? If so, consider giving your partner the same benefit of the doubt. If you discover that you would act harshly, ask if a harsh reaction would really be appropriate. If not, search for any values that might be making you less accepting of your own pleasurable fantasies. This sort of honest introspection can help you feel much more comfortable with yourself, as well as with approaching your partner. The results could lead you to a new era of your relationship, characterized by trust and intimacy that carries you both to higher and higher levels of sexual ecstasy.

When One of You Is Unavailable For your relationship to work optimally, you need to invest some time and energy to both maintain it and make it thrive. If either partner is unavailable to attend to the needs of the other or to the relationship as a whole, your relationship can begin to lose its luster. Anything that takes time and attention away from the relationship has the potential

you're not alone

Mindy (age 29) and Dan (age 28) had been married for six years and had two young children (ages 5 and 2). Mindy was working as a dental hygienist from 9 to 5 and Dan ran a print shop working from about 8 until 6. Mindy would drop the kids off at the sitter's in the morning on her way to work and pick them up after work. She would come home, attend to the children's needs, cook, and then help Dan clean up after dinner. By the time they got the kids to bed at 9, all Mindy wanted to do was unwind for a while by herself and then go to sleep around 10. Whenever Dan tried to initiate any sort of sexual activity at night, Mindy would reluctantly go along or roll over and fall asleep.

Eventually, Dan became upset enough to bring it to Mindy's attention. She explained that she was simply too exhausted during to breed unavailability: work, work-related travel, a focus on friends or other family members, fatigue, illness, an over-involvement with the kids, excessive drinking, hobbies, or even a lack of interest (which can relate to sex or any other part of the relationship). Unavailability can mean a physical absence or, more commonly, an emotional absence, typically expressed by some version of the feeling, "My partner's just not there for me."

If you feel as though your partner is unavailable, try to pin down specifically what it is you want—that is, what is it that's missing for you? What could your partner do to help you feel as though he or she were sufficiently available? Form specific, doable requests, such as spending two hours alone every Saturday afternoon or spending a weekend together every other month. Most importantly, know what would resolve this issue for you, ask for it, and then, if necessary, negotiate it.

Couples who are successful at addressing these issues take a flexible, creative approach to form a custom plan that applies specifically to their situation, needs, desires, and schedules. Nowa-days, you can find all sorts of successful long-term relationships—couples living on opposite coasts, taking separate vacations, living different lifestyles—but somehow many of these couples are able to work it out in a way that enables each of them to do their own thing and then come back and to attend to one another's needs in a way that satisfies them both.

the week to have sex and she really needed an hour or so to herself to unwind after work. Dan agreed that Mindy had to do much more in the evening than he did, so he offered to take the kids out for an hour or so after dinner to play, so that she could unwind. He also started to help her make everyone's lunch for the next day, which gave them both the added benefit of doing something together that was more fun and provided an opportunity for them to talk. They would put the kids to bed at nine and have an hour or so to relax together before bedtime. Mindy began to feel much less stressed, and the couple began to have sex more frequently and in a more relaxed way during the week.

Perhaps the biggest problem with availability is that some couples approach it with a defeatist attitude. They're both working, raising kids, and dealing with other time demands, and they don't feel as though they have any additional time to invest in the relationship. This is usually a sign that the couple needs to reevaluate how they spend their time, individually and together. If you're feeling that you don't have enough time for your relationship, the first step is to take an inventory of how much time you spend on various activities during a normal week. At the end of each day, fill out the time log on the next page, entering the amount of time you spend on each activity for that day.

At the end of the week, you should have a pretty good idea of how much time you spend on various activities. Now, try to identify activities that you could afford to trim to make time for your relationship. Set a goal for giving your relationship a *minimum* of five hours a week. For example, if you spend two hours every night watching TV, consider limiting TV viewing to every other night or watching TV for only an hour every night. If you spend most Friday nights out with friends, consider going on a date only with your partner every other Friday. Whenever you say or think, "I don't have the time," keep in mind that everyone has the same amount of time: 168 hours in a week, 60 minutes in an hour. How you choose to spend that time is another matter and is *entirely* your choice.

As you begin to budget time and space for your relationship, be sure to account for your own, individual needs as well. Some people need a lot of time alone—personal time and space to wind down, sort out their own thoughts and emotions, and engage in other important solitary activities. Without that crucial time alone, some people might be physically present but emotionally unavailable. If you ever feel that the constant presence of your partner is suffocating, you may find yourself looking for ways (whether consciously or not) to physically or emotionally flee, so it's almost certainly to the advantage of a partner who needs more attention to let the partner who needs more time alone

Time Table

	Monday	Tuesday	Wednesday	Thursday	Friday	Saturday	Sunday
Breakfast							
Commuting							
Working							
Lunch							
Dinner							
Study/Reading							
TV/Movies							
Computer/Internet							
Friends							
Community work							
Raising kids							
Other family							
Personal time							
Hobbies							
Conversation/ Support time							
Romance/Sex time							
Other							

have it. This doesn't mean that the one who needs more alone time loves the other one any less; or that the one who wants more time together is more in love. It's not about love. It's simply about personal preferences.

My partner comes home and wants to read her mail and e-mail before she even says hello. When this happens, I feel unloved and angry. How can I get her to change?

A common area of conflict for many couples is the time when they first arrive home at night. Some people look forward to seeing their partner at the end of the day to process the day; others need to come home, check their mail, shower, or just have a little quiet time before they can really be available. Both of you would be way better off understanding and accepting each other's needs and the fact that they may be different in this area. Never think that the amount of alone time your partner needs in and of itself has anything to do with her feelings toward you or her commitment to your relationship. It's simply about her preference in this aspect of life. So, we urge you to team up to create an environment in which you both have the time alone and together that will satisfy each of your needs. Resist the temptation to read more into it than that.

When Attraction Fades What do you do when passion completely leaves your relationship? When you feel indifferent toward your partner sexually, but you still have other sexual desires and feel unfulfilled? Do you seek additional help? Stay with your partner and hope it somehow works out? Or end the relationship and then seek someone else to provide you the sexual satisfaction that's lacking?

The relationship problems of anger, fear, and unavailability are less complex than the issue of indifference. You can choose to work on becoming less angry and on resolving issues, and, with the right amount of determination from both of you, you will succeed. The same is true of those fears related to revealing your most intimate desires. And you can certainly restructure your life to become more available to your partner. But when the passion is gone and you see no realistic hope of it returning, you might understandably ask, "What's the point?"

246

If you find yourself asking that question, you might first consider some of the other issues that might underlie your feeling disconnected from your partner. For example, anger can put so much distance between you that passion might *appear* to have disappeared, but is really still there to perhaps a greater degree than you might have thought.

Another factor that commonly contributes to a loss of passion is the aging process and how each of you deals with it. Over the course of a long-term relationship, sexual desire can begin to fade. First, the initial passion lessens as you become more comfortable with one another, and then as you age, physical changes can lead to diminished attraction. Decreased desire might be due to physiological changes that control desire, or your partner might undergo physical changes that you find less attractive. If you know that and can use the knowledge to adjust your expectations, you can better cope with those changes. In addition, your own aging and how you feel about it can play a role. If you have trouble coming to terms with getting older, you might feel turned off as your partner begins to show signs of aging, as well. So, part of the solution is to begin to accept who you are and realize that you and your partner can be and are sexual beings at all stages life. Another part of the solution is to learn to focus less on what turns you off and more on what turns you on.

Q&A

How can I be sure whether the passion is gone or merely whether our issues are obscuring it?

Here's one question to help figure out if sexual desire is really gone: "If we could magically resolve all of the issues that are standing between the two of us, what is left?" The idea is to explore whether is there still any attraction underneath all of that, or is there nothing at all? If the answer is that there is simply not enough, perhaps you might ultimately choose not to be together. On the other hand, if something good lies beneath those unresolved issues, there is something to work with. Your task then is to get to work on those issues that may be the obstacles (and any anger related to them) in order to see whether passion that could be restored is buried underneath.

Wandering Attraction Very few people are 100 percent *mentally* exclusive with their partners. In other words, most of us at times feel attracted and even turned on by other men or women we encounter in our day-to-day lives, in addition to those we see on the screen. Moreover, it is perfectly normal to have sexual fantasies involving people other than your partner. These thoughts and feelings are very natural and usually do not become a significant issue unless your partner finds out, becomes jealous, and chooses to make it an issue. However, if you become involved with another person in an undisclosed affair or in an intimate way, emotionally or physically (flirting, kissing, petting, a strong emotional connection, different types of sexual contact, and so on), some major soul-searching is in order. You need to question whether your relationship may have run its course, whether this connection to someone new has awakened something inside of you that has made you more aware of what you want to experience in your primary relationship, or even something in between.

If you are straying outside of your primary relationship, ask yourself what it is that you're getting out of it that you need but might not be getting from your primary partner. If you think, "I really wish I could have these feelings or experiences toward my partner," this could be a sign that you're hooked on the initial attraction—that powerful initial passion, which rarely, if ever, characterizes a long-term relationship. The first step is to realize that long-term relationships are entirely different than affairs. Also, be clear about not only what you might be gaining from this new relationship, but also what you risk losing by letting it become as important or more important to you than your long-term primary relationship.

Many people realize when they feel their passions stirred that they have let their long-term relationship go. You might become aware of what you're really looking for: "This other person pays a lot of attention to me … actually does sex the way I like it without me having to ask … is more receptive than my partner." Also ask yourself, "How do I feel about myself when I'm with this other person?" Often the answer is "Alive and accepted, again." If this resonates with you, what would you have to do to feel that way with your spouse or primary partner? What changes would you have to make in order to get what you need from your primary relationship? And perhaps most importantly, are you willing to do something to make those changes happen? We have seen many relationships over the years get stronger as a result of an outside liaison. If both partners choose to stay together, discuss it, and learn from it, they might see what's missing in their relationship, and then choose to begin attending to each other's needs once again.

Q&A

I made out with this guy at work, and now I feel guilty about it. Should I tell my husband?

Be very cautious about sharing with your partner anything about an affair—physical or emotional—that you might have had. You can always choose to say it; but once you do, you can't take it back; so if you do choose to tell, realize that there may be irreversible consequences. Many marriages and long-term relationships have ended abruptly that night when a partner says, "You know, I've been seeing someone else." The partner who was just informed might not wait around to hear what comes after the admission: "... but, I'm not seeing them anymore ... but, it'll never happen again ... but, it made me realize I want you ... but, I wish I hadn't done it." "It meant nothing to me," and so on. So be very cautious about what you reveal in this very sticky situation. Before you reveal anything you might regret, consider talking it over with somebody neutral to clarify your options and decide both whether and how best to broach the topic. Also, consider checking out some of the references we have included to supplement this topic in Appendixes B and C, including the book *Can Your Relationship Be Saved?*

Falling Out of Like For many, the old cliché "I *love* you, but I'm just not *in love* with you" pretty much summarizes the feeling of "falling out of love." It's common for people to compare the type of love they feel in a long-term relationship to that initial passion they felt when the relationship was brand new and then decide that the feeling of being *in love* is what they truly miss. However, if you ask most people who have had both what they would rather have, you will rarely hear someone say, "You know, I'd much rather have a passionate short-term relationship in which I'm infatuated than a long-term relationship where the feelings are not as intense all the time." Most people generally feel that, all things considered, the love, passion, and sex they experience in a long-term relationship where the connection is solid are ultimately more fulfilling than those intense feelings of initial passion that characterize a short-term relationship.

Falling out of *like* is a different matter and is usually more serious. This has a lot more to do with losing respect for one's partner, the sort of thing that might have triggered an immediate or inevitable breakup in a short-term relationship. Falling out of like has to do with disliking the way the person acts or reacts toward you, your children, other people, or toward the world as a whole, especially in the important non-sexual areas. Don't confuse this with certain behaviors that you might not like, such as a partner's penchant for spending money or telling corny jokes. Falling out of like is something that is far more serious and difficult to accept or repair.

you're not alone

Barb and Jeff, a couple in their early 40s, had been married about 3 years. Barb was a teacher, and Jeff sold insurance, but Barb never really knew the details of Jeff's job and never asked many questions about it early in their relationship. Eventually, she found out that what he really did was sell expensive insurance policies that he knew his customers didn't need, mostly to senior citizens who were naive and couldn't afford it. He was essentially engaging in a con job. When Barb became aware of this, she talked to Jeff about it and asked him, "How can you do that to people who are so vulnerable?" And Jeff replied, "Listen, these people are suckers. If I don't take their money, someone else will." Barb was repulsed by his attitude and realized that she could no longer respect him. After a period of about a year of reflection, she left him, realizing that she simply could no longer live with someone whom she could not respect as a person.

If you think you might have fallen out of like with your partner, ask yourself how significant to you are the characteristics that you find troubling (assuming they are clearly identifiable)? Is it something that you can let go of or is it something that your value system will not allow you to accept? Your choice is clear but not necessarily easy: You can either let your partner go or let go of the issues. Strategies for helping you to navigate these problem areas are available. You can consult with a professional or refer to Appendixes B and C for books and other resources.

Dealing with the Crunches

"We don't have time." "We're both exhausted." "We don't have the money to have a nice, romantic evening out." "The children might hear." All these excuses are ways to avoid dealing with the *crunches*—those day-to-day necessities and annoyances that can get in the way of having good sex … but only if you let them. Let's take a quick look at these common issues:

> **Not enough time**   Budget your time, as explained previously in this chapter, to give each of you the alone time you need, provide time for maintaining the "business" of your relationship, and set aside whatever time you need for intimacy and romance as well as sex. This probably means giving up other things. If you truly want to make good sex a priority, *act as if it is* by finding or making time for it.
>
> **Not enough energy**   Fatigue can be a very real issue, and it's important to have time to connect with your partner when you're both alert. Look at lifestyle issues. Do you drink? Do you smoke? Have you had a physical exam lately? If you have an iron deficiency, see what you can do about it. Maybe a little exercise can help you to feel more energetic. Do you like to stay up late and watch TV? Tape your favorite show and watch it the next evening. Then, instead of watching TV before bed, maybe you

can read erotica together. Are you a morning person? Then maybe having sex the first thing in the morning is an option (or earlier in the evening), or take a shower when you get home from work and have sex before or after dinner. Take "naps" together on the weekend. Think about opportunities that make sex something other than the last thing you do at night, which for many people is when their energy is lowest. Be creative about this together.

Not enough money   Having money to pay a sitter, so that you can go out to a movie or show or have dinner at your favorite restaurant, is great, but if your finances are tight, find other ways to get out and enjoy yourselves. For example, you can save money on sitters by trading off with other parents in the neighborhood. Instead of going out to eat, you might pack a picnic. You can rent a movie and cuddle up on the sofa. Spending time together does not necessarily mean having to spend lots of money. But it could mean investing your time and effort together to think up novel ways of connecting for free.

The children will hear   If couples stopped having sex when they had their first child, cities wouldn't feel so crowded. If this is a concern, all sorts of solutions are available. Lock your bedroom door. Move the bed away from the wall, so it won't bang. Find a place, if possible, in a different room,

GET PSYCHED

In her book, *50 Ways to Please Your Lover: While You Please Yourself,* Lonnie Barbach gives some tips for those who feel as though they are too tired to have sex:

- Come straight home from work, bring home takeout, and jump into bed with or without clothes. Talk while you picnic between the sheets.

- Keep the conversation on a positive note. Steer away from criticism and conflict.

- Express your loving feeling toward each other.

- Share hopes and long-term goals.

- Turn the lights low and savor your partner for dessert.

- Stay connected physically by touching arms, legs, and feet.

where the children are less likely to hear. Play music to drown out the sound. If appropriate, send the children out to play and instruct them to stay outside for one hour unless there is an emergency. Now, brainstorm some solutions of your own!

But I'm a mother/father now When you have a child, it's important to acknowledge your partner's role as a mother or father, but you also still want to see your partner as a lover and make sure that spending time alone as a couple never stops being a priority. Sometimes it helps a man to refer to his wife as his "girlfriend," so he can still feel that it's "okay" to find her attractive.

When it comes to crunches, the strategy is clear: Identify the crunch. Start with our list, and then add your own. (You may want to take a moment to do this now.) Together, figure out a way to work through it or around it, and then get past it in order to enjoy each other optimally. Don't let a crunch take away your pleasure. You owe it nothing, and you are way better off not letting your relationship suffer because of it. Each and every crunch is something you *can* probably work out. You only have to both want to.

Overcoming Communication Traps

In intimate relationships, communication calls for more than just saying what's on your mind, because you need to do more than express an idea or feeling. The challenge is to phrase a message in a way that your partner can be more receptive to it and that helps your partner hear your message as you intended it to be heard. Anything in the message that triggers a strong reaction in your partner can hinder your partner's ability to hear it, understand it, accept it, and respond to it in a way that is favorable to you. Effective communication also calls for you to reciprocate by listening when your partner wants to be heard.

One of the most important skills in carrying on a productive discussion has to do with giving feedback. Focus your feedback on specific behaviors or actions that can be changed, and phrase your feedback as observations, and not judgments or insults. For example, instead of telling your partner that she doesn't seem to care where or how you like to be touched, you might tell her what you like that she already does, "I love the way you kiss ..." and then tell her specifically how you liked to be touched, "... and I would love a lot of pressure when you're massaging me," or guide your partner's hands to the right places and moan softly when the touch is just right (almost like a Geiger counter). If you say your partner doesn't care, you're making a judgment about your partner based on an assumption rather than on a fact and you're just asking for a defensive response, which can trigger an argument. With positive and constructive feedback, you have much more of a chance of getting what you want, and your partner will feel a lot better about it.

I provide plenty of hints about what I would like, but my husband never picks up on them. Is there a more effective way?

Be assertive. Tell your partner very specifically what you want when you want it, *without the attitude that he should already know.* Otherwise, unspoken, unfulfilled desires can build up and collectively create a major issue that's a hundred times more significant than it needs to be. Express your needs with "I" statements. Instead of saying something like, "You don't seem to care that I'm too exhausted to make love at night," you might say, "I'm too exhausted to feel real turned-on at night; how about if we set a date to make love in the morning or afternoon when I can feel more energetic—which would you prefer?" Try to clarify reasons why, and perhaps you can even provide an alternative that could make it better for both of you. Also, make sure he understands that it benefits him to both listen to and be responsive to the things you are requesting.

When your partner is describing his or her feelings and offering feedback, keep in mind that statements of feelings are great sources of information about what is going on inside your partner. For example, if your partner says "I feel angry when you come to bed two hours late," whether or not you disagree, that is the way he or she feels. Hear it, and you become a bit more knowledgeable about your partner. Argue against it, and you have erected a barrier. By acknowledging the feeling, you at least provide your partner with some validation and a sign that you are willing to listen to his or her feedback. And by really listening, you can collect a wealth of information that can help you develop more empathy and then be able to more effectively provide what your partner desires.

When listening, really listen, not only to the literal words, but also to the spirit in which they are expressed and "listen" to your partner's body language. Listening in the true sense of the word does not mean offering unsolicited advice or waiting for an opportunity to interject a correction. It doesn't consist of soothing speech to gloss over feelings and avoid an uncomfortable conversation. When listening, really listening, simply take in what is being said and ask questions to clarify what your partner is saying. When responding, restate what your partner said so you can make sure you understand correctly, and respond only after you have truly taken in what your partner has communicated to you. Here's an exercise for honing your listening skills:

1. Set aside 15 to 20 minutes to talk and listen with your partner.

2. For the first five minutes, have your partner talk about something you would like to know or understand. During this period, limit your own responses, if any, to clarifying what your partner is saying. If you make any comments, do so at a time when a response is clearly requested.

3. After five minutes of listening, take a few minutes to share with your partner what you heard—summarize or paraphrase what you heard without offering any rebuttal.

4. Add a brief observation of how you thought your partner was feeling when he or she was talking. Was your partner

happy, sad, angry? Ask your partner how accurate your observations are—did you pick up on your partner's emotions? This can help you really focus on making a connection instead of just trying to get the words down.

5. Switch roles. Now, you're in control of the conversation for the next five minutes.

6. When you're done, have your partner share his or her summary of what was heard. Many couples are surprised at how differently one partner hears what the other one has actually said. This puts a spotlight on how important a role communication plays in what may be an on-going issue.

Consider following up on the exercise by talking about some of the things you learned with respect to each other and your individual listening styles. Start with something nonsexual before moving on to sexual issues. For example, see if it can help you to further clarify sexual preferences or what it is that each of you wants.

Addressing Sexual Desire Discrepancy

Sexual desire discrepancy is rarely a problem in a short-term relationship, when that initial passion serves to fuel a sufficient sex drive to satisfy both partners. When the initial passion wears off, however, few, if any, couples discover that sex means exactly the same thing to each of them or that they each like to experience the same amount of sex in exactly the same way. Sexual desire discrepancy does not mean that one partner is more or less in love or more or less committed to the relationship. It does not indicate that the partner who wants it more is a "bottomless pit" or "sex addict," or has "only one thing on his or her mind." Nor does it mean that the one who wants it less is frigid, prudish, less in love, or doesn't like sex. It has more to do with normal variations in the range of sexual desire—which as we have said earlier in the book—happens to be a fairly wide range.

Couples usually resolve this by working out a compromise over the long term in which both partners' needs are met. The partner who wants sex more might be satisfied with having it a little less frequently or accept different types of sexual activities that the less desirous partner is more willing to provide. The one who wants it less might be okay with having it a bit more frequently or stimulate the more desirous partner in other ways. However, for many couples, desire discrepancy often becomes a significant issue. Nearly 25 percent of couples who come in for treatment are there because of issues resulting from some degree of desire discrepancy.

What we see is usually the higher-desire person wanting the lower-desire person to have more desire. And when there's a *demand* for sex, it's not erotic, arousing, or seductive. It often results in pushing the lower-desire person farther away. Or, the lower-desire person will give in and have sex, but won't enjoy the lovemaking session and ends up having even less desire for sex the next time. Thus a vicious circle! This doesn't mean that the higher-desire person is necessarily at fault—the partner who has a lower desire usually is in ultimate control of the amount of sex that the couple is having. So this really is an issue that affects both partners and often in ways that even go beyond sex. So as you can see, if it is allowed to fester, it often begins to generate anger that can spread into many other areas of the relationship or even cause other sexual difficulties.

GET PSYCHED

"For me to expect my husband of many years to knock my socks off like he did in the beginning is unrealistic. It's not the way nature works. However, if I had a high testosterone level, I would be hot to trot on a regular basis. So people who walk around with this high desire level have an illusion that everybody is like that or that somehow 'if you loved me you would be this way … (and fill in the blanks).' A lot of it is understanding who you are. It's almost like a you-are-here map to describe it, here is the body I've been given. How I play it is really up to me and it's my bias and it's my responsibility to know what turns me on and to teach that to my partner and to negotiate for my needs, which may not seem like sexual needs to him."
—*Pat Love, Ed.D., marital therapist and author of* Hot Monogamy

Ilda Ficher, Ph.D., professor emeritus, Institute of Graduate Clinical Psychology at Widener University, who along with Dr. Marvin Zuckerman researched sensation seeking in couples, believes that many desire discrepancy issues are caused by the couple's different levels on the trait of sensation seeking. When she works with couples and explains to them that it is no different than having different appetites, it allows blame and anger to disappear and gives them a new appreciation of each other. Then couples can begin to negotiate a mutually satisfying sex life.

We asked relationship expert and author Michele Weiner-Davis the following question: What advice could you offer a low-desire person concerning sexual desire discrepancy?

"A lot of people who are less sexual don't understand what it means to the more highly-sexed spouse to be sexual. So many times I've heard people of low desire say, 'I'm not feeling close. We've been at odds. We haven't been spending time together.' And they offer themselves explanations, but the only explanation they come up with is that it must be because for him sex is just a biological urge, like having to sneeze. And that is gigantic myth—that sex is just about sex.

If you asked the average person on the street whether you should take your partner's feelings into consideration when it comes to deciding whether to have kids or where you're going to live or whether it's going to be a one- or two-career family or how you're going to spend the holidays, everyone would say, 'Absolutely, these are collaborative decisions. You do have to honor your spouse's feelings.' But conspicuously missing from the mix is knowing, finding out about, and caring about how your spouse feels about sex. I am a strong believer that this is wrong."

If a couple notices a real difference in the frequency of sex each of them wants, the first step is to discuss those differences *without judgment*. Here are some additional approaches to try:

- The partner with more desire can back off even for several weeks to a month in order to give the person with less sexual desire a chance to feel a bit more aroused and desirous and then possibly be the one to initiate sexual activity. It's important for the partner with higher desire to avoid forming any expectations or being so eager during this time that the plan fails.

- Talk about what sex means to each of you and what needs sex serves for each of you. Understand that sex is rarely just about sex; it can serve important emotional and psychological needs, as well. See whether some of these needs can be met in ways other than having sex, such as touching, talking, and massaging.

- Write down how often each of you wants sex and then trade notes. You might be surprised to find that your desire levels are in a range that may seem much more negotiable. When desire discrepancy begins to generate anger, you could form an exaggerated estimate of how often the partner wants sex, such as "never" (for low) or "three times a day" (for high). Be mindful of that common tendency.

- Look for ways that might help the lower-desire partner want to be more sexual. Engaging in sexual activity or massage doesn't necessarily need to lead to intercourse. Perhaps agree to remain sexual without intercourse for a period of time, or take the opposite approach and follow Michele Weiner-Davis's "Nike philosophy"—"*Just do it!*" With many women, arousal might trigger desire. Choose the approach that works best for both of you.

- Lonnie Barbach, Ph.D., recommends that couples check in with themselves three times a day (at times when they couldn't possibly have sex), to keep track of how much sexual desire they're feeling, on a scale of 1 to 10. This can help you track your fluctuations throughout the day and possibly reveal times of the day or situations that might be more conducive to sex.

Partners who feel very different levels of sexual desire can certainly experience sexual ecstasy and have a very fulfilling sexual relationship, if they are committed to acceptance and are willing to compromise. If desire discrepancy continues to be problematic, even after you've tried the exercises here, seek out additional resources and assistance. Most couples who understand what desire discrepancy is and who are able to work together to address it can accommodate their differences in desire. Remember, open discussion, in which both partners' needs are considered, can lead to more satisfying sexual encounters for both.

Bringing a Reluctant Partner on Board

A reluctance to work on improving sex is fairly common. Your partner might be perfectly satisfied with the frequency and type of sex that he or she is experiencing or think that sex isn't something that people should need to work at. Many very intelligent people might wonder why humans need to work on sex: Dogs and cats don't need to work on sex, so why should humans need to work on sex? The answer is that cats and dogs pretty much have sex one certain way, and they do it in a very primitive manner. Humans tend to place those things called expectations on sex and require more variation. They look upon sex as something that has the potential to deliver that wonderful state called ecstasy, and they appreciate sex as a means of closeness with a partner that can be highly fulfilling. When it isn't, most humans notice.

Whenever you are reluctant to improve, it's generally because you think either that the situation doesn't need improvement or that nothing can be done to make a difference. And when you think that nothing is going to make a difference, and you approach the situation with that attitude, anything you do probably is not going to make a difference. In other words, it becomes a self-fulfilling prophecy. So, the first step is either to demonstrate to the reluctant partner that something can make a difference, or show the partner that his or her cooperation has the potential of delivering something that he or she wants or needs.

If your partner is reluctant, it usually falls on you to take the initiative. For example, if you want your partner to go with you to therapy, you can choose first to see a therapist on your own. In some cases, your therapist might be able to help you improve your situation. Your partner might notice an improvement and thus see the value in becoming involved. Or, the therapist might help you demonstrate something to your partner that could possibly be lacking in his or her life that joint sessions could help your partner achieve.

Once you know what you specifically want and you have identified some potential benefits for your partner, schedule a time to talk it over. If your partner expresses a reluctance or says that your sex life is good enough as it is, you might share your feelings about wanting to be closer or wanting to experience more or experience something specific. If your partner says, "I'm okay with the sex we're having," the question becomes this: What could make it even better? Each of you can rate your sexual satisfaction on a scale of 1 to 10. If your partner gives it a 7 or 8, ask what you could do together to make it a 9 or 10.

If you hit a roadblock, express yourself more assertively: "I really value our relationship, and I'm not satisfied with the way things are sexually right now. I would like your help to make it better for me. I'm not blaming. I understand I could be more _____. I need your help to change things, would you be willing to ...?" Or "I really need you to be there with me when I talk with somebody about this."

Of course, some people are dead set against getting any help or treatment or therapy. They might feel threatened by it, feel that it won't work, or simply think it's just for crazy people. If you reach a point at which you realize that your partner will not go along with you under any circumstances, it's probably

WEB TALK: To find a therapist who can help you with relationship issues check out the following web sites:

➤ www.psychologytoday.com
www.helping.apa.org
www.therapistlocator.net

time to give up on trying to get your partner onboard. Then you need to ask yourself, "What options remain that I can do, without the cooperation of my partner?" You might be able to discover ways of getting what you're looking for, perhaps by slowly introducing some of the ingredients talked about in this book into the relationship. Sometimes, this can awaken the desire in your partner and help your partner realize that your relationship together can be a whole lot more than what it is now.

Getting Help

Throughout this chapter, we identified and explored many of the most common relationship issues that can act as barriers to sexual ecstasy. And, we have provided information and suggestions for dealing with them. However, if you have completed this chapter and issues still remain unresolved, don't give up yet. You can always do that, but when you are in a long-term relationship you value, leave no stone unturned when exploring your options.

You can find additional help in other resources (including books and tapes) that are devoted to helping couples overcome their relationship issues and improve their lives together. Relationship therapy, workshops, classes, and retreats are also readily available. If you and your partner are committed to teaming up to improve your relationship, keep searching for answers and working together to remove any and all obstacles that might still be getting in the way of your sexual ecstasy!

WEB TALK: For additional books and products that can help specifically with relationship issues, visit these websites:

www.rebt.org

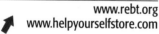 www.helpyourselfstore.com

What You Can Do

In this chapter, you have learned strategies to help remove relationship obstacles to sexual ecstasy. Here are some additional ideas that can apply to almost any area of your relationship:

☐ Each of you, on your own, make a list of those areas where you believe your relationship is working well.

☐ Each of you, on your own, make another list of areas where your relationship is not what it could be or where it could use some work.

☐ Exchange lists and thoroughly discuss the items only after you have completed them individually.

☐ Using your lists and whatever you discovered through your conversation, create a master list of what needs to be different. What is not working that needs to be working, and what is working that could be improved?

☐ What specific changes need to be made? Here you consider, *specifically,* what would need to change in order for each of you to have the things that you've identified become a reality. Think in terms of what changes you, *not your partner,* can make.

☐ If you and your partner are doing the exercises together, reflect on and talk about what changes each of you would like to see the other make. What behavior would you like to request that he or she change? All things considered, what exactly would you like to be different with respect to your partner from now on?

☐ Identify what you see as being the problems that you have communicating together. How do you avoid communicating? What is it you avoid communicating about? Once you are able to do that, see if you can redo the third and fourth exercises, communicating about your most difficult areas. Get in there and talk about them in a way you really haven't talked about them before. How can you make things genuinely different?

☐ Once you have identified problems, don't neglect the most important: switching your focus to solutions. Work together as a team—be as creative as you can be and have fun with this. Become less problem-oriented and more solution-oriented!

☐ Set goals for your relationship. Talk with each other about where it is that you would like to see the relationship go with respect to specific periods of time. Where would you like to see yourselves in a month, in six months, in a year, in five years, in ten years, ultimately? These goals can help you see what the potential truly is for your relationship.

☐ As you talk, pay special attention to the things that are standing in the way of the goals you've identified. How can you remove these barriers? Now concentrate on problem-solving together. If you can do this as a team you can get through virtually anything together you agree to work on— relationship issues, desire discrepancies, when to have sex, and so on.

Additional Barriers to Sexual Ecstasy

O
ver the course of your relationship, the path to sexual ecstasy provides many opportunities for you and your partner to draw upon your resourcefulness together as a couple. Early in your relationship, you might face the anxiety of discussing safer sex options with your partner. Some time later, a decision to have children might challenge you to find innovative ways to keep sex stimulating during pregnancy and through the many years of raising children. And as you enter your middle years and beyond, the physical changes that accompany aging can give you the impetus you need to explore new ways of experiencing sexual fulfillment.

All life changes that affect your sexual relationship call for you to learn more about each other's ever-evolving sexual makeup and to explore new ways to experience sexual ecstasy as well as all types of closeness and intimacy. They encourage you to develop new skills and experiment with the infinite variety of available sexual activities, and they provide opportunities to deepen your connection with your partner.

This chapter explores the various stages of a long-term sexual relationship, from dating to the golden years. We describe some of the issues that couples commonly encounter at each stage. Hopefully this will help you to form more realistic expectations of yourself and of each other. We also point out many of the options that are available for addressing these issues so that you can enhance and deepen the bond that is your foundation for sexual ecstasy.

Safer Sex: A Win-Win Proposition

Any discussion of safer-sex options in a long-term, monogamous relationship in which both of you are free of any sexually transmittable diseases would be fairly brief, because you're probably already experiencing sex in one of the safest settings available. In a long-term monogamous relationship in which neither partner has an STD (sexually transmitted disease), safer-sex options are rarely a concern.

The issue of safer sex usually comes up in the beginning of a relationship and can affect your sexual connection by making you hesitant to broach the topic with your partner. Bringing up the issue can suggest that you're voicing a suspicion that the other person might have engaged in high-risk sexual behavior. Of course, it's understandable that you might feel anxious about introducing a sensitive subject, but you really can't lose by broaching this subject. If you bring it up with a prospective new sex partner, and he or she becomes upset and is unwilling to consider your concern, you have learned something very important about this person, and it's a pretty good clue that you are probably on solid ground to walk away. Chances are that if you can't resolve the issue of safer sex, you probably will find little cooperation when it comes to other conflicts that might arise later. But if you can work together on this issue of safer sex, it can be the first one you've resolved together as a couple and that's a pretty good start for when you get to the point of sharing, for example, your sexual hot spots.

WEB TALK: For specific information on sexually transmitted diseases and safer sex practices, visit:

www.sexualhealth.com

Q&A

I have genital herpes, and whenever I have an outbreak, our sex life shuts down. Are there any ways we can keep having sex?

Yes, you can engage in any of several very safe and potentially very satisfying sexual activities, including hugging, massage, body-to-body rubbing (excluding parts of the body that are infected), mutual masturbation, exhibitionism and voyeurism (with consent), telephone or online sex chat, role playing, and stimulating each other using separate sex toys. Affection can also help fill the emotional and psychological needs of both you and your partner, so it's important to remain affectionate before, during, and after any outbreaks.

Be aware that herpes can spread even when no visible lesions are present, so to have safer sex, it is advisable to wear a condom for vaginal intercourse, even between outbreaks. Consult with your physician about options for clearing up any outbreaks as quickly and effectively as possible. Although herpes has no cure, several medications are available for effectively treating it.

We refer to "safe sex" as *safer sex*, because there really are very few ways of experiencing safe sex with a partner. The only way to have *absolutely guaranteed* safe sex with a partner is to share fantasies or masturbate in each other's presence without touching one another. Once any sort of body contact is involved, there is some risk, however minute, of passing viruses or bacteria. In this discussion, then, we refer to safer sex as it relates to having sexual intercourse in ways that are safer than having unprotected sex.

If you and your partner choose to engage in alternative lifestyles that involve other people, such as swinging, or you're single and dating, we strongly recommend that you do additional research to learn more about sexually transmitted diseases and available options for reducing the risks. We cannot possibly do the subject justice in one section of one chapter. Just keep in mind that you can choose to continue to experience sexual ecstasy with your partner, even while practicing safer sex, by remaining affectionate, sensual, and

WEB TALK: To learn more about preventing the spread of herpes and treating outbreaks, visit:

www.herpeshelp.com

sexual; by engaging in safer types of stimulating sexual activities; and by following any recommended precautions, in addition, of course, to the five ingredients for sexual ecstasy, when you and your partner choose to be sexual.

Making Contraception a Part of Foreplay

To experience sexual pleasure without procreation, give some thought to available contraceptive methods. A number of birth control options, including the pill and the *IUD* (*intrauterine device*), require little thought; however, other methods of birth control (including condoms, diaphragms, sponges, and spermicidal creams and gels) do require some preparation and some focus during lovemaking. Rather than letting them detract you from the process of arousal, you can choose to make your contraceptive of choice part of foreplay and thus a fun and stimulating part of lovemaking.

Condoms, for example, can function almost like sex toys. They come in a rainbow of colors and a variety of shapes and textures; some are even flavored! If you're using a condom for safer sex, be sure to use a latex condom with an appropriate spermicide. If you're using it for birth control, other types of condoms, including lambskin, are effective, especially when used with a spermicide. Condoms with ridges or dimples can help increase vaginal stimulation. To use a condom effectively, always put it on before penetration, not just before ejaculation; pre-ejaculatory fluid carries sperm as well as any virus or bacteria.

To make the condom part of foreplay, a woman might consider putting the condom on her male partner as part of a massage, or she can put it in her mouth and roll it out over his penis using her lips and tongue (avoid using your teeth, because they might puncture or tear the condom). The woman can fondle

WEB TALK: Try different types of condoms to see which work best for both of you. You can check out a wide assortment online at

➤ www.condomania.com

the testicles while putting on the condom, which can enhance the erection and make it more pleasurable for both partners. By making a condom part of your foreplay, you avoid having to stop in the middle of lovemaking to put it on. Putting it on can become a smooth and erotic transition from foreplay to intercourse. If the woman is using a diaphragm, female condom, or sponge, perhaps along with a spermicidal cream or gel, discuss with your partner ways of incorporating it as an erotic part of your lovemaking.

Birth control methods really are the responsibility of both partners, and there's no universal or pat solution for using the right one in the most erotic way, but couples who don't want to conceive can usually find ways to preserve or even enhance the pleasure for both partners. Just be sure to talk about it, so that you know what you and your partner find to be both effective and pleasurable. Then, you can not only have fun working around any limitations, but even use the novelty of contraceptives to generate some additional sexual energy!

I'm newly married and have been taking birth control pills for the last year. I have noticed that I'm not as interested in sexual activity as I was before my marriage. My husband believes that maybe now that we're married, I don't feel like I have to have sex, but it feels more to me like the urge isn't there physically. Could the birth control pills be contributing to my lack of sexual desire?

Certainly an adjustment to marriage can cause stress on your sexual relationship, but the first thing to do is talk with your gynecologist. Birth control pills have been known to decrease sexual desire in some individuals. Don't stop taking the pills, but talk to your doctor to see if you can stop for a while and try a different contraceptive method or switch to a pill that might not have the same effect. If the pill is an unlikely cause, talk with your husband about anything that might have changed in your relationship. Understand that people often do experience a lessening of passion in a long-term relationship.

Pregnancy, Child Birth, and Sexual Ecstasy

Pregnancy and childbirth, especially with a first child, can introduce dramatic changes to a long-term relationship. During a pregnancy, a woman's body and hormones are in constant flux, how she feels physically and emotionally can vary from day to day or throughout the day, and she might feel more or less sexually desirable and desirous through the course of her pregnancy. Her partner, although not experiencing the dramatic physical and physiological changes, also undergoes a transformation of sorts as he witnesses the progression of the pregnancy, realizes the shifting of priorities, and prepares himself emotionally and psychologically for his new role as a father. And once a child is born, the maintenance of the family adds another facet to the couple's relationship that demands its own time and focus.

Couples who are able to accept the changes and challenges that accompany pregnancy and children and can keep their relationship as a couple a top priority usually find that they feel more connected to one another, which is an important ingredient of sexual ecstasy. But in order to succeed, it helps to know what to expect and how to handle the changes.

Pregnancy No single rule governs pregnancy; how you will experience it, feel about it, or respond to it; or how it will affect you as a couple. So during pregnancy, it's usually helpful to approach it with no expectations, and if you experience a pleasant surprise, enjoy it.

Generally speaking, physical and hormonal changes experienced during the first trimester can cause nausea as well as decreased sexual desire for many women. During the second trimester, women typically feel better, and sometimes the increased estrogen can actually boost a woman's sex drive beyond its normal range; however, some women might still feel quite uncomfortable. During the third trimester, many women feel too physically uncomfortable to have much sexual desire, but you can still engage in enjoyable sexual activities, even involving intercourse if you choose, during this stage.

My wife is in her second trimester, and she still has no sex drive and tells me she feels nauseous during sex. Is she okay? We both miss sex, but she's really not interested and neither of us wants her to feel sick.

If your wife is physically ill during her pregnancy and you are concerned about her health or the health of the baby, consult with your wife's physician. Nausea and a loss of desire during pregnancy are very common. Simply knowing this and working through it with your wife can help you establish a deeper connection. According to Alex Robboy, M.S.W., sex therapist, and founder of howtohavegoodsex.com, "I know some women who had zero sex drive throughout their pregnancy, and every time they tried intercourse and were getting close to orgasm would throw up. With other women, their sex drives skyrocketed and they had the most orgasmic sex ever. It really varies a great deal with the individual and can even vary from one pregnancy to another.

"The advice that I would offer the husband is to acknowledge his wife as a sexual being, reminding her how beautiful she is as her body is going through these major transformations. She may not be feeling sexy or she may be feeling sexier. Be attentive to her needs, but be attentive to your own sexual needs, as well, and figure out ways to satisfy them in ways other than having intercourse. Remain receptive, and let your wife initiate sexual activity, if she so desires. Most importantly, keep an open dialogue and remain affectionate to one another."

During pregnancy, a woman's sex drive can increase, especially during the second trimester. Part of this is due to hormonal changes, but it's also the result of increased blood flow into the genital area. If both partners are on the same page with this, they can have incredible sex any time during pregnancy. In the third trimester, you and your partner will probably want to try some different positions—sometimes side-to-side or the woman on top—if you choose to continue having intercourse. If the man is concerned about hurting his partner, talk about that. In a pregnancy with no complications, there's really no reason not to have intercourse, as long as you're comfortable with it. But if you are not comfortable with intercourse, you can still engage in many other sexual activities. It's important to maintain your closeness during the pregnancy, and for the woman to consider her partner's needs as well as her own. As a couple, discuss your needs and attend to them, so that the pregnancy, and beyond, remains an overall positive experience for both of you.

The key to successfully navigating your way through a pregnancy while remaining sexually satisfied is to talk with your partner about what's going on in your body as well as changes you feel sexually, and talk with your gynecologist to make sure that there are no physical reasons to abstain from intercourse. Keep your expectations in check, too—realize that at least for this 9- to 10-month period in your life, you probably will experience changes in your sexual activity. With the right attitude and understanding, you can establish a deeper connection and perhaps even experience some of the most ecstatic sex you've ever had!

Childbirth Few things change a couple's relationship more than a first child. Partners go from being a couple to being a family. The newborn to some degree draws the attention and focus of the new parents and certainly demands some of their time and energy. The relationship often calls for a restructuring to provide for everyone's needs: those of the child, those of each partner, and those of the couple. With some innovative adjustments, most couples are able to accommodate the changes and provide themselves and each other with a suitable amount of attention, particularly when they know what to expect.

Most physicians recommend that women not have intercourse for at least four to six weeks after childbirth. But again, that doesn't mean you need to abstain from other kinds of sexual activities, including manual or oral sex, if you and your partner choose to, and it certainly doesn't mean that you should be any less loving or affectionate. If the mother has chosen to breastfeed, it's important to note the physiological effects that breastfeeding often has on desire. Women who breastfeed have high levels of the hormone prolactin, which acts as an antiandrogen (having the opposite effect of testosterone).

According to Carole Zawid, Ph.D., R.N., C.S., clinical nurse specialist and author of *Sexual Health, A Nurse's Guide,* during pregnancy, prolactin increases to 10 to 20 times the normal level and usually does not return to normal until a woman stops breastfeeding. High levels of prolactin can decrease sexual desire and arousal, sometimes leading to difficulty with lubrication and desire. This doesn't mean that a woman has fallen out of love with her man; it is a physiological change that might call for a couple to spend more time together in intimate ways to allow the woman to feel rested before she can become aroused. Talking or sharing in the care of the baby can be an additional aphrodisiac.

In addition to changes in hormones, a woman's body might take some time to repair itself from any physical trauma she may have experienced during the birth. According to Alex Robboy, some women feel wonderful six weeks after giving birth—everything is back to normal, everything is great. But others might actually experience some nerve damage in the vaginal canal, which can be painful. It can take up to 8 months to return to normal. Even if you experience no nerve damage, the pregnancy and birth can push things around inside, but don't be afraid of trying to have intercourse; take it slowly and gradually and be prudent at first. You might not feel as tight as you used to be; the body takes a while to shrink back to its normal size. Doing the Kegel exercises will almost certainly help.

As the woman's body returns to normal and as both of you adjust to a new child, give yourselves time as individuals and as a couple to transition into your new situation. Ask a friend or family member to take your baby every once in a while for a couple of hours or an evening, in order for you to spend some time at home by yourself, to have a date together, or even just to have sex with no likely disturbances. This gives you some time—without the baby in sight or in hearing range—to relax and unwind, to find your center, to return to your relationship, or to have sex without having to worry that the baby might need something. Work out a deal with your partner so that each of you can spend some time alone without the baby around. During this time, really take care of yourself—and make sure you give yourself whatever you may need to bypass burnout and exhaustion. Let yourself have time to relax and feel pleasure, so you can return to your partner and your child feeling more relaxed and refreshed. If you haven't set up date night yet, this is a good time to start. Keep up a continuing dialog with your partner on a frequent and regular basis to make sure your needs are being attended to and that your sexual relationship stays on at least one of the front burners!

Addressing Midlife Issues and Beyond

Few would dispute that as people age, they experience physical changes that affect their sex drive and their sensitivity to pleasure. But that doesn't mean that sexual ecstasy needs to be any more elusive as you get older. Most people can still achieve sexual satisfaction at any age if they remain optimistic and incorporate the ingredients of sexual ecstasy into their lovemaking. It also helps

you're not alone

Lauren (age 22) and Kyle (age 23) were six months past the birth of their first child and had not yet engaged in sexual activity again. Both of them were working, and their lives had become very hectic. Lauren had returned to work three months after the child's birth and was still breastfeeding and felt tired and somewhat guilty about having gone back to work so soon. Kyle felt ignored and was beginning

to think that once the baby came, Lauren was no longer interested in him; he was getting pretty angry about it. He was attracted to another woman at work, and although he hadn't acted on it, he did tell Lauren that he was interested in someone else and that he didn't think that Lauren loved him anymore.

In therapy, Kyle and Lauren began to learn about the changes that

most couples experience when they have their first child and they saw a lot of similarities to their own situation. They began to see that neither of them really had known what sorts of changes to expect with a pregnancy and birth, so when the changes happened, they didn't know what was going on. They learned that they needed to make adjustments to keep sex an important part of their relationship. Lauren to know about the physiological changes you're likely to experience as you get older, so you can be less concerned with recapturing the sexual feelings of youth and be more aware of the deep connection and unique sexual feelings that many couples begin to experience in midlife and beyond.

> **GET PSYCHED**
>
> It is not how old you are, but how you are old.
> –*Marie Dressler*

As people age, desire levels may begin to taper off and sex can start to feel less spontaneous. Men frequently have weaker erections, and women commonly experience less desire, arousal, and lubrication. The age at which these changes occur varies from person to person; sometimes they start in a person's 30s, but usually in their 40s or 50s. Once changes do begin, decreases in desire and arousal typically continue as people get older. It's important for couples to realize that desire may decrease with age and is not a sign that one has lost interest in sex or in one's partner or loves him or her any less; physiological changes normally result in decreased desire and arousal that can often be overcome by spending more time getting turned on.

asked Kyle for help around the house, and he agreed to come home a little earlier from work to care for the child, so that she could take a bath after work and relax after a long day. They also learned that while Lauren was breastfeeding she probably had a normal dip in sexual desire because of the elevated levels of prolactin, not because she loved Kyle any less or found him less attractive. This meant both of them needed to focus more on helping Lauren become aroused.

Kyle and Lauren agreed to set aside time for each other, particularly on the weekends when the baby napped, to do relaxing, sensual massage, which Lauren really enjoyed. They also decided to do massage a couple times during the week. Eventually, Lauren found that once a week or so, she would get really turned on during a massage and feel like having sex. The couple also started to go to bed a little earlier and began to feel more rested during the week. They added one date night a week to help them connect as a couple, and over time, they began engaging in sexual activities once or twice a week that they both found very satisfying.

The National Health and Social Life Survey found that for women, the prevalence of sexual problems tends to decrease with increasing age except for those who report trouble lubricating. For men, increasing age is positively correlated with the experience of erectile problems and the lack of desire for sex. The good news for men is that erectile dysfunction which becomes more prevalent with age responds well to good medical and psychological interventions.

Sandra Leiblum, Ph.D. sex researcher, co-author of *Getting the Sex You Want: A Woman's Guide to Becoming Proud, Passionate, and Pleased in Bed*, adds, "The re-conceptualization of the female sexual response cycle is very important. Even though women might feel less initial desire after menopause, delaying sex until you feel desire can be a mistake. Arousal often precedes desire, and you have to be willing to go into a sexual experience not feeling anything other than a kind of openness to see what happens. Being receptive and willing to see where it takes you can often, with adequate stimulation, lead to arousal and then desire."

Masters and Johnson, as well as other experts in the field, have studied and documented many of the physiological changes that both men and women experience as they age. One of the major changes is the decrease in testosterone levels in both men and women. Testosterone is the hormone that triggers sex drive—the physical urge to have sex. You don't need great amounts of it, but without enough to create a spark, your sex drive might never get started. A decrease in testosterone can cause a man to take longer to become aroused, to get erections, and to reach orgasm; it can weaken the ejaculatory response; and it can increase the refractory period (the time it takes a man to be able to orgasm again). Likewise, low levels of testosterone in women can lead to decreased desire and arousal and can make it take longer for a woman to reach orgasm. Decreases in estrogen can also decrease lubrication and cause physical changes to the vagina that might decrease sensation and sometimes lead to uncomfortable or painful intercourse.

If you begin to notice that your sex drive is diminished or that arousal takes longer, and sensation has changed, and you suspect that it might be related to your age, consider consulting a gynecologist or urologist who specializes in sexual health. A concerned and qualified specialist will be able to help identify specific causes and explain your options to you. Fortunately, this is an era in which many very effective treatment options are available to help both men and women remove any physical barriers to sexual ecstasy. We describe several of the treatments available later in the chapter, but more effective treatments are constantly being developed.

Dr. Gina Ogden's research on spirituality has found that as people age, there seems to be a greater occurrence of experiencing a spiritual component during sexual activity. One of the major findings of Ogden's survey was that sexual and spiritual experience become more integrated as respondents grow older. For instance, when asked: "Have you ever experienced God in a moment of sexual ecstasy?" 58 percent of the respondents 60 and older answered "Yes," as compared with only 23 percent of respondents 30 and under. Another major finding was that integrating sexual and spiritual experience contributes to the overall personal and relational health of respondents—that is, acceptance and love, oneness with one's partner, intense inner vitality, energy, and security as distinct from boredom, deception, and distance. Moreover, the survey letters provide a compelling body of evidence that late-life sexual relationships involve much more than physical performance. This narrative material reveals that eroticism is embedded in the totality of relationship—with self, with partner, and even with divine presence.

The survey responses reflect more gender convergences than differences. Both men and women indicate similar

GET PSYCHED

Be sexual now! Studies show that people who were more sexually active and really enjoyed sex in their younger years enjoy it more when they get older, too. So start investing now for those retirement years!

convictions that the essential ingredients of spiritual sex are love (almost 90 percent), commitment (about 65 percent), and safety (about 65 percent). Sharing deep feelings (more than 80 percent) is far and away the most important contributor to spiritual sex for both men and women.

So, though the experience of sexual ecstasy might be different, it needn't be any less intense or less ecstatic. By knowing that the experience of sexual ecstasy changes throughout the course of the relationship, you can begin to shed any expectations that it's supposed to be like it was in your youth (or any other time), and begin to appreciate it more for what it really is at this stage of your life. And once you know that, begin to experiment with other ways of having sex that you might find even more enjoyable than anything you may have previously experienced. Midlife and beyond is a time when couples can grow closer—when you have a little more free time and perhaps feel less inhibited. You need more time to become aroused, and chances are that you have more time, so enjoy!

Addressing Medical Problems

In this era of modern medicine, rarely can a disease, in and of itself, prevent you from being sexually active at all. A disease properly treated and followed up by your and your partner's commitment to restoring sexual satisfaction to your relationship usually enables you to attain some degree of sexual satisfaction in some form. If you believe that you're too weak or unable to have sex due to an illness, that can become a self-fulfilling prophecy. Instead of focusing on the problem, focus on the solution, and instead of focusing on what you can't do, focus on what you can do. Make this shift in attitude and you can almost always find ways to have very satisfying sex.

Any of several diseases can lead to a temporary cessation of sex, and the treatments for some conditions can also affect your sexual activity and the way you experience sex. Here are descriptions of some of the illnesses that can commonly change the way couples might approach sex, at least temporarily:

- Heart disease can limit sexual activity and perhaps even intercourse, but with proper treatment, most people find it possible, and even quite healthy, to return to their normal sexual activities.

- Cancer, both the depression and anxiety following diagnosis and some treatments for it, can lead to a general loss of interest in sex. For women, breast cancer or uterine cancer can change how they feel about their bodies. Men who have prostate problems or testicular cancer might experience some erectile difficulty, as well.

- Diabetes typically causes difficulties by limiting blood flow to the genitals or by causing neurological damage that can lead to a loss of sensation.

- Arthritis and illnesses like it can cause pain, stiffness, and limitation of movement, and can have negative effects on your self-esteem and body image. In many cases, it helps to schedule sex for a time when you're feeling more comfortable and then try different positions.

- Alcoholism often causes a temporary decrease in sensation and can even lead to neuropathy (neurological damage), which can affect arousal in both men and women, as well as erectile difficulties and the inability to ejaculate in men.

- Depression is a psychological or medical illness that can occur any time in a person's life and lead to a lessening of sex drive. This is usually related to a loss of interest in life and in most of life's activities, including sex. Unfortunately, some (but not all) of the medications that can treat depression, such as SSRI antidepressants, can also cause sexual difficulties as side effects.

Affection, love, and sex can often help lift depression.

WEB TALK: For more information on how to overcome sexual difficulties related to illness, visit:

www.sexualhealth.com

If you have an illness that diminishes your ability to enjoy sex, such as a heart attack, stroke, cancer, diabetes, or depression, talk with your doctor about what your options are and perhaps do some research on your own. Discuss your condition with your partner. Then, you can begin to work together as a team to figure out ways you can both enjoy being sexual together. If your doctor recommends that you abstain from any forms of strenuous activity, including sex, for a period of time, remain affectionate and never lose sight of your connection as a couple. It's not at all unusual that after a serious illness, such as a heart attack, a couple's sex life is reinvigorated by the realization of how valuable they really are to one another.

you're not alone

Herb and Janet, retired teachers in their mid 60s, had begun experiencing sexual problems. Herb was beginning to feel arthritis pain in his hips, which made sex so painful at times that he would lose his erection. This had been going on for about a year, and within that time the couple had completely stopped being sexual. Herb discussed his situation with his urologist, who recommended that Herb see a sex therapist before trying any medications, such as Viagra.

By the time the couple sought therapy, the problem was not only that Herb felt arthritis pain, but that he had become embarrassed and frustrated about his inability to obtain and maintain his erection. He then started to become less affectionate. Although Janet understood what was going on, she still felt some hurt and anger, because she missed the affection as much as the sex.

In therapy, they learned that at this stage in their lives, arthritis pain and other health-related issues could have a real impact on their sex life. The therapist recommended that they try different positions that might be less painful for Herb, as well as that they consider experimenting with oral stimulation, which neither of them had tried before. They were a little reluctant at first, but they soon began to feel more comfortable about trying some new things. They tested several positions and found a few that were comfortable for Herb and that Janet really enjoyed, and they learned ways of performing oral sex that were acceptable, as well as pleasurable, to both of them. They also found that having sexual contact in the morning or early afternoon made it easier for Herb to become aroused. Soon Herb began having erections again.

Medications, Herbs, and Other Aids

No magic sex pill or other aphrodisiac is guaranteed to turn you on and lead to ecstatic intercourse. However, medications and herbs can help remove some of the physiological barriers to sexual satisfaction and make it easier to bring ecstatic sex back into your relationship.

For both men and women, if testosterone levels are low, increasing testosterone to a level at which it can trigger desire and arousal can help. Ask your doctor to run a blood test to check the level of testosterone in your system. If you have low testosterone, have your doctor explain the benefits and possible side effects of testosterone replacement therapy. Testosterone patches and creams can make it convenient and painless to increase testosterone levels. DHEA—an over-the-counter supplement that can, once ingested, become converted into testosterone and estrogen—has been reported by some people to help, but some doctors caution about potentially dangerous side effects, and the quality of these supplements can vary greatly—so do some research. But remember, before you try testosterone replacement therapy or start taking DHEA, consult your physician and have your testosterone levels tested; if you already have adequate testosterone, any decrease in desire or arousal can probably be traced to some other cause.

In women, both estrogen and testosterone levels can affect sexual desire, arousal, and sensation. Some women have found that applying testosterone cream to the genitals increases sensation. For years, doctors have prescribed hormone replacement therapy (HRT) for women in menopause and post-menopause, but with the controversy now surrounding the effectiveness and possible negative impact of long-term use of HRT, doctors are becoming more cautious about recommending it. Estrogen creams, as well as Vagifem and the Estrace ring, have proven to be effective in treating vaginal dryness and pain associated with estrogen loss. Consult your doctor and do some research on your own to fully understand the options, benefits, and risks associated with their use.

Q&A

What do women and their partners need to know about sex and menopause to maintain a healthy sex life?

"Menopause is a physiological process that changes a woman's hormone levels and affects sexuality in a few ways. For many women, sex becomes uncomfortable and they might not be getting adequate lubrication. The vaginal lining is thinner and they can experience discomfort.

"Our advice for women is to use a water-soluble lubricant every single time—don't wait to figure out whether you're wet enough. If you're wondering whether you're wet enough or whether you're too dry, this can take away from your enjoyment in the moment; use a lubricant every time so you don't have to think about it. If you're experiencing pain and discomfort, talk with your doctor to find out if using some form of estrogen, vaginally, will help you.

"If you notice a significant decrease in your libido—maybe you were fantasizing fairly often and are no longer fantasizing—ask your doctor if you could possibly benefit from using a testosterone cream.

"Finally, it is important for the woman's partner to understand these changes, not blame himself or his partner." *—Lonnie Barbach, Ph.D., sex therapist, and author of* The Pause, Positive Approaches to Perimenopause and Menopause

PDE-5 inhibitors such as Viagra have also been reported by many men with erectile dysfunction to help with obtaining and maintaining their erections. However, some studies question the real effectiveness of PDE-5 inhibitors and suggest that much of their success is due to a placebo effect. It's interesting to note that about half the men who try PDE-5 inhibitors do not refill their prescriptions, possibly because the drug didn't work, the men regained their self-confidence, or they began having erections but their partners were not interested. Some clinicians have reported using Viagra with some success to help increase arousal in post-menopausal women and women who are experiencing a loss of arousal linked to other medications they are taking. However, formal studies of the effects of Viagra on women do not provide conclusive evidence that Viagra is any more effective for women than a placebo.

Q&A

What do men and their partners need to know about erectile dysfunction to maintain a healthy sex life?

"The PDE-5 inhibitors, including Viagra, can benefit men not only by helping them maintain their erections but also by helping them to regain some of the self-confidence they may have lost related to their erectile difficulties.

"However, having erections alone may not be enough to restore sexual functioning to a relationship. Many couples seek help after they have been without sex for years, and they have built up some barriers that can be difficult to remove." *—Stanley Althof, Ph.D., sex researcher and professor, Department of Psychology, Case Western Reserve University*

Some men and women have also found that an amino acid called L'Arginine can have similar effects to Viagra. L'Arginine increases nitric oxide in the bloodstream to promote better blood flow and perhaps even help lower blood pressure. Some women have found that using L'Arginine cream on the clitoris leads to an increase in sensation. VasoFem is a medication that contains phentolamine, which works to increase blood flow to the genitals. Again, the potential long-term side effects of these supplements are not yet fully known and there are no large-scale, well-designed studies that prove their effectiveness, but some people have found them helpful.

In some small studies, a few herbs including ginseng, kava kava, ginkgo biloba, and especially yohimbine have shown promise in helping alleviate some sexual dysfunctions. Yohimbine is the only such herb that has had any major research studies done on it. Obtained from the African yohimbine tree, this herb is reputed to be an age-old remedy for erectile problems, and research has shown that it can have a mildly positive effect on some individuals who suffer from erectile dysfunction. But again, yohimbine can have some unpleasant side effects, including sweating, agitation, hypertension, and sleeplessness. Yohimbine can increase blood flow, so it is contraindicated for certain cardiovascular and neurological conditions or for use with certain medications. It has sometimes been used to counteract the negative sexual side effects of some antidepressants, but consult your physician before adding this to your regimen.

Ginkgo biloba is another herb that some people have found to help with desire and arousal. It has also been used to treat peripheral vascular disease as well as to enhance cerebral blood flow. Some researchers suspect that it increases blood flow into the genitals, as well, which can help with mild sexual dysfunction. Ginkgo biloba has sometimes been used to counteract the effects of other medications, such as antidepressants. Ginseng, another Chinese medicine, has also been reported to increase libido and arousal in some individuals. Of course, any of these herbs, just as any medicine, can have negative side effects, so before you try an herbal remedy, check with your doctor and do your own research.

Some devices are available that are designed to stimulate the genitals and increase sensation. Most of these devices might serve as fun and stimulating sex toys, but their effectiveness in increasing sensation, creating erections, or increasing penis size is highly questionable. Pumps for increasing penis size might provide you with a temporary erection, but don't expect any permanent change in size or in your ability to obtain and maintain erections. Vacuums for pulling blood into the clitoris and labia can help during foreplay, but they probably won't make any long-term changes to a woman's desire level or ability to become aroused. One exception seems to be the EROS-CTD (Clitoral Therapy Device), which was developed by UroMetrics. This device is placed over the clitoris and surrounding tissue and provides general suction that the woman controls. Although it is not a vibrator, it can cause orgasm to occur for some women. Its purpose is to enhance arousal and engorgement in the clitoris and the labia by pulling blood into the area. Some believe that the increased blood flow can help prevent fibrosis of the clitoral and the labial arteries, which commonly occur with aging and menopause.

Although many medicines can help enhance a person's libido and arousal, many more can have a negative effect on desire.

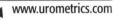

Antidepressants, which have helped many people overcome debilitating depression, can reduce libido and cause difficulty both in arousal and in orgasms for some individuals who take them. Antihistamines, sleeping pills, and other over-the-counter medications can reduce libido and also lessen the frequency and intensity of orgasms. Blood pressure medications, and even diuretics, can affect sexual functioning, particularly arousal. Even antibiotics and oral contraceptives can sometimes diminish a person's sex drive.

WEB TALK: For more information about the EROS-CTD and other medical products for supporting sexual and reproductive health visit: **www.urometrics.com**

If you begin taking a medication or herb and you notice a downturn in sexual activity and feeling, consult your physician. Don't suddenly stop taking a medication that your doctor has prescribed. Sometimes your doctor can switch the medication or add a medication or herb to lessen any negative side effects, or you might be able to switch the timing of the medication to correspond better with the time that you and your partner usually engage in sexual activity. Sometimes simply taking the medication after sex rather than just before bedtime can help.

The search for the perfect aphrodisiac continues, but don't expect a quick fix anytime soon. In the meantime, many medications out there can help remove or lessen the effects of any physiological obstacles to your sexual ecstasy.

Remember that the best aphrodisiacs are the ones you already have: love, fantasy, your connection with your partner, and the never-ending variety of sexual activities that you can choose to explore together. No medication, supplement, herb, or device can, by itself, create an overwhelming desire for your partner. Some can help, however, when your minds are in sync, but your bodies can use some tweaking. So play together and incorporate the five ingredients of sexual ecstasy into your lovemaking to whatever degree is possible, along with as many of the other secrets we have provided you, and then simply let sexual ecstasy happen for both you and your partner.

What You Can Do

As your relationship matures, it passes through normal developmental stages, each of which has its own unique challenges. If you experience any of the issues discussed in this chapter, here are a few actions you can take to continue experiencing sexual ecstasy with your partner:

☐ Talk with your partner about how you can work together to get around, through, over, or past whatever issue you're facing. Think of ways that can turn what might appear as a negative into a positive addition to your sexual activity and enjoyment.

☐ Keep in mind that working together to resolve an issue strengthens the connection between the two of you that is such an important component of sexual ecstasy.

☐ Research any issue you might be facing, whether it relates to safer sex, pregnancy, childbirth and child rearing, aging, or disease. Learn about any causes, any potential effects it might have on your sexuality, and any options that might improve the situation.

☐ Thoroughly discuss with your physician the sexual aspects of any health condition you might have or changes you have experienced in relation to sexual desire or arousal. If your doctor is not responsive or is unable to provide satisfactory advice or treatment, find another doctor, specialist, or therapist who is more sensitive, responsive, and knowledgeable. Obtain as many opinions as you need until you know that you're getting the most current information and options.

☐ Try something new from the suggestions we provided in this chapter as well as in the other chapters in this book.

☐ Connect with your partner to discuss additional ways that can make your lovemaking even more ecstatic. This is a lifelong process!

Even Sexual Ecstasy Can Become Boring, if You Let It!

Our lives are a work in process. You, your partner, and your relationship will continue to change over time, and that's a good thing! Change is what life is all about. It constantly challenges us to become more than what we are in every aspect of our lives. You and your partner have the potential to change and grow together perhaps to heights never before imagined! So, we urge you to honor your growth together and to use the skills and knowledge you have acquired throughout this book to expand your experience of sexual ecstasy and to deepen the connection that will make sexual ecstasy a stronger and stronger part of your relationship.

We have given you the tools needed for you and your partner to continue to design your path to sexual ecstasy. However, if for some reason sexual ecstasy begins to elude you, we urge you to review the five ingredients to see why:

- Do you need to give yourself more permission to allow your experience of sexual ecstasy to expand?
- Have you let the present moment slip away during lovemaking?
- We've given you many ways to connect with your partner. Have you let that connection begin to wane?
- Have you let your sensual side go?
- Have you been neglecting the lustful side of things? Is some novelty and newness in order?

If you and your partner can earnestly ask yourselves and each other those questions, chances are that the answers will become obvious. If you have experienced sexual ecstasy as the result of working and playing together to achieve it, you have learned some great secrets. We wish you nothing less than a lifetime of ecstatic experiences together. Keep it fresh and keep your connection alive and exciting. Remember how counter to ecstasy both expectations and sameness can be, and to remind each other to focus on connection and pleasure, not performance. Should one of you lose this perspective every once in a while, simply give that gentle reminder.

Using This Book as a Life-Long Resource

Most importantly, remember that the door is always open to come back and visit this book again any time one of you feels the desire. You might just find that something that didn't apply to you three months or two years ago is quite relevant now. It's never too late to try something new, and it's always too early to give up the journey.

We wish you much happiness, fulfillment, joy, and ecstasy in your life together!

Glossary

anorgasmic   The condition of being unable to reach orgasm. Women can be preorgasmic—never having had an orgasm—or secondary anorgasmic—able to experience orgasms through masturbation or other forms of stimulation, but rarely, if ever, with a partner.

aphrodisiac   A substance that increases or excites sexual desire. The word comes from the Greek, *aphrodisiakos*, which means sexual pleasure.

arousal   The physical reaction one experiences as a result of being turned on. Arousal is often accompanied by erection in the man and lubrication and swelling of the genital tissues in a woman, along with other physiological responses throughout the entire body.

attitude   An organized and enduring set of beliefs and feelings toward an object, person, or situation. Attitudes predispose people to the way they behave towards something or someone. Approaching sex with a less inhibited attitude is important for experiencing sexual ecstasy.

audiotherapy   A form of self help or a supplement to psychotherapy in which carefully selected resources recorded on CDs or audiotapes are used therapeutically to assist a client in learning about and resolving an issue. *See also* bibliotherapy.

bibliotherapy   A form of self-help or a supplement to psychotherapy in which carefully selected reading materials are used therapeutically to assist a client in learning about and resolving an issue. *See also* audiotherapy.

body image   A sense of how one feels about his or her own body.

bondage and discipline (B&D)   A sexual practice in which a person restrains or pretends to restrain or overpower his or her partner in some way. Bondage relates to restraining the partner. Discipline refers to power control—domination and submission.

climax   Another word for orgasm. *See* orgasm.

clitoris   An erectile organ of the female anatomy that has only one known function—to experience sexual sensation and erotic pleasure. The clitoris is made up of three parts: the clitoral gland, which is the tip or head and is the only visible part, resembling a small button; the clitoral hood, the fold of skin covering the clitoral shaft, sometimes referred to as the female foreskin; and the clitoral shaft, part of the external female genitalia, consisting of two small erectile bodies enclosed in a fibrous membrane and ending with the gland.

communication   An exchange of information verbally or nonverbally.

coronal ridge   The rim around the head of a penis that many men find particularly sensitive.

crunches   Day-to-day necessities and annoyances that can get in the way of a couple's ability to experience good sex, including time constraints, fatigue, and children.

cunnilingus   Oral sex performed on a woman. *See also* oral sex.

desire   An interest, drive, or craving to engage in sexual activity.

dyspareunia   *See* painful intercourse.

ejaculation   The reflex discharge of seminal fluid, including semen from the penis during the orgasm phase of the response.

empathy   Understanding how another person feels.

erectile dysfunction (ED)   Often referred to as impotence, a man's inability to obtain or maintain an erection. Global ED is characterized by an inability to have an erection under any condition. Situational ED is an inability to become erect during a specific sexual activity. Primary ED means never having had erections; secondary ED means not having erections after a period of time.

estrogen   A hormone present in both sexes but more so in the female that is produced in the ovaries and adrenal gland and is necessary for maintaining a healthy lining of the vagina.

expectation   An idea of how something will happen or how it will be or feel. Unrealistic expectations can often lead to disappointment.

fantasy   A mental image or scene. Sexual fantasies are usually pleasurable images of a sexual scene at its best. *See* scripted fantasy and sensory-type fantasy.

fantasy rehearsal   An exercise in which partners create a fantasy together, each taking turns to narrate the fantasy and contribute details. Partners can perform this exercise in each other's presence, over the phone, or using Internet chat.

fellatio   Oral sex performed on a man. *See also* oral sex.

fetish   An attraction to and need for an inanimate object or a part of the body that serves as the focus of sexual arousal.

G spot   *See* Graffenberg spot.

Graffenberg spot   Commonly known as the G spot, a structure said to lie on the front wall of the vagina that is reported to be an area of sexual pleasure and possibly female ejaculation when stimulated.

homeplay   Exercises for practicing and improving your sex life that are more fun than work. Just about everything related to improving one's sex life can be fun.

impotence   *See* erectile dysfunction.

inhibited sexual desire   The suppression of normal sexual desire in an intimate relationship. ISD can be categorized as global (not desiring sex in any form with anyone or even by yourself) or situational (not desiring sex in any form with one's partner). In order to be considered a dysfunction, it must cause distress in either the individual or the relationship.

initial passion   The infatuation and biological attraction a person often feels for a new partner early in a relationship.

intimacy   A feeling of closeness and acceptance that comes from knowing the other person, including knowing what the other person thinks and feels.

introject   To completely adopt a belief or value in its entirety without examining or questioning it.

Kama Sutra   A sex manual developed in India, circa the fourth or third century B.C.E., that presents sex as a way to attain greater spiritual fulfillment. (This book has legs; it is still popular today!)

labia   The outer two folds of skin on either side of the inner lips of the clitoris and the urethra and vaginal openings.

labia minora   The two inner folds of skin covering the urethra and vaginal openings.

long-term relationship   A connection between two individuals who are romantically or sexually involved, that involves some sense of commitment to continue indefinitely or at least past the point of initial passion.

lust   Intense sexual desire or need.

masturbation   The act of sexually pleasuring oneself.

ménage à trois   A sexual activity in which three people are involved in pleasuring one another at the same time.

menopause   The period of natural cessation of menstruation, which usually occurs between the mid 40s to 50s. It involves the natural decline in female sex hormones. *See also* estrogen, menstruation, perimenopause, postmenopause, and testosterone.

menstruation   The flow of blood from the lining of the uterus in women. It generally occurs once a month from puberty to the onset of menopause. *See also* menopause.

mons pubis   The mound of fatty tissue over the female pubic bone, which is covered with pubic hair.

myth   An ill–founded belief.

oral sex   A sexual activity that consists of using one or more parts of the mouth to stimulate the partner's genitals. *See also* cunnilingus, fellatio, and sixty-nine position.

orgasm   A total body response, which involves intense sensation during the peak of sexual arousal and the discharge of accumulated sexual tension.

orgasmic disorder A woman's inability to climax with one's partner or through other forms of sexual stimulation. *See also* anorgasmic and preorgasmic.

painful intercourse Also known as dyspareunia, any sexual activity in which penetration causes pain. This condition is far more prevalent in women but can affect men as well.

PDE-5 inhibitor A medication that is commonly used to treat erectile dysfunction in men. PDE-5 inhibitors do not trigger erections—sexual stimulation of some form must be present for the penis to become erect—but it allows the erection to stay. The first and most famous of the PDE-5 inhibitors is Viagra.

penis The male sex organ, which consists primarily of three cylinders, spongy tissue, and many thin-walled blood vessels. It is the male organ of copulation as well as urination.

performance anxiety Any concern that one might not be able to perform sexually at a given level of expectation.

perimenopause A period 8 to 10 years before menopause when many women begin to experience some of the changes related to menopause. *See also* menopause.

perineum The hairless area of skin between the vagina and the anus in the female and between the scrotum and the anus in the male, which, when stimulated, can produce pleasurable sensations.

pheromone A chemical that a creature can emit to influence the behavior or development of others of the same species. Pheromones often serve to attract members of the opposite sex.

pleasure anxiety Self-consciousness or guilt about feeling sexual pleasure that prevents one from fully experiencing pleasurable sensations or sexual fulfillment.

postmenopause The years that follow menopause, during which women typically experience a lessening of symptoms, such as hot flashes, that are associated with menopause.

premature ejaculation Sometimes called rapid ejaculation, the inability to exercise conscious or voluntary control over the timing of one's ejaculation. It's not considered a problem unless it interferes with the sexual satisfaction of one or both partners.

preorgasmic The condition of never having experienced a noticeable orgasm. It must cause distress in either the individual or the relationship in order to be considered problematic.

prostate gland A part of the male anatomy that surrounds the urethra at the base of the bladder, controls the release of urine, and secretes a fluid, which is a major constituent of semen. Many men find stimulation of the prostate gland to be very sexually arousing, but others might find it uncomfortable or even painful. The prostate gland is sometimes referred to as the male G spot.

psychopathology The study of psychological and behavioral disorders.

psychotherapy The treatment of psychological issues using a variety of techniques designed to clarify conflicts, foster insight into problems; change beliefs, attitudes and behavior; resolve emotional conflicts; and enhance personal development.

pubococcygeal muscle Also referred to as the P.C. muscle, this is a pelvic muscle present in both men and women that can often contribute to making sex more pleasurable. In women, the pubococcygeal muscle surrounds the vaginal opening and is the main muscle that contracts during orgasm.

reframe To adjust your perspective in order to view your reality in a different way. People can often improve their attitudes about themselves, others, their situations, or their beliefs and values through reframing.

retarded ejaculation An inability to ejaculate for an inordinate amount of time or at all once obtaining an erection.

sadomasochism (S&M) Sexual practices in which a person inflicts pain on another person (sadism) or receives pain (masochism) for erotic purposes.

safer sex Any sexual activity that poses less of a risk to the physical well-being of you and your partner.

scripted fantasy Pleasurable scenarios that play out in one's mind, like plots in a book or movie.

scrotum The loose sac of skin that holds the testes and contains a layer of muscle fiber.

self talk   The internal thoughts and dialogue, positive or negative, that play in one's mind.

sensate focus   A series of massage-like exercises, originally designed by Masters and Johnson to teach nonverbal communication skills and reduce anxiety.

sensory-type fantasy   Pleasurable mental images, pictures, or sensations.

sex drive   A biological impulse to engage in sex.

sexologist   A professional in the field of sexuality. *See also* sexuality.

sexual arousal disorder   A persistent or recurring inability for a woman to obtain adequate lubrication of the genitals or experience physiological changes associated with arousal, including swelling of the genital tissues, increased clitoral or labia sensation, or increased nipple sensitivity.

sexual aversion   A phobic response to engaging in sexual activity.

sexual desire discrepancy   A situation in which one person in a relationship wants sex significantly more than the other person *and* it interferes with the ability for one or both partners to feel sexually satisfied.

sexual dysfunction   The condition in which the ordinary physical responses of sexual arousal or orgasms are impaired, for either psychological or physical reasons. To be considered a dysfunction, the condition must cause distress in either the individual or the relationship.

sexual response cycle   A model that describes how a person responds and feels leading up to, during, and after sexual activity.

sexuality   A general term that encompasses the various aspects of being and feeling sexual.

short-term relationship   A connection between two individuals who are romantically or sexually involved that is usually fueled by initial passion.

sixty-nine (69) position   The position assumed by a couple when performing oral sex simultaneously on one another.

spectatoring   The process of evaluating yourself and your performance during sexual activity, usually negatively.

swinging   An alternative lifestyle in which two or more couples agree to trade partners, allow each other to seek out other partners for sex, or have group sex together. It can include ménages à trois.

Tantra   A mystical approach to understanding and experiencing the universe through meditation. Tantric sex encourages couples to establish a more spiritual connection during lovemaking by incorporating eye contact and meditative breathing into their lovemaking and by viewing each other as physical forms of divinity.

testes   The male gonads—sex glands that are responsible for the production of sperm and certain male hormones.

testosterone   A hormone in men and women that needs to be present to some degree for the person to experience sex drive.

thought-stopping   A technique in which a person chooses to end a negative or disturbing thought or replace it with a positive, pleasurable one. Thought-stopping is effective for blocking out thoughts and feelings that produce such things as anger, guilt, jealousy, and spectatoring.

trust   A sense that one can be open to freely express thoughts and feelings without the fear of any sort of negative consequences.

unprotected sex   Engaging in any sexual activity that involves the exchange of bodily fluids without taking any precautions to avoid transferring a bacteria or virus.

urethra   The tube from the urinary bladder to the exterior of the body that carries urine in females and urine and semen in males.

vagina   The hollow muscular internal organ in the female, situated between the urinary bladder and the rectum that receives the penis during intercourse, becomes part of the birth canal, and is capable of expansion and contraction.

vaginal introitus   The opening of the vagina.

vaginismus   A female sexual dysfunction in which the vagina experiences involuntary spasms, which prevents penetration.

visceral empathy   Understanding what feels or might feel physically pleasurable to one's partner.

vulva   External genitals of the female.

Additional Sources of Help

Many excellent resources are available to help you in your quest for sexual ecstasy. Here, we describe some of the resources that we have found to be most helpful and show you where to find them on the web.

Tips on Professional Consultations

There are several ways to find a therapist who specializes either in the area of couples or sex therapy: The best is through word of mouth by someone you know who has successfully been helped by that person and was satisfied with his or her services. The second, particularly in the area of sexuality, would be from another mental health professional, a physician, gynecologist, urologist, or other helping professional. The third-best source is referral from a professional organization that verifies credentials and lists its members by specialty, a number of which are described below:

Albert Ellis Institute

www.rebt.org

The Albert Ellis Institute has an excellent international referral list of mental health professionals trained in Rational Emotive Behavior Therapy (REBT), which is an extremely effective short-term, results-oriented, cognitive behavioral approach to relationship and sexuality issues, anxiety, depression, anger, and all matters concerning life change. The Institute offers a comprehensive free catalogue of workshops and seminars, books, audio and video programs, and other self-help materials. Contact the Albert Ellis Institute in New York (45 East 65th Street, New York, NY 10021, 212-535-0822 or 800-323-4738) or visit its website for more information or to locate a center near you.

The American Association for Marriage and Family Therapy

www.therapistlocator.net

This website offers a search tool for helping visitors find marital and family therapists in the United States, Canada, and overseas. It also features a collection of helpful articles. Visit the website or call 703-838-9808 for more information.

The American Association of Sex Educators, Counselors and Therapists (AASECT)

www.aasect.org

AASECT's website features a therapist locator as well as a list of frequently asked questions about human sexuality, links to other sites, and information about how to become a certified sex educator, counselor, or therapist. Visit the website or call 800-644-3288 for more information.

American Board of Sexology

www.sexologist.org

Provides a list of certified sex therapists as well as information about the history of sexology and research in the field.

The American Psychological Association (APA) Help Center

www.helping.apa.org

APA's help center provides advice to help you decide when to seek help, explanations of what psychologists and therapists can do to help you, and a search tool for finding a certified or licensed practitioner in your area. For more general information about psychology, check out APA's home page at www.apa.org.

Psychology Today

www.psychologytoday.com

Find a therapist on *Psychology Today's* online Therapy Directory. Choose from thousands of profiles in your area. See specialties, profiles, prices, and other information. Obtain help determining which therapist is best for you.

Helpful Information and Approaches from Other Experts

A number of professionals do intensive workshops, coaching, and talks to the public in the area of couples and sex therapy. Here are some of the best websites that we have mentioned in this book:

DivorceBusting.com

www.divorcebusting.com

Michele Weiner-Davis, M.S.W., provides information, coaching, quizzes, and articles on relationships. At Michele's online store, you can order CDs and videos and learn how to obtain counseling over the phone.

Gottman Institute

www.gottman.com

The Gottman Institute offers weekend and week-long workshops for couples. The website includes quizzes and tips on relationships and an online store where you can shop for books, audiocassettes, videos, and other helpful products.

HealthySex.com

www.healthysex.com

Wendy Maltz, M.S.W., offers information and articles about healthy sexuality, sexual fantasies, midlife sexuality, sex abuse, and more. You can also order books and tapes online.

HowToHaveGoodSex.com

www.howtohavegoodsex.com

Founded by Alex Robboy, L.C.S.W., this site provides sex education and tips, a dictionary of common terms, questions and answers, and more, plus information about workshops and an online store where you can order videos and toys.

The Marriage and Family Health Center

www.passionatemarriage.com

This is the website of David Schnarch, Ph.D., who offers weekend and week-long intensive workshops for couples: Passionate Marriage, Constructing the Love Crucible, and Resurrecting Sex. You can learn more about his approach at this site.

Pat Love & Associates

www.patlove.com

This is the home page of Dr. Pat Love, author of *Hot Monogamy*. At this site, you can learn more about Love and her approach, pull up information about current studies on relationships and sexuality, take relationship quizzes, and learn more about available seminars and workshops.

Woman Spirit

www.Womanspirit.net

The information available at this site has been compiled by Dr. Gina Ogden, author of *Women Who Love Sex: An Inquiry into the Expanding Spirit of Women's Erotic Experience*. This site provides information on female sexuality and spirituality. Here, you also can join a reader's forum to exchange ideas with others, find a calendar of events and information about books and articles, access resources for counseling, and check out links to other websites. You can even add to important new research by completing the online survey.

Additional Helpful Information

To find more general information about human sexuality and obtain additional advice, consult the following organizations:

The Sexuality Information and Education Council of the U.S.

www.siecus.com

SIECUS is a national, nonprofit organization which affirms that "sexuality is a natural and healthy part of life." SIECUS develops, collects, and disseminates information, promotes comprehensive education about sexuality, and advocates the right of individuals to make responsible sexual choices. The SIECUS website provides a good collection of accurate and useful information about human sexuality.

Planned Parenthood

www.plannedparenthood.org

Planned Parenthood provides excellent resources and help related to sexual health, birth control, and family planning.

SexHealth.com

www.sexualhealth.com

This site offers information and education on various sexual issues, including chronic illness and disability. It also features an online store where you can shop for sexual products and videos.

Network for Women's Sexual Health

www.newshe.com

This is the official website of Drs. Jennifer and Laura Berman, experts in female sexual dysfunction and other areas of human sexuality that specifically affect women.

SexWithoutPain.com

www.sexwithoutpain.com

This site takes a multidisciplinary approach to the causes and treatments of pain associated with sexual intercourse.

His and Her Health

www.hisandherhealth.com

This site has up-to-date information for both men and women on issues of sexual functioning and sexual dysfunctions.

Helen Fisher

www.helenfisher.com

This site discusses Dr. Fisher's findings on love, sex, and evolution.

American Social Health Association

www.ashastd.org

The ASHA is dedicated to developing and delivering accurate, medically reliable information about STDs, and this site provides easy access to most of that information.

Center for Disease Control

www.cdc.gov/nchstp/dstd/disease_info.htm

The CDC is a government organization responsible for disease prevention. This particular area of the CDC website provides information relating specifically to STDs and features helpful advice for preventing the spread of STDs. You can also call the National STD hotline (1-800-227-8922).

SexHelp.com

www.sexhelp.com

This is the home page of Dr. Patrick Carnes, nationally renowned expert on the topic of sexual addiction. Here, you can take an online screening to determine if you have an addiction. You can also read articles on how to recover from a sexual addiction and get help.

Sexual Products and Toys

You can locate a host of online stores that carry sex toys and other products by searching for "sex toys," but here are some that we have found to be quite good:

www.howtohavegoodsex.com

www.sexualhealthhealth.com

www.evesgarden.com

www.goodvibes.com

www.condomania.com

Alternative Lifestyles

To learn more about alternative lifestyles, including swinging, S&M, and B&D, the following sites provide some useful information:

> www.lifestyles.org
>
> www.NASCA.com
>
> www.tes.com

Films and Tapes

To shop for how-to videos on sensual massage and other sexually related activity, visit these websites:

> www.nudemuse.com/massage.htm
>
> www.bettersex.com

Tantric Sex

For information about and products relating to Tantric sex, visit the following sites:

> www.tantric.com

The Authors

To contact the authors and obtain information about their professional services; workshops for couples; seminars for psychologists, psychiatrists, clinical social workers, and other helping professionals; books, audio programs, and other self-help materials:

> Michael S. Broder, Ph.D. 215-545-7000
> mb@drmichaelbroder.com
> 1420 Locust Street
> Suite 7G
> Philadelphia, PA 19102

> Arlene Goldman, Ph.D. 215-545-7014
> drarlenegoldman@aol.com
> 255 South 17th Street
> Suite 2900
> Philadelphia, PA 19103

> Call toll free: 1-800-434-8255

Or visit our website: www.DrMichaelBroder.com

Bibliography

Because sexual ecstasy can be so many things to so many people, no one book can cover all facets of it. Here we list dozens of books that can enrich your vision and experience of sexual ecstasy.

Couples—Relationships

Barbach, Lonnie, and David L. Geisinger. *Going The Distance: Finding and Keeping Lifelong Love.* New York, NY: Plume, 1993.

Ellis, Albert, and Ted Crawford. *Making Intimate Connections: Seven Guidelines for Great Relationships and Better Communication.* Atascadero, Calif.: Impact Publishers, 2000.

Fisher, Helen. *Anatomy of Love: The Natural History of Mating, Marriage, and Why We Stray.* New York: Ballantine Books, 1994.

———. *Why We Love: The Nature and Chemistry of Romantic Love.* New York: Henry Holt, 2004.

Gottman, John, and Nan Silver. *The Seven Principles for Making Marriage Work.* New York: Crown Publishing, 1999.

Love, Pat. *The Truth About Love: The Highs, the Lows, and How You Can Make It Last Forever.* New York, Simon & Schuster, 2001.

McCarthy, Barry W., and Emily J. McCarthy. *Getting It Right the First Time: Creating a Healthy Marriage.* New York: Brunner-Routledge, 2004.

Schnarch, David. *Passionate Marriage: Keeping Love and Intimacy Alive in Emotionally Committed Relationships.* New York: W.W. Norton & Company, 1997.

Weiner-Davis, Michele. *Divorce Busting: A Step-by-Step Approach to Making Your Marriage Loving Again.* New York: Simon & Shuster, 1992.

———. *The Divorce Remedy: Proven Seven-Step Program for Saving Your Marriage.* New York: Simon & Shuster, 2002.

Couples—Sexuality

Barbach, Lonnie. *For Each Other: Sharing Sexual Intimacy.* New York: Signet, 2001.

Levine, Stephen B. *Sexuality in Mid-Life.* New York: Plenum Press, 1998.

Love, Pat. *Hot Monogamy: Essential Steps to More Passionate Intimate Lovemaking.* New York: Dutton, 1994.

McCarthy, Barry W., and Emily J. McCarthy. *Couple Sexual Awareness: Building Sexual Happiness.* New York: Carroll & Graf, 1998.

———. *Sexual Awareness: Enhancing Sexual Pleasure.* New York: Carroll and Graf, 1998.

Sexuality (General)

Ellis, Albert. *Sex Without Guilt in the 21st Century.* Fort Lee, N.J.: Barricade Books, Inc., 2003.

Sexual Techniques and Sexual Play

Barbach, Lonnie. *Turn Ons: Pleasing Yourself While You Please Your Lover.* New York: Plume, 1998.

Cane, William. *The Art of Kissing.* New York, N.Y.: St. Martin's Press, 1995.

Comfort, Alex. *The Joy of Sex: Fully Revised and Completely Updated for the 21st Century.* New York: Crown Publishers, 2002.

Corn, Laura. *52 Invitations to Great Sex.* Santa Monica, Calif.: Park Avenue Publishers, 1999.

———. *101 Nights Of Grrreat Sex: Secret Sealed Seductions for Fun-Loving Couples.* Santa Monica, Calif.: Park Avenue Publishers, 2000.

Joannides, Paul. *The Guide to Getting It On*. West Hollywood, Calif.: The Goofy Foot Press, 1999.

Male Sexuality

Metz, Michael E., and Barry W. McCarthy. *Coping with Premature Ejaculation: How to Overcome PE, Please Your Partner and Have Great Sex*, Oakland, Calif.: New Harbinger, 2003.

Milsten, Richard, and Julian Slowinski. *The Sexual Male, Problems and Solutions*. New York: W.W. Norton, 1999.

Zilbergeld, Bernie. *The New Male Sexuality*. New York: Bantam Doubleday Dell, 1999.

Women's Sexuality

Barbach, Lonnie. *For Yourself: The Fulfillment of Female Sexuality*. New York: Signet, 2000.

Berman, Jennifer L., and Laura Berman. *For Women Only, A Revolutionary Guide to Overcoming Sexual Dysfunction and Reclaiming Your Sex Life*. New York: Henry Holt & Co., 2001.

Boston Women's Health Collective. *Our Bodies, Ourselves for the New Century*. New York: Simon & Schuster, 1998.

Dodson, Betty. *Sex for One, The Joy of Self Loving*. New York: Random House, 1995.

Ellison, Carol, and Beverly Whipple. *Women's Sexualities; Generations of Women Share Intimate Secrets of Sexual Self-Acceptance*. Oakland, Calif.: New Harbinger Publications, 2000.

Ladas, Alice Kahn, Beverly Whipple, and John D. Perry. *The G-Spot, and Other Recent Discoveries About Human Sexuality*. New York: Holt, Rinehart, and Winston, 1982.

Leiblum, Sandra, and Judith Sachs. *Getting the Sex You Want: A Woman's Guide to Becoming Proud, Passionate and Pleased in Bed*, Lincoln, Nebr.: ASJA Press—IUniverse, 2003.

Ogden, Gina. *Women Who Love Sex: An Inquiry into the Expanding Spirit of Women's Erotic Experience*. New York: Pocket Books, 1994.

Inhibited Sexual Desire

McCarthy, Barry W., and Emily J. McCarthy. *Rekindling Desire: A Step-by-Step Program to Help Low-Sex and No-Sex Marriages.* New York: Brunner-Routledge, 2003.

Schnarch, David. *Resurrecting Sex: Resolving Sexual Problems and Rejuvenating Your Relationship.* New York: HarperCollins, 2002.

Weiner-Davis, Michele. *The Sex-Starved Marriage: A Couple's Guide to Boosting Their Marriage Libido.* New York: Simon & Shuster, 2003.

Sexual Poetry

Maltz, Wendy, ed. *Intimate Kisses: The Poetry of Sexual Pleasure.* Novato, Calif.: New World Library, 2001.

————. *Passionate Hearts: The Poetry of Sexual Love.* Novato, Calif.: New World Library, 1996.

Fantasies and Erotica

Maltz, Wendy, and Suzie Boss. *Sexual Fantasies: Private Thoughts Exploring the Power of Women's Sexual Fantasies.* Novato, Calif.: New World Library, 2001.

By Lonnie Barbach

The Erotic Edge, Erotica for Couples. New York: Plume, 1996.

Erotic Interludes: Tales Told By Women. New York: Plume, 1995.

Pleasures: Women Write Erotica. New York: HarperCollins, 1985.

Seductions: Tales of Erotic Persuasion. New York: Dutton, 1999.

By Nancy Friday

Forbidden Flowers. New York: Pocket Books, 1991.

Men in Love. New York: Dell Publishing, 1998.

My Secret Garden. New York: Pocket Books, 1998.

Women on Top. New York: Simon & Schuster, 1991.

Classics

Cleland, John. *Fanny Hill.*

Lawrence, D. H. *Lady Chatterley's Lover.*

Miller, Henry. *Tropic of Cancer.*

Nin, Anais. *Delta Of Venus.*

———. *Little Birds.*

Regea, Pauline. *The Story of O* (B&D, S&M).

Body Image

Cash, Thomas. *The Body Image Workbook: An Eight-Step Program for Learning to Like Your Looks.* Oakland, Calif.: New Harbinger Publications, 1997.

Hirschmann, Jane R., and Carol Munter. *When Women Stop Hating Their Bodies.* New York: Fawcett Columbine, 1995.

Maine, Margo. *Body Wars: Making Peace with Women's Bodies: An Activist's Guide.* Carlsbad, Calif.: Gürze Books, 2000.

Sexual Abuse

Maltz, Wendy. *Sexual Healing Journey: A Guide for Survivors of Sexual Abuse*, Revised Edition. New York: Quill, 2001.

Tantric Sexuality

Anand, Margot, and Leandra Hussey, ill. *The Art of Sexual Ecstasy; The Path of Sacred Sexuality for Western Lovers.* Los Angeles, Calif.: J. P. Tarcher, 1989.

Muir, Charles, and Caroline Muir. *Tantra: The Art of Conscious Loving.* San Francisco: Mercury House, 1990.

Alternative Lifestyles

Bellemeade, Kaye. *Swinging for Beginners: An Introduction to the Lifestyle.* New Traditions, 2003.

Brame, Gloria, Jon Jacobs, and William Brame. *Different Loving: A Complete Exploration of the World of Sexual Dominance and Submission.* New York: Villard Books, 1993.

Califia-Rice, Patrick. *Sensuous Magic: A Guide to S/M for Adventurous Couples.* Cleis, 2001.

Wiseman, Jay. *SM 101: A Realistic Introduction.* San Francisco: Greenery Press, 1996.

Selected Books and Audiotapes by Dr. Broder

The Art of Living Single. New York: Avon, 1990.

The Art of Staying Together. New York: Hyperion, 1993.

Can Your Relationship Be Saved? How to Know Whether to Stay or Go. Atascadero, Calif.: Impact Publishers, 2002.

Help Yourself Audiotherapy Series. Philadelphia: Media Psychology Associates, 2000 (rev.):

    Can Your Relationship Be Saved?

    How to Develop Self-Confidence and a Positive Self-Image

    How to Develop the Ingredients for Staying Together

    How to Enhance Passion and Sexual Satisfaction

    How to Find A New Love Relationship That Will Work for You

    How to Manage Stress and Make It Work for You

    Letting Go of Your Ended Love Relationship

    Making Crucial Choices and Major Life Changes

    Overcoming Your Anger: In the Shortest Possible Period of Time

    Overcoming Your Anxiety: In the Shortest Possible Period of Time

    Overcoming Your Depression: In the Shortest Possible Period of Time

    The Single Life: How to Love It With or Without a Relationship

Living Single After the Sexual Revolution. New York: Macmillan, 1988.

Positive Attitude Training. Chicago: Nightingale Conant, 1992. Audio.

Self Actualization: Reaching Your Full Potential. Chicago: Nightingale Conant, 1993. Audio.

All available at DrMichaelBroder.com or 1-800-434-8255.

Index

attachment, 27
attitudes, 4
  history, 4-5
  personal, 15
  shifting, 60-61
  simplifying, 7-8
attraction, 42
  brain chemicals, 27
  wandering, 248-249
audiotherapy, 209
availability of partners, 242-246
average, 10
awareness, 81

B

B&D (bondage and discipline),
  101
barriers (sexual desires), 69-70
bibliotherapy, 209
birth control, 268-269
bodies
  awareness, 81
  G spots, 179-180
  hot spots, 173, 176-178
  image, 74-75
    acceptance, 74-77
    activity, 79-80
    feeling sexy, 78
    genitalia size, 78-79
    obsessing, 74
    weight, 75
  kegels, 187-188
  self-conscious, 49
  skin, 81

bondage and discipline
  (B&D), 101
boredom, 49
brain
  as sex organ, 56-57
  attitude shifts, 60-61
  chemicals, 64
  experiencing present
    moment, 61-63
  love, 27
  mindset, 57
  negative thoughts, 60
  self-talk, 57
  sensations, 59-60
  sexual desires, 63-65
    anticipation, 71
    barriers, 69-70
    brain chemicals, 64
    circular model, 65
    enhancing, 70-71
    motivation, 64
    myths, 66-67
    novelty, 71
    self-enhancement, 71-72
    self-image, 69
    sex drive, 64
    stress, 69
    truths, 68-69
    wish, 64
  values, 57-58
breasts
  sensitivity, 176
  size, 78-79
busy lifestyles, 51

Internet fantasies, 106
intimacy
  defined, 23
  enhancing, 23
  long-term relationships,
    113-114
intrauterine device (IUD), 268
introjecting, 58
inventory of sexual satisfaction, 35-38
  amount of sex, 41, 49
  arousal, 52
  attraction, 42
  boredom, 49
  busy lifestyles, 51
  closing of eyes, 42
  communication, 42, 49
  connections, 46
  distractions, 40
  emotional connections, 51
  erections, 47
  fantasies, 39, 44, 50
  functioning, 48
  G spots, 43
  guilt, 40
  inhibitions, 48
  initiating sex, 41, 50
  long-term relationships, 46
  lubricating, 47
  mental exclusivity, 45
  novelties, 41
  oral sex, 43
  orgasms, 39

partner interest, 47
partner satisfaction, 40, 46
post-childbirth, 45
premature ejaculation, 51
romantic connections, 42
self-acceptance, 39
self-arousal, 44
self-conscious, 49
sensual stimulations, 48
sexiness, 39
sexual interest, 40
sexual play, 44
spiritual connections, 47
spontaneity, 43
statements, 36-38
talking, 45
tension, 46
touching, 47
trying new things, 50
variety, 43
vision, 52
withholding sex, 51
ISD (Inhibited Sexual Desire),
  217-218
IUD (intrauterine device), 268

K

Kama Sutra, 202-203
Kegel, Dr. Arnold, 187
kegels, 187-188
Kinsey, Alfred, 5
kissing, 151-153

pleasure
anxiety, 213
delaying, 150
positions, 185-187
69, 180
missionary, 185
post-childbirth sex, 45
pregnancy, 270-272
premature ejaculation, 51,
220-221
preorgasmic disorder, 228
present moment, experiencing,
61-63
prolactin, 273
pubococcygeal (P.C.) muscle,
187
pumps (penis), 284

quality (orgasms), 39

R

rapid ejaculation, 220-221
realistic expectations (long-
term relationships), 117-118
relationships
assessing, 15
communication, 253-256
feedback, 254
listening, 255
crunches, 251
feelings toward partners, 233
anger, 234, 237-240
anxiety/fears, 240-242

availability, 242-246
falling out of love,
249-251
passion, 246-247
wandering attraction,
248-249
Gottman website, 117
help, 262
initial passion, 26-28
long-term, 29
childbirth, 272-274
comfort, 111
components, 115-117
contraception, 268-269
downsides, 285
empathy, 114
herbs, 283-284
illnesses, 278-280
intimacy, 113-114
love, 46
medications, 281-283
midlife issues, 274-278
partner connections, 110
passion, 110
pregnancy, 270-272
realistic expectations,
117-118
romance, 120-123
safer sex, 266-268
sex, 119-120
transitions, 30-32
trust, 112
physiology, 27

size (genitalia), 78-79
skin sensations, 81
smell, 170-171
sounds (sensual), 171-172
special occasions (sex as), 147
spectatoring, 57
spirituality
  connections, 47
  defined, 200
  Kama Sutra, 202-203
  midlife issues, 277
  orgasms, 199-201
  tantric sex, 201-202
  Western religions, 203
spontaneity, 43
stimulating senses, 48
stress, 69
swinging, 102

T–U

talk (sex), 45, 150
tantric sex, 201-202
taste, 170
Tenderness Openness
  Understanding Chemistry
  Honesty (TOUCH), 138
tension, 46
testosterone
  medications, 281
  midlife issues, 276
therapists websites, 261
thought stopping, 238
time, 251

touch, 47
  G spots, 179-180
  mutual erotic touching, 173,
    177-178
  sensual massage, 166-169
TOUCH (Tenderness Openness
  Understanding Chemistry
  Honesty), 138
toys (sex), 158
trust, 112
truths, 68-69

V

vacuums, 284
vaginas
  EROS-CTD, 284
  sensitivity, 177
  vacuums, 284
vaginismus, 230
values, 57-58
variety of sex, 43
VasoFem, 283
Viagra, 282

W–X

websites
  Albert Ellis Institute, 60
  body image, 77
  condoms, 268
  Dr. Ava Cadell, 183
  Dr. Gina Ogden, 200
  ED (Erectile Dysfunction),
    224

Y-Z

psychologytoday.com

You want to talk to someone ...

but how do you find the right person?

FIND A THERAPIST

PROFILES | SPECIALTIES | PHOTOS | FIND THE THERAPIST WHO SUITS YOU

* Review profiles, photos and fees

* Explore therapists' specialties, in their own words

* Thousands of professionals listed